# PREPARING TEACHERS
## BUILDING EVIDENCE FOR SOUND POLICY

Committee on the Study of Teacher Preparation Programs
in the United States

Center for Education

Division of Behavioral and Social Sciences and Education

NATIONAL RESEARCH COUNCIL
*OF THE NATIONAL ACADEMIES*

THE NATIONAL ACADEMIES PRESS
Washington, D.C.
**www.nap.edu**

THE NATIONAL ACADEMIES PRESS   500 Fifth Street, N.W.   Washington, DC 20001

NOTICE: The project that is the subject of this report was approved by the Governing Board of the National Research Council, whose members are drawn from the councils of the National Academy of Sciences, the National Academy of Engineering, and the Institute of Medicine. The members of the committee responsible for the report were chosen for their special competences and with regard for appropriate balance.

This study was supported by Contract No. ED-05-CO-0012 between the National Academy of Sciences and the U.S. Department of Education; by Contract No. 20060517 with the Ewing Marion Kauffman Foundation; by Contract No. D07001 with the Carnegie Corporation of New York; by Contract No. 200700087 with The Spencer Foundation; and by the President's Fund of the National Research Council. Any opinions, findings, conclusions, or recommendations expressed in this publication are those of the author(s) and do not necessarily reflect the views of the organizations or agencies that provided support for the project.

**Library of Congress Cataloging-in-Publication Data**

Preparing teachers : building evidence for sound policy.
    p. cm.
    "Committee on the Study of Teacher Preparation Programs in the United States, Center for Education Division of Behavioral and Social Sciences and Education."
    Includes bibliographical references.
    ISBN 978-0-309-12805-6 (pbk.) — ISBN 978-0-309-12996-1 (pdf)  1.
Teachers—Training of—United States.
    LB1715.P727 2010
    370.71'173—dc21

                        2010014539

Additional copies of this report are available from the National Academies Press, 500 Fifth Street, N.W., Lockbox 285, Washington, DC 20055; (800) 624-6242 or (202) 334-3313 (in the Washington metropolitan area); Internet, http://www.nap.edu.

Copyright 2010 by the National Academy of Sciences. All rights reserved.

Printed in the United States of America

Suggested citation: National Research Council. (2010). *Preparing teachers: Building evidence for sound policy.* Committee on the Study of Teacher Preparation Programs in the United States, Center for Education. Division of Behavioral and Social Sciences and Education. Washington, DC: The National Academies Press.

# THE NATIONAL ACADEMIES
*Advisers to the Nation on Science, Engineering, and Medicine*

The **National Academy of Sciences** is a private, nonprofit, self-perpetuating society of distinguished scholars engaged in scientific and engineering research, dedicated to the furtherance of science and technology and to their use for the general welfare. Upon the authority of the charter granted to it by the Congress in 1863, the Academy has a mandate that requires it to advise the federal government on scientific and technical matters. Dr. Ralph J. Cicerone is president of the National Academy of Sciences.

The **National Academy of Engineering** was established in 1964, under the charter of the National Academy of Sciences, as a parallel organization of outstanding engineers. It is autonomous in its administration and in the selection of its members, sharing with the National Academy of Sciences the responsibility for advising the federal government. The National Academy of Engineering also sponsors engineering programs aimed at meeting national needs, encourages education and research, and recognizes the superior achievements of engineers. Dr. Charles M. Vest is president of the National Academy of Engineering.

The **Institute of Medicine** was established in 1970 by the National Academy of Sciences to secure the services of eminent members of appropriate professions in the examination of policy matters pertaining to the health of the public. The Institute acts under the responsibility given to the National Academy of Sciences by its congressional charter to be an adviser to the federal government and, upon its own initiative, to identify issues of medical care, research, and education. Dr. Harvey V. Fineberg is president of the Institute of Medicine.

The **National Research Council** was organized by the National Academy of Sciences in 1916 to associate the broad community of science and technology with the Academy's purposes of furthering knowledge and advising the federal government. Functioning in accordance with general policies determined by the Academy, the Council has become the principal operating agency of both the National Academy of Sciences and the National Academy of Engineering in providing services to the government, the public, and the scientific and engineering communities. The Council is administered jointly by both Academies and the Institute of Medicine. Dr. Ralph J. Cicerone and Dr. Charles M. Vest are chair and vice chair, respectively, of the National Research Council.

**www.national-academies.org**

COMMITTEE ON THE STUDY OF TEACHER
PREPARATION PROGRAMS IN THE UNITED STATES


ELLEN CONDLIFFE LAGEMANN* (*Cochair*), Levy Economics Institute,
    Bard College
KENNETH SHINE** (*Cochair*), Department of Health Affairs, University of
    Texas
HERBERT K. BRUNKHORST, Department of Science, Mathematics, and
    Technology Education, California State University at San Bernardino
MARGARITA CALDERÓN, Center for Research and Reform in Education,
    Johns Hopkins University
MARILYN COCHRAN-SMITH, Lynch School of Education, Boston College
JANICE DOLE, Department of Teaching and Learning, University of Utah
DONALD N. LANGENBERG, Department of Physics, University of
    Maryland
RONALD LATANISION, Exponent Consulting, Natwick, MA
JAMES LEWIS, Mathematics Department and Center for Science,
    Mathematics, and Computer Education, University of Nebraska at Lincoln
DAVID H. MONK, College of Education, Pennsylvania State University
ANNEMARIE SULLIVAN PALINCSAR, School of Education, University of
    Michigan
MICHAEL PODGURSKY, Department of Economics, University of Missouri
ANDREW PORTER, Graduate School of Education, University of
    Pennsylvania
EDWARD SILVER, School of Education, University of Michigan
DOROTHY STRICKLAND, Graduate School of Education, Rutgers
    University
SUZANNE WILSON, College of Education, Michigan State University
HUNG-HSI WU, Department of Mathematics, University of California,
    Berkeley
JAMES WYCKOFF, Curry School of Education, University of Virginia


LYN COUNTRYMAN (liaison from Teacher Advisory Council), Price
    Laboratory School, University of Northern Iowa
MICHAEL ALLEN, *Study Director (to 2006)*
LISA TOWNE, *Study Director (2006-2008)*
STUART ELLIOTT, *Study Director (since 2006)*
ALEXANDRA BEATTY, *Senior Program Officer (since 2008)*
TINA WINTERS, *Senior Research Associate (to 2008)*
PATRICIA HARVEY, *Project Assistant*

---

*Chair, starting January 2009.
**Resigned January 2009.

# Preface

The quality of teachers is increasingly recognized as critical to student learning. Holding schools and teachers accountable for student performance is a key element of plans for improving public education and is likely to remain so as the No Child Left Behind legislation is updated. Yet while the education of public school teachers has been the subject of concern, it has not been a primary focus of standards-based reform efforts. This study was mandated by Congress to answer basic questions about teacher education and the research that supports it and to highlight the way forward.

The study had two objectives: (1) to pull together a disparate and uneven research base, so that policy makers can see clearly what is and is not known and (2) to propose a research agenda to fill the gaps in that knowledge base. Our focus was clearly defined: we examined initial preparation for reading, mathematics, and science teachers. That is, although teacher learning is best understood as a process that continues throughout teachers' careers—for example, through induction, mentoring, in-service professional development, and professional collaboration—our focus was the ingredients essential to preparing "well-started beginners."

While preparation is undeniably important, other factors have significant influence on the strength of the nation's teaching force. The incentives that attract aspiring teachers, the status of the field, the compensation teachers can expect, the conditions in which they do their work, and their opportunities for professional advancement are just a few of the factors that affect who becomes a teacher and who stays in the field. In a report more than 20 years ago, the Carnegie Task Force on Teaching as a Profession made a number of recommendations regarding teacher preparation, but it also clearly articulated the importance of seeing it as tightly integrated with other aspects of teachers' professional lives and other elements of the education system. Although our report is not intended to address all the issues related to teacher quality, we emphasize that effective teacher education is one necessary condition for ensuring the quality of the teaching force, but is neither the only condition nor a sufficient one.

Teacher preparation programs are turning out more than 200,000 new teachers every year, and those teachers are badly needed to fill vacancies in a field that has high turnover and a particular need for teachers prepared and willing to work with the neediest children. It is important to strengthen teacher preparation, not just because teachers make up one of the largest occupational groups in the United States, but also because they are asked to serve every child and family in the country. Their work is a basis for democratic citizenship, and they are at the heart of one of the central experiences of growing up—schooling. Nevertheless, teaching has never attained the same status as law or medicine, and the uneven quality of teacher preparation is a reflection of the ambivalence with which university scholars and others have historically viewed this female-dominated field. If that is to change, improving teacher preparation is vital.

We found many gaps in the knowledge base, but it is important also to highlight the considerable grounding we found for many types of guidance regarding the preparation of reading, mathematics, and science teachers. Our goal was to provide a dispassionate summary and objective analysis that will help policy makers debate alternatives and help teacher educators provide stronger preparation, while also providing guidance for much-needed research. Teacher education deserves careful, balanced scrutiny, and that is what we have worked to provide.

A number of individuals assisted us in our information gathering and analysis and we are very grateful for their thoughtful input and their time. At our first meeting, several people provided us with a variety of perspectives and information about a range of questions related to our charge: Joan Baratz-Snowden of the American Federation of Teachers; Vicki Bernstein of the New York City Department of Education and the New York Teaching Fellows Program; Jean Braxton, dean of the School of Education of Norfolk State University; Daniel Fallon of the Carnegie Corporation; Mary Hatwood Futrell of the School of Education and Human Development of George Washington University; Frederick Hess of the American Enterprise Institute; Deborah McGriff of Edison Schools; and Jon Snyder of the Bank

Street College. At another of our meetings several individuals assisted us in exploring methodological issues: Pamela Grossman, Nomellini Olivier professor of education at Stanford University; Karen Hammerness, a post-doctoral fellow at Stanford University; Raven McCrory of the Division of Science and Mathematics Education at Michigan State University; Susan Moore-Johnson, professor of teaching and learning at Harvard University; Stephen Raudenbush of the Department of Sociology at the University of Chicago; Kate Walsh, president of the National Council on Teacher Quality; and Robert Yinger, professor of educational studies and teacher education at the University of Cincinnati and research director for the Ohio Teacher Quality Partnership.

We held workshops to explore several issues in depth. The first addressed both teacher licensure and program accreditation and we gratefully acknowledge the assistance of presenters: Dan Goldhaber of the Center on Reinventing Public Education at the University of Washington; Peter McWalters of the Rhode Island Department of Education; Frank Murray, president of the Teacher Education Accreditation Council; Kara Schmitt, formerly of the Michigan Department of Consumer and Industry Services; Kathy Sullivan of the North Carolina Department of Public Instruction; J. Fredericks Volkwein of the Penn State Center for the Study of Higher Education; Judith Watkins of the Council for Higher Education Accreditation; and Arthur Wise, president of the National Council for the Accreditation of Teacher Education.

At our second workshop we explored two issues. One was the preparation of mathematics and science teachers, and we thank: Sybilla Beckmann, a professor of mathematics at the University of Georgia; Rodger Bybee of the Biological Sciences Curriculum Study; Elizabeth Davis of the Department of Applied Economics at the University of Michigan; James Hiebert of the School of Education at the University of Delaware; Barbara Miller of the Education Development Center; Paul Sally, director of undergraduate mathematics education at the University of Chicago; Mark Windschitl of the College of Education at the University of Washington; and Robert Yager of the College of Education at the University of Iowa. The second issue was perspectives on professions in the United States, and we thank: Steven Brint, a professor of sociology at the University of California, Riverside, and Lee Shulman of the Carnegie Foundation for the Advancement of Teaching.

We explored several state and regional analyses of teacher preparation by commissioning two studies, and we extend our sincere thanks to Tim Sass of Florida State University and to Pamela Grossman and her colleagues for their investigations of data from Florida and New York City, respectively. We also thank Douglas Harris of the University of Wisconsin at Madison;

George Noell of Louisiana State University; Kent Seidel and Robert Yinger, both of the University of Cincinnati; and David Wright of the California State University System for their contributions to the workshop.

Finally, the intellectual leadership demonstrated by costudy directors Lisa Towne and Stuart Elliott in guiding the committee's work was outstanding. The substantive and editorial contributions of Alexandra Beatty were of the highest quality and added significantly to the shape and eloquence of the report. The combined administrative support and responsiveness of Tina Winters and Patricia Harvey were also of the highest quality, and we are extremely grateful for all they did throughout the committee process. We would have no report without them. We also wish to note that the views expressed in this report are those of the committee, not the sponsors who generously supported our work.

This report has been reviewed in draft form by individuals chosen for their diverse perspectives and technical expertise, in accordance with procedures approved by the Report Review Committee of the National Research Council. The purpose of this independent review is to provide candid and critical comments that will assist the institution in making its published report as sound as possible and to ensure that the report meets institutional standards for objectivity, evidence, and responsiveness to the study charge. The review comments and draft manuscript remain confidential to protect the integrity of the deliberative process.

We thank the following individuals for their review of this report: Deborah H. Cunningham, Educational Management Services, New York State Education Department; Robert E. Floden, Institute for Research on Teaching and Learning College of Education, Michigan State University; Carolyn D. Herrington, Department of Educational Leadership and Policy Studies, Florida State University; Paul W. Holland, Paul Holland Consulting Corporation; Kenneth Howe, School of Education, University of Colorado at Boulder; Roger Howe, Department of Mathematics, Yale University; Joseph Krajcik, School of Education, University of Michigan; Henry M. Levin, Economics and Education, Teachers College, Columbia University; P. David Pearson, Graduate School of Education, University of California, Berkeley; Penelope L. Peterson, School of Education and Social Policy, Northwestern; and Steven Rivkin, Department of Economics, Amherst College.

Although the reviewers listed above have provided many constructive comments and suggestions, they were not asked to endorse the conclusions or recommendations nor did they see the final draft of the report before its release. The review of this report was overseen by Diana Pullin, School of Education, Boston College, and Burton Singer, Emerging Pathogens Institute, University of Florida. Appointed by the National Research Council, they were responsible for making certain that an independent examination of this report was carried out in accordance with institutional procedures and that all review comments were carefully considered. Responsibility for the final content of this report rests entirely with the authoring committee and the institution.

Ellen Condliffe Lagemann, *Chair*
Committee on the Study of Teacher
Preparation Programs in the United States

# Contents

# Summary

Teachers make a difference. The success of any plan for improving educational outcomes depends on the teachers who carry it out and thus on the abilities of those attracted to the field and their preparation. Yet there are many questions about how teachers are being prepared and how they ought to be prepared. As mandated by Congress, the U.S. Department of Education requested that the National Research Council conduct a study of teacher preparation with specific attention to reading, mathematics, and science. The Committee on the Study of Teacher Preparation Programs in the United States was charged to address four questions:

1.  What are the characteristics of the candidates who enter teacher preparation programs?
2.  What sorts of instruction and experiences do teacher candidates receive in preparation programs of various types?
3.  To what extent are the required instruction and experiences consistent with converging scientific evidence?
4.  What model for data collection would provide valid and reliable information about the content knowledge, pedagogical competence, and effectiveness of graduates from the various kinds of teacher preparation programs?

We examined many aspects of the complex and diverse network through which the majority of the nation's teachers are prepared. It was exceptionally difficult to assemble a clear picture of teacher preparation because there have been no systematic efforts to collect the necessary data; thus, we can provide only partial answers to the first three questions in our charge. However, we did find many sources for conclusions about the skills and knowledge most likely to be valuable to beginning teachers, as well as clear indications of the research that is most needed to build a base of knowledge to guide improvements to teacher education.

## HOW TEACHERS ARE PREPARED AND CERTIFIED

The lack of data related to the first two questions in our charge, about the characteristics of teacher candidates and how they are prepared, is surprising—at the very least because of the huge scale of the enterprise. There are approximately 3.6 million public school elementary and secondary teachers in 90,000 public schools in the United States. More than 200,000 students complete a teacher preparation program each year. Little is known about these teacher candidates except that they are predominantly female and white.

Aspiring teachers in the United States are prepared in many different kinds of programs, which in turn reflect many different kinds of career pathways. Between 70 and 80 percent are enrolled in "traditional" programs housed in postsecondary institutions; the rest enter the profession through one of the approximately 130 "alternative" routes.

Yet however they are designated, teacher preparation programs are extremely diverse along almost any dimension of interest: the selectivity of programs, the quantity and content of what they require, and the duration and timing of coursework and fieldwork. Any pathway is likely to entail tradeoffs among selectivity, the intensity of the training, and the obstacles it presents to teacher candidates. More selective pathways, and those that require greater effort and time to complete, may have the disadvantage of yielding fewer teachers to fill vacancies, for example, but the teachers they do produce may be more highly qualified.

There is some research that suggests that there are differences in the characteristics of teacher candidates who are attracted to different pathways and types of programs. There is also some research comparing the outcomes for graduates of different kinds of programs. However, the distinctions among pathways and programs are not clear-cut and there is more variation within the "traditional" and "alternative" categories than there is between these categories. We found no evidence that any one pathway into teaching is the best way to attract and prepare desirable candidates and guide them into the teaching force. This finding does not mean that the characteristics of pathways do not matter; rather, it suggests that research on the sources of the variation in preparation, such as selectivity, timing, and specific components and characteristics, is needed.

The wide variety in teacher education programs led us to consider the current mechanisms for accountability and quality control in teacher education, which strongly affect the ways that teachers are prepared. These mechanisms are a patchwork of mandatory and voluntary processes, including state program approval, program accreditation, and teacher licensure and certification. These mechanisms are not effectively linked in a coherent, outcomes-driven accountability system, and they are not grounded in solid empirical research about which program elements or accountability mechanisms are most effective, partly because such research is not available. Thus, they neither achieve the goal of a true accountability system nor provide evidence about the value of different mechanisms for producing effective teachers. In view of this lack of information, the committee recommends that the U.S. Department of Education undertake an independent evaluation of teacher education approval and accreditation in the United States.

## HIGH-QUALITY PREPARATION

For the third question in our charge, about the extent to which current practices in the preparation of mathematics, reading, and science teachers are consistent with converging scientific evidence, we found a range of potential relevant material. This material included a relatively small body of evidence about the effects of particular kinds of instruction and an even smaller body of evidence about the effects of particular approaches to teacher preparation. Other available research included descriptive and qualitative studies about many aspects of teaching and learning in the three subjects and a substantial body of empirical work on learning and cognition. In addition, the relevant professional organizations have drawn on the available research and their own intellectual traditions and experience as educators to develop content and achievement standards for students and for teachers and, in some cases, for teacher education.

These sources together provide the basis for conclusions about:

- what successful students know about the subject,
- what instructional opportunities are necessary to support successful students,
- what successful teachers know about the subject and how to teach it, and
- what instructional opportunities are necessary to prepare successful teachers.

In analyzing the available evidence, we were mindful of the need to distinguish the basis for different sorts of claims and arguments, even as we synthesized the most important points for policy makers and teacher educators and highlighted questions that have yet to be answered.

There has been an extraordinary amount of work, from a variety of fields, on questions about the factors that influence the effectiveness of teaching, but this work is only a starting point. There is little firm empirical evidence to support conclusions about the effectiveness of specific approaches to teacher preparation. However, we found no reason to question the recommendations professional societies have made about what is important for teachers to know. Moreover, those recommendations integrate well with the relatively small body of empirical work. The research base is strongest for reading and least strong for science, and our conclusions about preparation in the three fields reflect these differences.

In general, the evidence base supports conclusions about the characteristics it is valuable for teachers to have, but not conclusions about how teacher preparation programs can most effectively develop those characteristics. For all three fields, we conclude that both strong content knowledge (a body of conceptual and factual knowledge) and pedagogical content knowledge (understanding of how learners acquire knowledge in a given subject) are important.

For teachers of reading, it is important to (1) understand that students must master the foundational skills of reading (which include a firm grasp of phonics and comprehension strategies), and (2) possess a range of approaches for helping all students develop this mastery.

In mathematics, it is important for teachers to be able to foster students' understanding of the core elements of mathematical proficiency (which include conceptual understanding, procedural fluency, and capacity for reasoning and problem solving). This capacity requires not only mathematical knowledge, but also understanding of how mathematics learning develops and of the variation in cognitive approaches to mathematical thinking.

In science, the key points are similar to those for mathematics teachers: a grounding in college-level study of the science disciplines suitable to the age groups and subjects they intend to teach; understanding of the objectives for students' science learning; understanding of the way students develop science proficiency; and command of an array of instructional approaches designed to develop students' learning of the content, intellectual conventions, and other attributes essential to science proficiency.

This was the picture we found of the evidence relevant to teacher preparation. There is very little systematic research regarding the specific ways teachers of reading, mathematics, and science are currently being prepared that we could use to make comparisons with that picture. The limited information we found does not support conclusions about the current nature and content of teacher preparation programs.

## EVALUATING EFFECTIVENESS

Ideally, teacher education programs would be evaluated on the basis of the demonstrated ability of their graduates to improve the educational outcomes of the students they teach. Unfortunately, the data needed for such evaluation do not exist, although there has been some promising work. More such research is needed, but identifying and measuring the relationship between teacher preparation and student outcomes poses methodological difficulties.

First, it is difficult to measure teacher effectiveness in valid and reliable ways. Assessments of K-12 student learning are the most readily available quantitative measures of educational outcomes. These types of measures serve important purposes, but they do not address the full range of outcomes of concern to policy makers. Indeed, much of the K-12 curriculum is not addressed by such tests. The assessment community has made important strides in developing richer measures of achievement but these are not yet at the stage where they could be easily used for systematic analysis of teacher effectiveness.

Second, establishing clear causal links between aspects of teacher preparation and outcomes for students is extremely difficult. The effects of teacher preparation are hard to disentangle from other factors, such as school, curriculum, community, and family influences. Efforts to establish causal links are also hobbled by the relative lack of data on the characteristics of teachers and their preparation; the dearth of robust measures of teachers' knowledge and practice; and difficulties in linking student achievement to instruction or to what teachers know. And, there is considerable distance in time and place between teachers' preparation and the effects their teaching may later have on student achievement.

These obstacles partly account for the paucity of strong empirical evidence regarding the effects of teacher preparation. Yet we believe that building knowledge about teacher preparation, as in any field of scholarly inquiry, requires ambitious and creative approaches to empirically examining causal relationships. It is very important to connect what occurs in preparation programs to characteristics of their graduates, to the ways those teacher-graduates interact with their students, and to learning outcomes for those students.

## A MODEL FOR FUTURE RESEARCH

Because the information about teacher preparation and its effectiveness is so limited, high-stakes policy debates about the most effective ways to recruit, train, and retain a high-quality teacher workforce remain muddled. If the base of empirical knowledge about teacher preparation is thin, the way forward is to build on what has been done by drawing on the professional consensus in each academic field for hypotheses about which features of teacher preparation are most promising and to subject those hypotheses to rigorous research. We were asked to develop an approach to future research that would provide a firmer foundation for policy and practice in the future. We organized our response around two overarching needs:

1. improved understanding of the relationships between characteristics of teacher preparation and student learning, and
2. a comprehensive, coherent system for collecting data about teacher preparation.

## High-Priority Research Questions

The primary need is to build a body of evidence, developed from multiple perspectives and using an array of research designs, that establishes links between teacher preparation and learning—both teachers' learning and K-12 students' learning. Particularly valuable will be research that identifies and explains

- the features that make programs attractive to academically accomplished teacher candidates,
- the ways teachers' knowledge affects outcomes for students, and
- the characteristics of clinical experiences that affect outcomes for the students teacher candidates will later teach.

## Data Collection

A comprehensive data collection system would provide not only baseline information for identifying and monitoring trends in teacher preparation, but also the necessary infrastructure for research into complex questions about teacher preparation.

A comprehensive data system for teacher preparation would provide meaningful information about teacher candidates, preparation programs, practicing teachers, the schools where those teachers teach, and the students they teach: that is, it would incorporate indicators beyond standardized test scores, degree title, courses taken, or certification category. These data would be integrated so that information about teacher candidates and their preparation can be connected with their knowledge, teaching practices, career paths, school environments, and student outcomes. One key to integration will be consistent definitions of key indicators so that data from states can be compared and used for research.

As states pursue strategies for sharing data and making it more accessible through web-based systems, possibilities for research in teacher preparation will expand. The federal government can play a critical role in coordinating states' efforts and encouraging them to move in this direction.

## CONCLUSION

The quality of the nation's teachers has been the subject of sharp critiques, and so have many preparation programs. Yet, teacher preparation is often treated as an afterthought in discussions of improving the public education system. Federal and state policy makers need reliable, outcomes-based information to make sound decisions, and teacher educators need to know how best to contribute to the development of effective teachers. Clearer understanding of the content and character of effective teacher preparation is critical to improving it and to ensuring that the same critiques and questions are not being repeated 10 years from now.

# 1

# Introduction

Teachers make a difference. Indeed, of all the factors that education leaders can control, the quality of teaching has perhaps the greatest potential effect (see, e.g., Wenglinsky, 2002; Rockoff, 2004; Rivkin, Hanushek, and Kain, 2005; Clotfelter, Ladd, and Vigdor, 2007). Policy has begun to reflect this perspective, most prominently in the provision of the No Child Left Behind Act of 2001 (NCLB) that requires that all public school teachers in core academic areas be highly qualified by 2012. Teacher qualifications and preparation are likely to remain in focus even as the policy environment for education reform shifts. Yet many questions about what it takes to produce highly qualified teachers, and about how teachers are currently prepared, do not have clear answers. Who enters teaching and what educational options are available to aspiring teachers? What should teachers be required to study? Should all teachers be required to complete a program of professional education, culminating in a university degree? Are U.S. teachers provided with real opportunities to develop the necessary competence, and what is known about the institutions that prepare them? Is there high-quality research to support current methods of preparing teachers or to guide improvements?

## COMMITTEE TASK AND REPORT

In response to a mandate from Congress for an objective and comprehensive synthesis of the available evidence on key questions about teacher preparation that could be used as the basis for future policy making, the

Institute of Education Sciences of the U.S. Department of Education asked the National Research Council (NRC) to conduct the required study. With additional support from the Kaufmann Foundation, the Carnegie Corporation of New York, and the Spencer Foundation, the NRC established the Committee on the Study of Teacher Preparation Programs in the United States to carry out this work. The committee's charge was to answer four questions:

1. Who enters teacher preparation programs (preservice, graduate, and alternative)? What is their academic preparation? What is their educational background?
2. What type of instruction and experiences do participants receive in the preparation program? Who delivers it? To what extent is there commonality in content and experiences?
3. To what extent is the required coursework and experiences in reading, mathematics, and science across teacher preparation programs consistent with converging scientific evidence?
4. What model for data collection would provide valid and reliable information about the content knowledge, pedagogical competence, and effectiveness of graduates from the various kinds of teacher preparation programs?

We interpreted this charge as focusing on public school teachers both because they are the objects of public policy and because the majority of the research on teacher quality and teacher preparation also focuses on them. We recognize the vital contribution that private school teachers make, but more than 85 percent of students in the United States attend public schools.[1]

Broadly viewed, our charge was to review the scientific evidence that pertains to teacher preparation and to consider the data collection that will best support improvements to this critical element of the public education system. The goal, implicit in our charge, was to rely on findings that are the product of responsible scholarship. We faced several challenges, however. First, the available data relevant to our charge are patchy. Second, the task of applying empirical evidence to some of the questions raised complex conceptual issues, such as the challenge of linking teacher characteristics and preparation to measures of student outcomes. In pursuit of answers,

---

[1]In 2006, more than 49 million students were enrolled in public schools, just over 6 million were enrolled in private schools, and another 1.5 million were home schooled (see http://nces. ed.gov/quicktables/ [January 2010]). Career pathways and preparation for private school teachers may differ in significant ways from those of public school teachers, but these differences are not well documented.

we explored a wide range of materials, held searching discussions about what inferences could be drawn from different sorts of evidence, and commissioned reports to delve more deeply into specific questions.

The committee had six formal meetings and a range of other interactions in the course of our study. We considered presentations from people with a range of expertise and perspectives on methodological issues; on what knowledge, skills, and attributes teachers should have; on the nature of teacher preparation in a variety of jurisdictions; and on the nature of professions. We also held two workshops, one on teacher certification and licensure and the accreditation of teacher preparation programs, and the other on evidence related to the preparation of teachers of mathematics and science.

In order to probe more deeply into several of our study questions, we commissioned three additional analyses, two on teacher preparation programs and career pathways in two jurisdictions and one related to data collection. Grossman and colleagues (2008) investigated the specific characteristics of teacher preparation and the impact they may have on student achievement in New York City, and Sass (2008) conducted a similar analysis for Florida. Crowe (2007) provided an overview of the current state of data systems, data collection, and data quality relevant to the knowledge, skills, and effectiveness of program graduates, which assisted us in responding to the part of our charge that requested recommendations regarding a model for future data collection.

Our response to our charge has several parts. The remainder of this chapter provides an overview, covering the characteristics of those who enter the field, a brief history of teacher preparation designed to provide context for current pressing policy and research questions, and a few key points about the circumstances in which today's teachers work. We were asked a number of factual questions about the current state of scholarship on how teachers ought to be prepared, as well as what is known about how they are currently being prepared. Most of that information is presented in Chapters 3 through 8.

Since we were also asked to review the status of data collection and other kinds of research and to develop a framework to guide future work, we turn to that issue first in Chapter 2. The nature of the available literature, as well as conceptual questions about the sorts of inferences the committee could make from different kinds of material, were the subject of far more of the committee's deliberations than we had expected. These issues are important not only to our own deliberations, but also to a clear understanding of what it will take to improve teacher preparation.

In Chapter 3 we present what we have learned about the career pathways open to teacher candidates and the programs in which they are educated. In Chapters 4 through 7 we present our findings related to content preparation, in response to the second and third questions in our charge. Chapter 4 is an overview of issues that cut across the three school subjects we addressed. Chapters 5, 6, and 7 describe our findings related to reading, mathematics, and science, respectively. Chapter 8 examines the issues of accountability and quality control in teaching and their effect on teacher preparation.

In Chapter 9 we return to the issues raised in Chapter 2 in presenting our research agenda for the future and our concluding thoughts. A dissent to our report from committee member Michael Podgursky is Appendix A.

## ONE OF THE LARGEST OCCUPATIONS IN THE UNITED STATES

The 3.6 million elementary and secondary public school teachers working in the United States in 2006 made up more than 8.5 percent of all college-educated workers aged 25 to 64 years old (National Center for Education Statistics, http://nces.ed.gov/programs/digest/d08/tables/dt08_064. asp [November 2009]). By way of comparison, there were approximately 888,000 physicians, 1.0 million lawyers, and 2.9 million registered nurses practicing in the United States in 2007. Approximately 200,000 new teachers graduate each year, a pace that far outpaces that in any other profession. For example, just over 16,468 new doctors graduated from 128 medical schools in 2009 (http://www.aamc.org/data/facts/enrollmentgraduate/start. htm [January 2010]).

Although professional training is still not a universal requirement for aspiring teachers, by the 1950s it was common for public school teachers to receive at least some preservice professional education in a college or university setting (Fraser, 2007). Yet teacher education has never been standardized as it has been for some other occupations. Teaching has frequently been regarded as less than a full profession, and both the study of pedagogy and teacher preparation have been accorded less status than other professional or academic pursuits (National Research Council, 2008a). States' requirements for teacher qualifications and their governance of teacher preparation vary markedly, as we discuss in later chapters. Thus, like the public education system it serves, teacher preparation continues to be characterized by variation rather than standardization (Labaree, 2004; Fraser, 2007).

It is a substantial enterprise nevertheless. In 2004, more than 220,000 students completed a teacher preparation program (U.S. Department of Education, 2006). In 2006, 174,620 master's degrees were awarded in education, accounting for 29.4 percent of all the master's degrees awarded that year (National Center for Education Statistics, 2007); master's degrees in business were the second most numerous, at 142,617. An additional 107,238 education students earned bachelor's degrees that year, accounting for 7.2 percent of all bachelor's degrees that year (National Center for Education Statistics, 2007), and many more so-called alternative programs augment the numbers of new teachers.[2] Teach for America, a program that recruits recent graduates of the nation's most elite colleges and universities and provides them with training both before and after they enter the classroom, is perhaps the best known of these. Many school districts have established fellows' programs, which usually combine expedited entrance into teaching with tuition-supported enrollment in graduate study in education. There are numerous other models as well—by one count there are 130 pathways identified as "alternative" in the 50 states and the District of Columbia (U.S. Department of Education, 2006).

Yet universities still dominate: 70-80 percent of students who completed teacher preparation programs were enrolled in one of 1,096 programs situated in postsecondary institutions (U.S. Department of Education, 2006).[3] These programs typically include 4-year bachelor's degree programs and 1-year postbaccalaureate programs (see Chapter 3).

## CHARACTERISTICS OF TEACHERS

We were asked about the characteristics of those who enter teacher preparation programs and the extent to which their characteristics may vary across programs. We found little systematic information about teacher candidates as they enter preparation programs (see Chapters 5-7 for some program-specific research); more research attention has been paid to the characteristics of new teachers who enter the field. The National Center for Education Statistics recently initiated a longitudinal study of beginning teachers (see http://nces.ed.gov/surveys/btls/ [November 2009]), which will eventually provide information about the career pathways of teachers who have been prepared in different ways.

Other sources provide demographic data about teacher education students and the current public school teaching work force: these data were summarized by Zumwalt and Craig (2005). Confining their attention to studies and survey data published between 1985 and 2004 that used sample sizes and methodologies that were clearly described and strong enough to support their reported conclusions, Zumwalt and Craig were able to assemble a general picture of current teachers. We note that although this summary reflects data available through 2004, much of the information is from the 1980s and 1990s; we were not able to locate more up-to-date

---

[2]Distinguishing between "alternative" and "traditional" programs is so complex that the labels are no longer useful; see Chapter 3.

[3]Chapter 3 includes a more detailed discussion of the challenges of counting teacher preparation programs.

data. Zumwalt and Craig note that there is a significant time lag in the collection, release, and analysis of data about teachers and that there are significant gaps between data collection points. Because there is no comprehensive effort to collect data about teacher candidates, information about their characteristics is not precise. For example, Zumwalt and Craig note that because classifications of ethnic groups have changed over the years, they have little confidence even in the limited information they found on this characteristic.

The teaching work force remains overwhelmingly female: 75 percent in 2000. Although the percentage of female college graduates choosing to enter teaching dropped from 40 percent in 1970 to 11 percent in 1990, females are likely to continue dominating the field because they make up an even higher proportion (84 percent) of teachers in their 20s. Teacher education students are also overwhelmingly female, and aspiring elementary teachers are more likely to be female than aspiring secondary teachers. Available data provide varying estimates—between 67 and 80 percent—of all teacher education students.

Teachers are also predominantly white (84 percent); 7.8 percent are African American, 5.7 percent are Hispanic, 1.6 percent are Asian American, and 0.8 percent are Native American. Zumwalt and Craig (2005, p. 114) note that while these proportions have fluctuated slightly, "the diversity gap between students and teachers is large and widening." This claim is supported by the limited data that are available, which show, for example, that the number of nonwhite students earning bachelor's degrees in education declined by 50 percent between 1975 and 1982.

The proportions of teacher candidates of different ethnic backgrounds differ across regions and institutions: some studies show that alternative programs may attract higher proportions of African American students than traditional programs do. Because students tend to look for postsecondary options close to home, the distribution of population subgroups among teacher preparation programs partly reflects the make-up of the regions in which they live. African American students, whose families' incomes are lower than those of white students, are more likely to attend 2-year programs.

In terms of other characteristics, the average age of teacher education students has been increasing slightly, likely reflecting a greater number of postgraduate and alternative options. Teachers' socioeconomic status, as measured by their parents' educational attainment, has edged up, as has that of teacher education students, but this trend may simply reflect the increase in overall educational attainment in the United States over time. Data collected by the National Center for Education Statistics (1999) show that almost all teachers have a bachelor's degree, and that 45 percent have a master's degree. High school teachers are the most likely to have a degree in an academic field, rather than an education degree: 66 percent of high school teachers, 44 percent of middle school teachers, and 22 percent of elementary school teachers.

## A BRIEF HISTORY OF TEACHER EDUCATION

The scale of initial teacher preparation is daunting and highlights the policy challenge of increasing teacher quality. Many of the newer pathways that are now part of the nation's teacher preparation system were created in response to concerns about teacher quality. But much of the innovation in teacher preparation, whether in university-based programs or in other settings, has not been well documented, and, as discussed below, data have not been systematically collected to support firm conclusions about which programs produce effective teachers.

The extreme variation in the way U.S. teachers are prepared reflects the overlapping layers of authority and oversight in a system that has placed education firmly in the jurisdiction of state and local governments. Since Horace Mann took charge of the first state department of education in the Commonwealth of Massachusetts in the 1840s, state departments have added their authority on top of those of local school authorities. Passage of the Elementary and Secondary Education Act of 1965 (ESEA) broke through long-standing opposition to federal involvement in public education, and, more recently, NCLB, a revision of ESEA, greatly enlarged the federal role. However, the federal government has had little direct involvement in or influence on teacher preparation.

A brief look at the historical roots of teacher preparation in the United States sheds some light on its current nature and structure. Formal teacher training began with the establishment of normal schools during the mid-19th century. Between 1839 and 1865, 15 normal schools began operation; by 1890, there were 92 such schools (Lagemann, 2002; Ogren, 2005).[4] Beginning in 1879, colleges and universities also started to appoint special professors of pedagogy, and by the turn of the 20th century, universities that supported schools and colleges of education began to compete with normal schools for both aspiring teachers and state funds. Eventually, universities became dominant and normal schools either were incorporated into universities or began their slow evolution into state universities (Jencks and Reisman, 1967; Judge, 1982; Clifford and Guthrie, 1988; Herbst, 1989; Labaree, 2004; Fraser, 2007).

Complaints about teachers' lack of competence—and even ridicule of their shortcomings—date as far back as the colonial era (and are still heard regularly today) (Elsbree, 1939; Sedlak, 1989; Lagemann, 2002). Yet few

---

[4]Normal schools were those set up to prepare high school graduates to be teachers.

formal studies of teacher education appeared until early in the 20th century (many sponsored by private philanthropic organizations), and the quality of teaching did not become a matter of intense public policy concern until the 1950s and 1960s. In those years, concern about the lack of rigor in public schools led to challenges to the progressive educational practices that had been adopted in the 1930s. Such books as *Educational Wastelands: The Retreat from Learning in Our Public Schools* (Bestor, 1953), *The Diminished Mind* (Smith, 1954), *Education and Freedom* (Rickover, 1959), and *The Miseducation of American Teachers* (Koerner, 1965) offered a pessimistic view of teachers and their preparation. One response came from John W. Gardner, president of the Carnegie Corporation, who asked former Harvard University President James B. Conant to study teacher preparation and other aspects of public education. Conant (1963) concluded that the problem lay with the education classes teachers were required to take. He advocated that teachers be educated in master's degree programs, similar to one he had established at Harvard, in which students would study the liberal arts and experience supervised practice teaching (Lagemann, 1989).

The publication of *A Nation at Risk* (National Commission on Excellence in Education, 1983) initiated the longest sustained period of attention to public education in the nation's history and ignited a new wave of interest in teacher preparation. Using an alarmist style, the report described deficiencies in the public schools. Although diagnoses of the problem have shifted since the report was published, a consensus emerged that instruction was critical to student achievement and that both teacher quality and preparation needed to be addressed.

As a follow-up to that report, the Carnegie Task Force on Teaching as a Profession (1986) issued a report that made a number of recommendations designed to improve the quality of the nation's teaching force, one of which was to "develop a new professional curriculum in graduate schools of education leading to a Master's in Teaching degree, based on systematic knowledge of teaching and including internships and residencies in schools (p. 3). The report also called for the establishment of the National Board for Professional Teaching Standards (NBPTS), a body that would certify practicing teachers who meet standards of accomplished teaching (that is, teachers who have moved beyond entry-level skills and knowledge) as part of its broad goal of establishing a more professional environment for teachers and a career trajectory that would reward them for pursuing excellence.

The NBPTS has been operating for more than 20 years, but the Carnegie Task Force's recommendations for teacher education—like those Conant had made earlier—have not been systematically pursued (National Research Council, 2008a). Many other individuals and groups have also made recommendations about teacher preparation, yet it remains extremely varied and, as we discuss in subsequent chapters, difficult to characterize.

## A CHANGING STUDENT POPULATION

As views of how teachers ought to be prepared have shifted over time, other changes have affected the demands on practicing teachers—and, in turn, expectations for their preparation. We cannot address all of these changes here, but changes in the population of U.S. public school students and in views about the public schools' responsibility to students with varying needs have had particularly broad implications for teachers' work. Three changes have been particularly important: a commitment to high standards and college for all, increasing population diversity, and the Individuals with Disabilities Education Act (IDEA) of 1975.

The commitment to educate all students—particularly including those from historically underserved groups, such as minorities and students from low-income families—to high standards has had profound implications for public school teachers. The proportion of students graduating from high school grew from less than 10 percent in 1900 to about 75 percent by the 1970s. Today educators are expected to prepare every child to go on to postsecondary education—an idea that would have seemed preposterous 100 years ago (National Research Council, 2001c).

Some important implications of this commitment are evident when one contemplates the numbers of children who are living in poverty, including some who are homeless, and the ways in which their circumstances may affect their education.[5] High-poverty students are the most likely to be taught by teachers who are not well qualified, in part because high-poverty schools tend to see high teacher turnover (Clotfelter, Ladd, and Vigdor, 2007). Although some teacher preparation programs may focus attention on the needs of poor and homeless children, there are no systematically collected data on the subject.

With respect to the nation's fast-changing demographics, the word "diversity" may have lost some of its impact through overuse, but its implications for public education are very concrete. As the United States has experienced significant increases in immigration in recent decades, the number of young people for whom English is not their first language has grown, as has the geographic dispersion of those young people. Language and cultural diversity is not a new feature of U.S. schools. Education historians point

---

[5]In 2006, for example, 17 percent of children were living in families with incomes below the poverty line (see http://www.childtrendsdatabank.org/indicators/4Poverty.cfm [January 2010]), and it is estimated that between 5 and 8 percent of school-age children are homeless (see http://www.endhomelessness.org/content/article/detail/1659 [January 2010]).

to large numbers of immigrants in the first decades of the 20th century, especially in urban schools, and note that they had a significant influence on goals for public schooling, such as teaching citizenship, promoting student health, and providing vocational education (Editorial Projects in Education, 2000). However, the numbers, percentages, and geographical distribution of students who are immigrants or the children of recent immigrants have all expanded significantly in recent decades. In 2000, 20 percent of all children under 18 (11 million of the 58 million school-age children) in the United States had parents who were recent immigrants (Capps et al., 2005). As has historically been the case, the children of immigrants are concentrated in the largest states: California currently has the largest percentage of such children (47 percent), and New York and Texas also have significant percentages of such children and long immigrant traditions (Capps et al., 2005). But other states in regions that had previously had only very small numbers have seen dramatic increases in a very short time. Between 1990 and 2000, for example, Georgia, Illinois, Minnesota, Nevada, and North Carolina saw increases in their language-minority populations of more than 100 percent, and in some cases more than 200 percent. More than half of these students, 55 percent, come from Spanish-speaking countries; the next largest group, 25 percent, is from Asia; and 4 percent are from Africa (Capps et al., 2005).

The children of immigrants bring to the classroom a wide range of language and cultural traditions. Teachers may see these traditions as potential assets, rather than as deficits for learning, but these students nevertheless present challenges for teaching. These children vary in the educational experiences they have had prior to entering U.S. schools (if they are immigrants themselves), in their parents' level of education, and many other factors. A significant number have had their education interrupted—and are now identified as a distinct group, students with interrupted formal education. The majority of students who are English-language learners both live in linguistically isolated families (that is, families in which the adults are also English-language learners) and attend linguistically segregated schools. At the same time, however, many communities are home to students from multiple linguistic backgrounds, so teachers might be responsible for children who are speakers of several different languages in one class.

Speakers of dialects in regions around the country also present a challenge for many teachers; that is, some native students speak a "nonstandard" English that significantly affects their education. Like English-language learners, these students are likely to be reading below grade level and to lack the necessary vocabulary to succeed in academic subjects. Results from the National Assessment of Educational Progress and other education indicators consistently show that these students do not perform as well academically as their peers, and many studies document the deficiencies in their educational opportunities (Banks et al., 2005).

Though many would argue that every form of teacher preparation should incorporate the knowledge and skills needed to teach these students (Lucas and Grinberg, 2008), preparation in this domain is uneven at present. One study of the 1.2 million teachers (about 43 percent of all teachers) with "emergent bilinguals" (students not yet fluent in English) in their classrooms found that only 11 percent were certified in bilingual education; another 18 percent were certified in teaching English as a second language. On average, these 1.2 millions teachers had received 4 hours of in-service training for working with emergent bilinguals over the previous 5 years (Zehler et al., 2003). (Only 15 percent of these teachers were fluent in another language.) Although there are many challenges that complicate teachers' work, the diversity of the 21st-century classroom is a central one. The needs of English-language learners are of particular importance to teachers of reading, as we discuss in Chapter 5.

The inclusion of many more children with disabilities has been another very significant change for U.S. schools. Between 1984 and 1997, high school graduation rates for children with disabilities increased significantly (see http://www.ed.gov/policy/speced/leg/idea/history.html [November 2009]). Public schools have also moved from accommodating almost no students with disabilities to accommodating most of them. For these students, 1975 was a landmark year: passage of the Education for All Handicapped Children Act, which mandated that children who were deaf, blind, emotionally disturbed, or mentally retarded could no longer be excluded from neighborhood schools.

Today, the legislation governing students with disabilities requires specified educational services, mostly provided within a regular school setting. Prior to its enactment, children with disabilities were more likely to be excluded from public education or given only limited access to it. The law was designed to address specific challenges to providing an equitable education for these students, by, for example, requiring the development of individual education plans to meet students' needs, training for teachers, and programs designed to be relevant for families of different cultural backgrounds with disabled children (U.S. Office of Special Education Programs, no date). In the 2006-2007 school year, 6.7 million children, approximately 9 percent of the population aged 3 to 21 in the United States, were receiving educational services as required by IDEA, and these students comprised approximately 11.5 percent of students enrolled in prekindergarten through 12th grade (National Research Council, 2004; see http://nces.ed.gov/fastfacts/display. asp?id=59 [February 2010]).

The needs of the students with disabilities who are served by public schools vary dramatically. One-half have some sort of learning disability, ranging from mild to quite severe. Other disabilities include speech or language impairments, physical disabilities, cognitive disabilities, mild to severe medical and emotional disabilities, and injuries (National Research Council, 2004). Although states and districts vary in their criteria for diagnosing disabilities and in the specific policies through which they implement the IDEA requirements, it is clear that teachers face far different challenges than they did prior to IDEA and that many teachers are responsible for students with a wide range of disabilities. Overall, the work of teachers has become more and more complex as the nation pursues the goal of equal, and equally high-quality, education for all students.

# 2

# Seeking Strong Evidence

The committee's charge was to consider the scientific evidence on teacher preparation and to design an agenda for the research that is needed to provide the knowledge for improving that preparation. We found many different kinds of evidence that relate to teacher preparation: as we sifted through the available work, we repeatedly confronted questions about evidentiary standards. At times we struggled to agree on whether particular kinds of information constituted evidence and on the sorts of inferences that could be drawn from different kinds of evidence. This chapter describes the issues we identified and our approach to them.

## APPROACHES TO RESEARCH DESIGN AND EVIDENCE

Much has been written about the problems of conducting research in education, specifically about the appropriateness of various research designs and methods and ways to interpret their results. In general, we are in agreement with the approach to research in education described in the National Research Council (NRC) (2002a) report *Scientific Research in Education*. In particular, that report identified six principles that should guide, but not dictate, the design of research in education:

1. Pose significant questions that can be investigated empirically.
2. Link research to relevant theory.
3. Use methods that permit direct investigation of the question.
4. Provide a coherent and explicit chain of reasoning.

5.  Replicate and generalize across studies.
6.  Disclose research to encourage professional scrutiny and critique.

The application of these principles to questions about teacher preparation poses particular conceptual and empirical challenges:

- There are no well-formed theories that link teacher preparation to student outcomes.
- The complex nature of schooling children makes it difficult to identify empirically the role of teacher preparation among the many intertwined influences on student outcomes.
- The use of strict experimental design principles can be problematic in some educational settings. Teacher candidates are sorted into teacher preparation programs in nonrandom ways, just as beginning teachers are nonrandomly sorted into schools and groups of students: consequently, it is difficult to control for all the important factors that are likely to influence student outcomes.

Improving learning outcomes for children is a complex process. Both common sense and sophisticated research (e.g., Sanders and Rivers, 1996; Aaronson, Barrow, and Sander, 2003; Rockoff, 2004; Rivkin, Hanushek, and Kain, 2005; Kane, Rockoff, and Staiger, 2006) indicate that teachers have enormously important effects on children's learning and that the quality of teaching explains a meaningful proportion of the variation in achievement among children. However, understanding that teachers are important to student outcomes and understanding how and why teachers influence outcomes are very different; our charge required us to think carefully about the *evidence* of the effects of teacher preparation. Student learning is affected by numerous factors besides teaching, many of which are beyond the control of the educational system. Even the factors that are affected by education policy involve intricate interactions among teachers, administrators, students, and their peers.[1]

Disentangling the role that *teachers* play in influencing student outcomes is difficult, and understanding the ways in which *teacher education* influences student outcomes is much more difficult. The design and the delivery of teacher education are connected to outcomes for K-12 students through a series of choices made by teacher educators and by teacher candidates in their roles as students and, later, as teachers. Identifying the empirical effects of teacher preparation on student outcomes poses many

---

[1] We note the progress that has been made in exploring causal relationships in education in new work supported by the Department of Education and in work synthesized by the What Works Clearinghouse (see http://ies.ed.gov/ncee/wwc/ [September 2009]).

of the problems that arise in most social science research, including: (1) the development of empirical measures of the important constructs, (2) accounting for the heterogeneous behavioral responses of individuals, and (3) the nonrandom assignment of treatments (teacher preparation) in the observable data. As in other social science research, the challenge of developing convincing evidence of the causal relationship between the preparation of teacher candidates and the outcomes of their K-12 students places strong demands on theory, research designs, and empirical models.

Some of these challenges are illustrated in Figure 2-1. Teacher candidates bring certain abilities, knowledge, and experiences with them as they enter teacher preparation programs. These differences likely vary within and across programs. The candidates then experience a variety of learning opportunities as part of their teacher education. Again, these experiences and the resulting knowledge and skills likely vary within and across programs. After completing their training, candidates who pursue teaching likely enter classrooms that vary greatly within and across schools on a variety of dimensions, including the characteristics of students, the curriculum, the school climate, and the neighborhood climate. Each source of variation affects individual student achievement: taken together, they com-

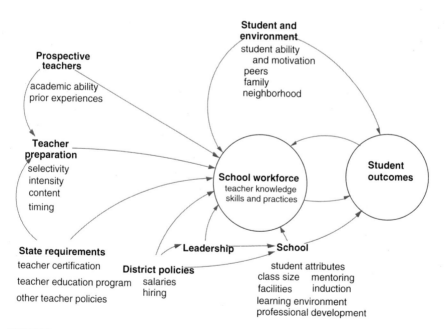

FIGURE 2-1 A model of the effects of teacher preparation on student achievement.
SOURCE: Adapted from Boyd et al. (2006, p. 159).

plicate the search for the empirical relationship between teacher education and student outcomes.

We note that establishing the chain of causation is a challenge not only in the field of education. Researchers and policy makers in medicine and in many other social science fields struggle to design studies that yield dependable results when carried out in real-world circumstances and to make sound decisions in the absence of a clear or complete evidentiary base (see, e.g., Sackett et al., 1996; Murnane and Nelson, 2007; Kilburn and Karoly, 2008; Leigh, 2009). Common to many fields is the challenge of thinking systematically about different sorts of evidence related to a question involving complex interactions of human behavior, which may not only vary in strength, but also vary in the mechanisms (or potential causes) about which they provide information. It is also the case that in many social science fields, as well as education, researchers have worked creatively to develop quasi-experimental research designs and other ways of making use of available data in order to examine empirical questions in complex real-world circumstances. Understanding of the nature of scientific evidence in education (and other fields) is evolving, and the diverse methodological backgrounds of the committee members enabled us to consider the issues broadly.[2] We considered all of these issues as we weighed different kinds of studies and other available resources related to teacher preparation.

## CAUSAL EVIDENCE

At the heart of many differences of opinion about the available research on teacher preparation (as on many topics in education) are questions about the strength of causal inferences to be made from it. One important purpose of research on teacher preparation is to provide an empirical basis for changes to policy and practice regarding the structure, content, and timing of teacher preparation, and many research methods can contribute to causal understanding. Causal understanding is built upon a body of research that usually begins with descriptive analysis and empirical efforts to identify correlations, and the development of competing theories of behavior. Refinements and adjustments are made to theoretical and empirical

---

[2]Katz and Singer (2007) developed an approach that uses abductive reasoning to integrate complex sets of qualitative and quantitative evidence related to a set of competing hypotheses. This approach integrates the different types of evidence by considering both their relative empirical strength and their relevance to the different hypotheses. The result is a systematic account of the overall strength of the evidentiary base for each of the competing hypotheses, which may clearly identify the hypothesis with the strongest overall explanatory power. This approach was developed in the context of the literature on expert systems and has been applied in military intelligence, medical diagnosis, and molecular biology, among other fields, but has not been widely used in the social sciences (see also Singer, 2008).

models as alternative explanations are explored. Causal understanding is built on a converging body of evidence that includes research designs that support causal inference, such as random assignment of subjects to treatment and control.

Although there has rightly been much focus recently on research that uses random assignment and other methods that produce direct causal evidence, qualitative and other quantitative methods that describe institutions, participants, and outcomes also provide valuable information. Descriptive methods (whether qualitative or quantitative) shed light on the factors and forces that may affect student outcomes. Correlation does not necessarily imply cause, but it may provide useful guidance in ruling out competing alternative explanations. When combined with theory, such methods contribute to the identification and development of research hypotheses and point to methods that can identify a causal relationship between a policy and an outcome. In addition, descriptive analyses can provide information that explains the chain of behaviors that lead to various student outcomes. Because different methods have different strengths and weaknesses, it is important to seek converging evidence that draws on multiple methods. We expand below on the challenges of identifying causal pathways—as well as the strengths and weaknesses of different research methods—in the context of a hypothetical example about the impact of coursework on teachers of mathematics.

## The Complexity of Analysis: An Example

Suppose policy makers are interested in understanding whether teacher preparation that includes rigorous mathematics coursework leads to higher mathematics achievement among students. There are a variety of research designs that could be used to explore this relationship. One would be to identify the teacher preparation programs in which math content is more rigorous than in other programs and compare the math achievement of the students taught by the graduates of the more rigorous program with the students taught by the teachers who completed the less rigorous math programs. However, without careful statistical controls, this simple comparison may well yield a misleading result because the other characteristics of teachers, their students, and schools that influence achievement outcomes may themselves be correlated with teachers' mathematics preparation.

To see how misleading results can occur, consider that parents have control over which schools their children attend; teachers have control over the schools in which they choose to work; and principals have control over the teachers they hire. Each of these choices influences which teachers teach which students, and there is evidence that these choices lead to quite different outcomes across schools in a variety of settings (see, e.g., Betts, Reuben, and Danenberg, 2000; Lankford et al., 2002; Clotfelter et al., 2006; Peske and Haycock, 2006). Teachers who score higher on measures of academic ability and teacher preparation are usually found in schools in which students come from more advantaged backgrounds and score better on achievement tests. This nonrandom sorting of teachers and their characteristics to students with systematically different achievement complicates the identification of the effect of preparation on student outcomes. Thus, one may not be able to draw valid conclusions about the effects of treatments from studies that do not adequately control for these confounding effects.

Researchers sometimes propose the inclusion of readily available measures in a statistical model to control for these kinds of differences, but this approach may not resolve the uncertainty. A variety of other important but very difficult-to-measure characteristics of students, teachers, or schools can also confound the understanding of teachers' mathematics preparation. For example, parents who believe that education is very important to their children are likely not only to seek out schools where they believe their children will receive the best education, but also to provide other advantages that improve their children's achievement. Teachers also make choices about how they approach their teaching, and those who make investments in rigorous mathematics preparation may also be more likely to engage in other activities (such as professional development) that support their students' learning. Many teachers find it rewarding to work in schools where students are inquisitive and have good study skills. Principals in these schools will have strong applicant pools for vacancies and will hire the most qualified applicants. As a result, one cannot determine whether better prepared teachers lead to better student outcomes or whether the presence of students who are very likely to succeed is among the school characteristics that attract and retain better prepared teachers. Because rigorous math preparation is correlated with such difficult-to-measure attributes of teachers, students, and schools, isolating the causal effect of rigorous mathematics preparation is very difficult. The difficulty may not be overcome even with the assistance of multiple regression models that control for a long list of readily available variables. This is the challenge that often leads researchers to turn to various other research designs.

## Randomized and Quasi-Experimental Designs

The strongest case for a causal relationship can often be made when randomization is used to control for differences that cannot be easily measured and controlled for statistically. In the context of our example about the impact of the teachers' mathematics coursework, the ideal case would be to randomly assign teacher candidates to different forms of mathematics coursework and then to randomly assign those teachers to different schools and students. If such a research design were both feasible and implemented well, a strong evaluation of the effectiveness of rigorous math preparation would be possible. When assignment is truly random, any possible effects of variation in the treatment (e.g., in the rigor of mathematics content preparation) will be evident despite variation in all of the other possible influences on student achievement. That is, any observed effect of the treatment on the outcome could be assumed to be a result of the treatment, rather than of other factors that may be unmeasured but are correlated with the treatment. For many research questions and contexts, random assignment experimental designs provide very strong internal validity when implemented well, and they are thus sometimes referred to as the "gold standard" of evaluation techniques.

However, randomized experimental designs have some potential shortcomings. Most significant is that such designs are not a feasible or appropriate research design in some education settings. To continue the example above, experimentally manipulating the extent of mathematics content preparation a teacher receives may be difficult, but it is possible. Randomly assigning those teachers across a wide range of student abilities may prove more difficult. Random assignment is also susceptible to other potentially confounding factors, such as when some parents respond to their perceptions about teacher quality by adjusting other factors, such as their own contribution toward student achievement. Also troubling is the challenge of accounting for the important individualized interactions that occur between teachers and students that lead to high student achievement. Finally, many experiments are designed tightly around a particular treatment and counterfactual case (that is, hypotheses about what the circumstances would be without the treatment). If well executed, the experiment provides very strong evidence for this specific question, but typically such experiments have limited ability to generalize to other settings (external validity) (Shadish, Cook, and Campbell, 2002; Morgan and Winship, 2007). In addition, random assignment experiments are expensive and time-consuming to carry out, which places practical constraints on the information this method has been able to provide. In general, random assignment is an important and underused research design in education; however, its strength—possibly providing clearer information about causal relationships—must be weighed against the difficulties in carrying out and generalizing from such studies.

Other research designs, often called quasi-experimental, use observational data to capitalize on naturally occurring variation (Campbell and Stanley, 1963; Cook and Campbell, 1986). These methods use varying approaches to attempt to mimic the ways in which randomized designs control the variation.[3] For example, a technique called regression discontinuity analysis, an alternative method developed for the evaluation of social programs and more recently applied to educational interventions, uses statistical procedures to correct for possible selection bias and support an estimate of causal impact (see, e.g., Bloom et al., 2005). Such approaches work well when they can convincingly rule out competing explanations for changes in student achievement that might otherwise be identified as an effect of the factor being investigated. Thus these approaches work best when researchers have a strong understanding of the underlying process (in this case, both the content of teacher preparation and the other forces that shape the relationship between teacher preparation and K-12 student achievement) and can explore the validity of competing explanations (National Research Council, 2002a, p. 113; Morgan and Winship, 2007). Theory and descriptive analysis, including quantitative and qualitative studies, as well as the opinions of experts, all contribute to such an understanding.

A method that attempts to control for many alternative explanations and is receiving increasing attention especially in examining issues of teacher preparation is the value-added model of student achievement. We examine this method in a bit more detail.

## Value-Added Models

Value-added modeling is a method for using data about changes in student achievement over time as a measure of the value that teachers or schools have added to their students' learning. The appeal of value-added methods is the promise they offer of using statistical techniques to adjust for unmeasured differences across students. Doing so would make it possible to identify a measure of student learning that can be attributed to individual teachers and schools. This approach generally requires very large databases because researchers must statistically isolate the student achievement data from data on other student attributes that could affect achievement (such as the students' prior achievement or the characteristics of their peers) to control for the confounding factors identified in Figure 2-1. The models typically include a variety of controls intended to account for many of the competing explanations of the link between teacher preparation and student achievement. The recent availability of district and statewide databases that link teachers to their students' achievement scores (Crowe, 2007) has made this analysis feasible. However, there is substantial debate in the research community about this approach (Kane and Staiger, 2002; McCaffery et al., 2003; Rivkin, 2007; National Research Council, 2010).

---

[3]For a more detailed discussion of quasi-experimental designs, see Shadish, Cook, and Campbell (2002); Morgan and Winship (2007).

There are concerns that value-added methods do not adequately disentangle the role of individual teachers or their characteristics from other factors that influence student achievement. That is, they may not statistically control for the full range of potential confounding factors depicted in Figure 2-1 (Rothstein, 2009). Accurate identification of these effects is complicated by the nonrandom assignment of teachers to schools and students, both across and within schools. In addition, there are concerns about measures of student outcomes and accurate measurement of teacher preparation attributes. For example, there is concern that commonly used measures of student achievement may assess only a portion of the knowledge and skills that are viewed as important for students to learn. It may also be the case that currently available measures of what constitutes teacher preparation are inadequate representations of the underlying concepts. Another concern is that student achievement tests developed in the context of high-stakes accountability goals may provide a distorted understanding of the factors that influence student achievement. While the tests themselves may be well designed, the stakes attached to their results may cause teachers to focus disproportionately on students who are scoring near the cut-points associated with high stakes, at the expense of students who are performing substantially above or below those thresholds.

All of these are important concerns that may affect the ability to draw inferences from the estimated model. As with any research design, value-added models may provide convincing evidence or limited insights, depending on how well the model fits the research question and how well it is implemented. Value-added models may provide valuable information about effective teacher preparation, but not definitive conclusions, and are best considered together with other evidence from a variety of perspectives.

## Qualitative and Descriptive Analyses

Qualitative and descriptive analyses also have much to contribute. Proper interpretation of the outcomes of experimental designs and the statistical approaches described above are dependent on the clear identification of the treatment and its faithful implementation. Theory, case studies, interpretive research, descriptive quantitative analysis, expert judgment, interviews, and observational protocols all help to identify promising treatments and can provide important insights about the mechanisms by which a treatment may lead to improved student outcomes. For example, if it appears that stronger mathematics preparation for teachers is associated with improved math outcomes for students, there is good reason to broaden and deepen the analysis with additional descriptive evidence from other contexts and ultimately to develop research designs to investigate the potential causal links.

As detailed in later chapters, there is more descriptive research available concerning teacher education than other forms of information. Indeed, many policy and program initiatives related to teacher quality and preparation have emerged in the past 20 years, and there has been a great deal of interest in the content and effects of teacher education. Professional societies in the academic disciplines have taken seriously their responsibility to offer guidance both about what students should learn and the knowledge and skills teachers need in order to develop that learning in their students, and they have drawn on both research and the intellectual traditions of their fields in doing so. We return in subsequent chapters to questions about what can be concluded from this literature, but these contributions to the discourse on teacher preparation have identified promising approaches and pointed to the mechanisms that seem likely to have the greatest influence on teacher quality. They also allow the field to refine testable hypotheses and to develop sophisticated, nuanced questions for empirical study.

## CONCLUSION

Although there has been a great deal of research on teacher education (for summaries, see Wilson, Floden, and Ferrini-Mundy, 2001; Cochran-Smith and Zeichner, 2005; Darling-Hammond and Bransford, 2005), few issues are considered settled. As a result, the field has produced many exciting research projects that are exploring a variety of ways of gaining evidence. For many questions, researchers are grappling with fundamental issues of theory development, formulating testable hypotheses, developing research designs to empirically test these theories, trying to collect the necessary data, and examining the properties of a variety of emerging empirical models.

Given the dynamic state of the research, we chose to examine a range of research designs, bearing in mind the norms of social science research, and to assess the accumulated evidence. Some research methods have greater internal or external validity than others, but each has limitations; polarized discussions that focus only on the strengths or weaknesses of a particular method have contributed little to understanding of important research questions. We concluded that the accumulated evidence from diverse methods applied in diverse settings would increase our confidence in any particular findings.

Ideally, policy makers would base policy on a body of strong empirical evidence that clearly converges on particular courses of action. In practice, policy decisions are often needed before the research has reached that state. Public scrutiny of deficiencies in teacher preparation has inspired many new program and policy initiatives that have, in turn, generated a great deal of information. Unfortunately, like most innovations in education, many of these initiatives have not been coupled with rigorous research programs to collect good data on these programs, the fidelity of their implementation, or their effects. Thus, although policy makers may need to make decisions with incomplete information, the weaker the causal evidence, the more cautiously they should approach these decisions and the more insistent they should be about supporting research efforts to study policy experiments. We return to this point in Chapter 9 in our discussion of a proposed research agenda.

# 3

# Pathways to Teaching and Teacher Preparation Programs

To understand how teachers are prepared, it is necessary to understand not only the nature of the education they receive in formal programs, but also the broader pathways through which they can enter the profession, which generally include some kind of teaching experience. We begin our overview of these two aspects of preparation with two observations. First, comprehensive data on U.S. teacher preparation in general are scant (Corcoran et al., 2004; Corcoran, 2007; Crowe, 2007). Thus, many basic questions about programs and pathways were surprisingly difficult to answer.

Second, although there are federal mandates related to teachers and their preparation—the most well known of which is the "highly qualified teacher" provision in the 2001 No Child Left Behind Act—states have the primary responsibility for policies pertaining to teachers. The states set standards for teachers as well as the requirements for teacher certification[1] (National Association of State Directors of Teacher Education and Certification, 2000). States are also responsible for approving or accrediting teacher education programs and for authorizing, sponsoring, and monitoring newer pathways into teaching, often labeled "alternative" (Johnson et al., 2005; Feistritzer and Haar, 2008). States' approaches to each of these responsibilities vary significantly, so that the options available to aspiring

---

[1]We use the terms licensure, certification, and credentialing interchangeably because states are not consistent in their usage. We discuss this aspect of teacher preparation in more detail in Chapter 8.

teachers look very different from one state to the next. This variety has complicated others' efforts to collect data and conduct comparative analyses, and it has also complicated our work.

We have drawn on a range of sources for our description of pathways and programs, and two recent major reports were particularly useful for this and subsequent chapters. A committee formed by the National Academy of Education was asked to articulate the knowledge base for teaching and to make research-based recommendations about how core knowledge could be incorporated into the curricula of teacher education programs and to develop "professional and scholarly consensus based on research about learning, teacher learning, and teacher education." The resulting report (Darling-Hammond and Bransford, 2005)—which drew on basic research on learning, research on the influences of different conditions on learning, research on the kinds of teacher education that are associated with particular instructional practices or student learning, and research on how teachers learn—described what kinds of teacher knowledge and experiences appear to be most valuable in promoting student learning.

Another report issued in 2005 focused on the somewhat different challenge of synthesizing the research on a variety of policies and practices in teacher preparation programs. Developed by a committee of the American Educational Research Association (AERA), the study (Cochran-Smith and Zeichner, 2005) considered such issues as the characteristics and demographics of student populations, coursework in both the arts and sciences and in pedagogy, field experiences and pedagogical approaches, means of preparing teachers to work with diverse student populations, among others. The chapter authors drew on the expertise of many scholars to assess the research base in each area, applying a consistent set of criteria for evaluating the studies available, and to provide critical summaries of the findings. These two volumes, together with some promising new lines of research on teacher preparation, have begun to lay the groundwork for a research base on teacher education, and we have drawn on them throughout our report.[2]

## PATHWAYS TO TEACHING

We look first at teachers' career pathways, the routes by which teacher candidates can obtain a license to teach. The distinction between programs and pathways is not precise, but in general pathways refers to broad categories of preparation, while programs are specific courses of study or experiences sponsored by a particular institution. There are numerous path-

---

[2]Of particular note is the Pathways Project, a collaboration among economists and teacher educators at the University at Albany and Stanford University: see http://www.teacherpolicy research.org/TeacherPathwaysProject/tabid/81/Default.aspx [September 2009].

ways into teaching, and this has long been the case (Fraser, 2007). Many types of educational institutions—including normal schools and school districts—were offering varied teacher training programs more than 100 years ago. The range of pathways has expanded recently, and a shorthand distinction has come into common usage between "traditional" and "alternative" pathways and programs. The former generally refers to those that are housed in colleges and universities and lead to a BA or an MA degree (and are thus sometimes referred to as "college recommending"). The latter is a catch-all for other pathways, particularly newer ones that have been designed to bring candidates who lack certain credentials into teaching.

The distinction arose in part because many of the newer pathways are viewed, in a political sense, as challenges to a stagnant *status quo*. It has not proved very useful, however, because there is considerable overlap in practice between the two categories, and there can be as much variation within pathways as across them (Wilson, Floden, and Ferrini-Mundy, 2001; Zeichner and Conklin, 2005; Humphrey, Weschler, and Hough, 2008). And many of the putative distinctions between alternative and traditional pathways are blurred at the program level. In one recent study, for example, aptly titled "Alternative Certification Isn't Alternative," the authors (Walsh and Jacobs, 2007) concluded that the required coursework and other educational experiences of an alternative pathway often take place in schools of education and are similar if not exactly the same as traditional pathways in many states.

## Variety Within and Among States

Examples from several states illustrate the variation among states in their definitions of pathways and in the characteristics of their pathways. Pathways may vary in the way teacher candidates are selected (and in the rigor of the entry requirements), their intensity, and the duration of the training required. For example, Texas has established an Alternative Teacher Certification (ATC) route—a pathway that is in many ways distinct from the one that takes students through state college and university programs. But the ATC authorizes a variety of institutions, including school districts, higher education institutions, and state-run regional education service centers, to design and run certain certification programs. Each ATC program may determine its entry requirements, the duration of the training, and other factors (Mayer et al., 2003). Similarly, in Louisiana, the Board of Elementary and Secondary Education sets parameters for its approved alternative pathways into teaching, but the individual programs differ substantially (Noell, 2008).

New York State has defined several pathways for prospective teachers, as shown in Table 3-1. In practice, there is overlap among these pathways.

**TABLE 3-1** Career Pathways for Teachers in New York State

| Pathway | Requirements |
|---|---|
| Undergraduate or Graduate College- or University-Based Programs | Programs require an average of 40 coursework credits and field experience hours, as well as independent student teaching (with a minimum of 32 credits completed prior to student teaching). |
| Individual Evaluations | Also known as transcript review, it is designed for people who are changing careers, people educated outside the United States, and others who choose not to enroll in a more formal preparation program. The state confirms that candidates have completed required coursework, examinations, and experience. |
| Temporary License | Temporary licenses, which were made available in response to teacher shortages, required little preservice preparation through September 2003. Modified temporary licenses, which required completion of the Liberal Arts and Science Test (LAST) and at least 27 hours of coursework in the content or pedagogical core for the certificate subject, were available for the 2003-2004 and 2004-2005 school years. |
| Transition B Certificates | Created to replace temporary licenses, this requires candidates to be enrolled in an alternative route program, such as NYC Teaching Fellows, Teach for America, Troops to Teachers, and the Teacher Opportunity Program, among others. Candidates complete summer preservice experience, including coursework and field experience, before becoming teachers of record and must complete additional certification requirements within 3 years. |

SOURCE: Information from Grossman et al. (2008).

For instance, a New York City Teaching Fellow would likely complete his or her MA degree at one of the same institutions at which aspiring teachers can complete a "traditional" program. Overall, the content of the coursework and experiences a prospective teacher has may be identical or very similar across different pathways.

Florida also offers numerous pathways, as shown in Table 3-2. In addition to temporary certificates, which are valid for 3 years and not renewable, there are multiple pathways to a professional teaching certificate.

Like New York and Florida, most states now offer an array of pathways for teacher candidates. A database maintained by a group that advocates for alternative teaching pathways, the National Center for Alternative Certification, shows the options available in each state (see http://www.

**TABLE 3-2** Career Pathways for Teachers in Florida

| Pathway | Certificate Requirement Options |
|---|---|
| Graduation from Florida Teacher Preparation Program | Candidates earn a BA or MA degree in teacher preparation program in a Florida college or university and pass certification exam. |
| Course Analysis | Candidates with a degree in a field other than education earn certification through approved college professional training or professional preparation college courses. Candidates must complete core education courses, obtain teaching experience, and pass certification exams. |
| Certification from Another State | Florida has full reciprocity with other states, recognizing their certification, as well as NBPTS[a] certification. |
| Graduation from an Out-of-State Teacher Preparation Program | Candidates earn a BA or MA degree in a teacher preparation program from a college or university in another state and pass the Florida certification exams. |
| District-Level Alternative Certification Program | Candidates complete district-level program and pass Florida certification exam. |
| Other | Candidates with a BA degree may earn certification with one of the following:<br>• ABCTE[b] passport certificate;<br>• two semesters of full-time college teaching experience and passing the Florida subject certification exam in their field; or<br>• a certificate from an Educator Preparation Institute, typically based in a community college and passing the Florida certification exams.<br>This new pathway was designed to help districts fill vacancies. |

[a]National Board for Professional Teaching Standards.
[b]American Board for Certification of Teacher Excellence.
SOURCES: Data from Sass (2008) and Florida Department of Education (see http://www.fldoe.org/administrators/educatorcertification.asp [April 2010]).

teach-now.org/map.html [September 2009]). Many of the newer options were developed to attract new candidates in areas where there are shortages (see http://www.bls.gov/oco/ocos069.htm#training [September 2009]); others are designed to recruit candidates who might not otherwise have considered teaching. Some—such as Teach for America (TFA), the American Board for Certification of Teacher Excellence (ABCTE) Program, or Troops to Teachers—are national. Others are developed in states; most states also have reciprocity arrangements, which allow relocating teachers to bypass some requirements.

## Variety Within Pathways

There is considerable variation within as well as between pathways. College- or university-based programs, for example, can be 4 or 5 years in duration; they may offer a baccalaureate or master's degree or both; they may include many institutional partners, both on and off campus; they may enroll handfuls or hundreds of prospective teachers; they may train elementary or middle or secondary teachers for a range of subject-matter teaching certificates; they have different philosophies about and approaches to teaching and teacher education.

Community colleges have become increasingly pivotal players in teacher education, as more and more prospective teachers obtain their first 2 years of general training at these institutions. For example, in 2006, more than half of the teachers graduating from traditional teacher education programs in Florida were transfers from community colleges (Coulter and Vandal, 2007). In addition, some alternative programs are housed in community colleges, at which post-baccalaureate students who have noneducation degrees can enroll in 2-year programs to earn the credit hours necessary for teacher licensure in their state (Coulter and Vandal, 2007).

There is at least as much variety among alternative pathways (Feistritzer, 2006; Walsh and Jacobs, 2007; Humphrey, Weschler, and Hough, 2008). In the 1980s, states started providing what amounted to emergency certification to fill classroom vacancies in specific fields (e.g., mathematics or special education) or in types of schools (e.g., those in urban or rural locations), and these emergency certification routes came to be labeled "alternative." Over time, however, these newer routes to certification have become a vehicle for state innovation in teacher credentialing—what has been called a "national experiment in how best to attract, prepare and train teachers" (Boyd et al., 2005, p. 212).

In sum, "alternative" pathways—such as the Teaching Fellows Program, TFA, or state approaches to issuing temporary licenses—differ quite substantially in structure, requirements, and candidate pools (Johnson et al., 2005; Walsh and Jacobs, 2007). The National Center for Alternative Certification developed 11 classifications for these programs, covering in purpose, admissions criteria, and other features. For example, one category includes "those routes that enable a person who has some 'special' qualifications, such as a well-known author or Nobel Prize winner, to teach certain subjects," while another includes "post-baccalaureate programs based at an institution of higher education" (see http://www.teach-now.org/classes.html [November 2009]). These classifications illustrate the range available, and, depending on state policy, a particular program might be labeled traditional in one state and alternative in another. And as noted above, many alternative programs are closely linked to postsecondary institutions: for example, in New York, participants in both the Teaching Fellows and TFA programs complete their coursework in universities.

## The Effects of Pathways

Empirical evidence has demonstrated the commonsense observation that all K-12 teachers are not equally effective (Sanders and Rivers, 1996; Aaronson, Barrow and Sander, 2003; Rockoff, 2004; Rivkin, Hanushek, and Kane, 2005; Kane, Rockoff, and Staiger, 2006), and so it seems reasonable to ask whether some pathways produce better, that is, more effective, teachers. In particular, observers of the various teacher preparation options have wondered whether less traditional pathways yield less prepared teachers, or, alternatively, whether such pathways attract excellent teachers who would otherwise not have entered the field. But because the distinctions among pathways are not distinct, high-stakes policy debates about the most effective ways to recruit, train, and retain high-quality teachers remain muddled.

To date, only a handful of studies have attempted to explore whether teachers prepared in "traditional" pathways are more or less effective than those prepared in "alternative" pathways. The evidence from this limited research base is mixed. Summaries of studies using a range of designs suggest little to no difference between the two (Wilson, Floden, and Ferrini-Mundy, 2001; Allen, 2003; Zeichner and Conklin, 2005), but several studies, including one that used a randomized control design (Glazerman, Meyer, and Decker, 2006), have identified small differences (Boyd et al., 2005; Xu, Hannaway, and Taylor, 2008).

A newly released study from the National Center for Education Evaluation (Constantine et al., 2009), in which students were randomly assigned to teachers trained through traditional or alternative routes (defined as those who do or do not complete all their training before they began teaching) also found little difference. The study reported no statistically significant difference in student outcomes that could be correlated with the type of training the teachers had received or the amount of coursework they had completed. The study did find that the students of teachers who were taking courses while teaching performed slightly less well on mathematics tests. The study also confirmed that there is considerable diversity within pathways, and the authors concluded that they could not identify aspects of preparation pathways that account for observed differences in teachers' effects on students' achievement.

In another study that used a randomized control design, Glazerman, Meyer, and Decker (2006) compared outcomes for teachers trained by TFA with outcomes for a control group of teachers who were not—a group that included teachers certified through "traditional" and other "alternative" programs, as well as teachers who were not certified. They found small improvements in the mathematics scores for the students of TFA teachers, but they also found more reports of behavior and other classroom management problems for the TFA teachers. Their conclusion was that TFA provides policy makers with a useful way of recruiting teachers for hard-to-staff schools and does not appear to lower teacher quality in those schools. We note that because the control group in this study distinguished only certified and noncertified teachers, and thus mixed several types of non-TFA teachers—those who came through traditional and other alternative paths, for example—the findings are not clear. For example, the finding that TFA teachers had students with slightly better mathematics scores could have resulted from those teachers having much stronger mathematics preparation prior to their teacher training, rather than from differences between the TFA and other training.

Finally, there have also been a number of studies that examined possible differences in the effectiveness of teachers who do or do not earn master's degrees. In two separate reviews and summaries of this work, Harris and Sass (2008) and Hanushek (2003) found little overall difference in the effectiveness of teachers who do and do not have this degree. Clotfelter, Ladd, and Vigdor (2007) conducted a study of the relative effectiveness of teachers with different academic credentials (including years of experience, test scores, certification status, and undergraduate and graduate degrees) in North Carolina (using statistical procedures to help overcome the fact that teachers are not randomly assigned to different sorts of students). They found that a graduate degree by itself was not predictive of higher achievement for students (though possession of any degree from a highly competitive institution was associated with greater effectiveness). However, the students of teachers who had stronger combinations of credentials, including educational credentials, had higher levels of achievement.

In general, this body of work seems to be moving toward the conclusion that, like the "traditional" and "alternative" designations, an MA in education is too broad and heterogeneous a degree category to be meaningful for the purpose of making comparisons. That is, it is quite possible that the preparation offered in different master's programs is very different, and that distinctions among them, and differing results for their graduates, would be obscured in analyses that treated them as a single group. The policy question at issue—what sorts of incentives states ought to have to encourage teacher candidates to pursue different sorts of credentials—is a pressing one. A detailed examination of the labor market for teachers was beyond our charge, but we discuss the tradeoffs between more stringent requirements and teacher supply below.

The availability of detailed state-level data on teachers and students, coupled with recent advances in research methodology, has enabled researchers to make some progress in identifying the extent to which various teacher characteristics influence learning outcomes. Value-added research, though not without limitations (see Chapter 2), can provide useful information, and we had hoped that it might help to answer questions about the various available pathways. Thus, the committee commissioned analyses in New York City and Florida to examine whether the state-specific pathways followed by prospective elementary teachers make a difference in terms of their pupils' achievement on state tests in reading and mathematics (Grossman et al., 2008; Sass, 2008). We also looked carefully at a similar analysis for Louisiana (Noell, 2008). Despite our concerns about the utility of the labels traditional and alternative, we believed it would be useful to investigate the pathways as they are defined by the states.

With slight variations related to differences in available data, the analyses for the three locations used value-added models to estimate the effect of entering through a particular pathway on new elementary school teachers' contributions to their students' learning in reading, English/language arts, and mathematics. The Florida research revealed limited and inconsistent differences among traditional, alternative, and out-of-state pathways, depending on the analysis and the subject area (English/language arts or mathematics). A similar analysis conducted in Louisiana showed no difference among teachers entering the profession through the three broad pathway categories (traditional, alternative, and out-of-state).

In the analysis of New York City schools, the researchers differentiated among the roughly half-dozen major pathways available to prospective teachers. This analysis found that elementary teachers with emergency licenses (i.e., uncertified) performed less well than traditionally trained teachers in helping their students succeed on mathematics tests, and, to a lesser extent, on English/language arts tests. There were no significant differences between the "traditional" pathway and the "alternative" pathways in New York. These results were consistent with those from another study of New York City teachers (Boyd et al., 2005).

In sum, results from the three state analyses of pathway effects support the conclusion that the pathway a teacher takes into the field has little to no effect on the contribution he or she makes to student learning.

What should be inferred from these findings? Some policy analysts have interpreted a lack of difference among pathways to mean that traditional programs are ineffective or unnecessary (Hess, 2002; Feistritzer, 2007). We note, however, that researchers are unlikely to be able to randomly assign teacher candidates to preparation programs so that any observed effects are likely to reflect the combination of training and the initial characteristics of the candidates. Though there is ample room for debate on how much and what kind of education is best for preparing effective teachers, inferring that one type of preparation does or does not yield better outcomes for students is not warranted by the evidence. An alternative hypothesis consistent with these findings is that the categories that have been used—alternative and traditional—do not capture important differences in teacher preparation. To explore this hypothesis, different empirically testable questions about differences among pathways could be identified and tested in rigorous future research.

In the last section of this chapter, we consider what such alternative distinctions might be. Before doing so, however, we examine what is known about the teacher preparation programs themselves, within different pathways, in order to consider whether their characteristics might better explain the variability in the quality of teacher preparation.

## PROGRAMS WITHIN PATHWAYS

The individual programs of study designed to prepare prospective K-12 teachers that are offered by institutions are just as diverse as the many pathways into teaching; unfortunately, however, there are relatively few data to support detailed analysis (Corcoran et al., 2004; Crowe, 2007). The U.S. Office of Education conducted a representative survey in the 1930s; the next attempt to characterize these programs comprehensively did not take place for another 50 years (Goodlad et al., 1990; Goodlad, 1994). More recent data exist, but in general, what is available is disparate descriptive information from which it is difficult to draw a coherent picture.

Even obtaining a precise count of teacher preparation programs is complicated by the lack of a precise definition of what constitutes a program.[3] For example, though most programs include both academic and classroom experience components, one institution may house multiple programs, and some programs operate in multiple institutions. At the next level, obtaining a quantitative picture of the features and general requirements of the programs is very difficult, and constructing a qualitative and nuanced picture of their content and character is nearly impossible.

The information that is available suggests that there are significant differences among programs. Just as states specify the pathways through which teachers can enter the profession, they also set policies related to program content, sometimes in surprising detail. Often buried in state administrative code, these policies take many forms. States may dictate minimum admissions criteria for programs or prescribe minimum credit hours for different types of coursework (e.g., education or pedagogy and subject matter), effectively setting a floor for the courses that state-approved teacher education programs must offer their students. States may also pro-

---

[3]Counts include 1,206 (U.S. Department of Education, 2006); 1,191 (Levine, 2006); and "over 1,300" (Schmidt et al., 2007).

hibit or limit the number of courses of a particular type, effectively setting a ceiling for what those programs can offer.

For example, the Annual California Education Code (§44320; see http://www.aroundthecapitol.com/code/getcode.html?file=./edc/44001-45000/44320-44324 [July 2009]) details the maximum number of credits prospective teachers are required to complete before beginning student teaching: "No more than nine semester units, or the equivalent, of professional education courses may be designated as prerequisites for purposes of admission to student teaching [except to satisfy English language requirements]." The code also specifies program length by providing that "in each program of preparation, support, and assessment, the postsecondary institution shall make it possible for each candidate to complete all requirements for a valid teaching credential in the equivalent of one year of full-time study."[4]

The content of required courses is also often mandated by a state, and even states with few course requirements may specify the topics to which prospective teachers in particular majors (such as general education, liberal arts and sciences education, disciplinary majors, and professional preparation) should be exposed.

These sorts of requirements are most evident when state departments require that programs demonstrate their alignment to state standards for new or practicing teachers during program review or accreditation. Yet there is enormous variability, for just as the United States has no centralized definition of what constitutes a high-quality education, there is also little agreement on what knowledge and skills teachers ought to acquire in the early stages of their careers. Many states accept or model their standards and expectations on those of national organizations—such as NCATE (National Council for Accreditation of Teacher Education) or TEAC (Teacher Education Accreditation Council)—but most states also have a set of requirements for teacher certification that have accumulated across years of legislation and are more patchwork in nature. (Accreditation and the role of NCATE and TEAC are discussed in Chapter 8.)

Our primary conclusion from an examination of the information available on teacher preparation programs is that they are extremely diverse. Because it is so difficult to generalize about programs, we could determine very little about their quality. Despite states' efforts to align the primary elements of K-12 systems to coherent standards, teacher preparation programs and pathways do not seem to have been brought into the fold (Cohen and Spillane, 1992). If one considers the situation from the perspective of an

---

[4]One reason for these requirements may be that teacher preparation programs are squeezed between university requirements for general education and disciplinary studies and university caps for maximum credits required for undergraduate degrees.

aspiring teacher weighing the options for preservice preparation, it is clear that the onus is on the aspirant to identify goals and the best avenue for meeting them.

## FEATURES OF TEACHER PREPARATION PROGRAMS

There may be little basis for drawing conclusions about teacher preparation programs, but there is no shortage of prescriptions as to what they should look like. During the 1910s and 1920s, the dean of Teachers College, James Earl Russell, laid out a basic model curriculum for teacher preparation, which included: "general culture" (general knowledge), "special scholarship" (learning across several disciplines), "professional knowledge" (a systematic inquiry into the theory and practice of education), and "technical skills" (practical pedagogical skills) (Cremin, 1978). Teacher education curricula have been strongly influenced by this model, and most of them are still organized around some combination of general, disciplinary, professional, pedagogical, and practical knowledge (Cochran-Smith and Fries, 2005).

For much of the 20th century and into the 21st, even more answers have been proposed to questions about the features teacher preparation programs ought to have. Wilson, Floden, and Ferrini-Mundy (2001) examined questions on the issue posed by the U.S. Department of Education, as did Allen (2003) on behalf of the Council of Chief State School Officers. The National Academy of Education's Committee on Teacher Education (Darling-Hammond and Bransford, 2005) and a panel of the AERA (Cochran-Smith and Zeichner, 2005) also sought to articulate the most important features of teacher preparation programs. In these reports, five broad domains are consistently identified as important:

1.  program purpose,
2.  requirements for subject-matter knowledge,
3.  requirements for pedagogical and other professional knowledge,
4.  field and clinical experiences, and
5.  faculty and staff qualifications.

We discuss each of these briefly.

### Program Purpose

All teacher preparation programs presumably have the goal of preparing excellent teachers, but a surprising variation is evident in their stated missions. For example, the mission of a teacher education program at the University of California at Los Angeles is to "Provide high-quality preservice education and radically improve urban schooling for California's racially, culturally, and linguistically diverse children" (see http://centerx. gseis.ucla.edu/mission.php [September 2009]). At the Massachusetts Institute of Technology, teacher education is designed to recruit the next generation of mathematics and science teachers and to offer them "sophisticated knowledge of subject matter, high-level analytical thinking skills, abilities to confront and play with complex problems, and the enjoyment of grappling with the surprise of unexpected outcomes" (see http://education.mit. edu/drupal/tep/mission [September 2009]). The Mississippi Teacher Corps, modeled on the Peace Corps, recruits prospective teachers nationwide to teach in high-need schools in the Mississippi delta (see http://www.olemiss. edu/programs/mtc/about [September 2009]), and TFA recruits prospective teachers committed to "eliminat[ing] educational inequity" (see http://www. teachforamerica.org/mission/index.htm [September 2009]). This aspect of preparation programs is not so much a subject for empirical research as a factor to be considered in evaluating a program's effectiveness in meeting its own goals.

## Requirements for Subject-Matter Knowledge

Programs vary significantly with respect to their requirements for subject-matter preparation (see Chapters 5, 6, and 7). Some require that prospective teachers complete majors in the subject matter they will teach; others require that teachers take a broad array of courses (this is especially true in programs for elementary teachers) that roughly map onto the school subjects. Subject-matter courses for teachers also vary in level and rigor of instruction. In some universities, faculty from teacher education and disciplinary departments work together to align the experiences that prospective teachers have, and in some programs faculty coteach courses across content and pedagogy (Heaton and Lewis, 2002). In other cases, there is less alignment. Data collected by Boyd and colleagues (2008) show that 25 states require that secondary teachers have majored in the subject they plan to teach and that they pass an exam in that subject; 6 require only the major; and 18 require only the exam. In addition, the authors note that there is a good deal of variability in the requirements for a major and in what is required to pass the exams.

Given the lack of centralized information about teacher preparation programs, however, it is not clear how extensive the variability is or whether the variability is associated with differences in new teachers' effectiveness. Simply documenting the range of requirements and summarizing existing variations is a challenge. Thus, even questions that seem straightforward—such as "How many courses in mathematics do elementary and secondary teachers have to take?"—are difficult to answer. And a more in-depth look at the substance of required courses is even more elusive.

Although there is no centralized information to draw on, the Conference Board of the Mathematical Sciences (CBMS) compiles a report that examines the status of undergraduate mathematics and statistics in U.S. colleges and universities every 5 years. As part of that survey, they collect information from teacher preparation programs. The most recent survey (Conference Board of the Mathematical Sciences, 2005) shows that 4 percent of K-8 certification programs require no mathematics courses, 26 percent require one course, 37 percent require two courses, and 22 percent require three courses. The average number of required classes is just over two.

The required courses themselves vary: between 59 and 70 percent of programs require a two-course sequence for elementary mathematics majors, and between 40 and 56 percent of programs require college algebra. Some programs include precalculus, an introduction to mathematical modeling, mathematics for the liberal arts, finite mathematics, mathematics history, calculus, geometry, and elementary statistics.

The Conference Board survey did not include the subject-matter requirements of programs not housed in colleges or universities, and so even these data are incomplete. Furthermore, because the survey does not include data about state requirements, organizational arrangements, institutional commitments, or measures of graduating teachers' knowledge, the data cannot be used to examine the relative effectiveness of programs in producing high-quality teachers or the amount of subject-matter knowledge of graduates. Nor do the available data support analysis of the effects of state regulations on program quality or effectiveness.

Relatively little information about subject-matter preparation in alternative programs is available, though Johnson and colleagues (2005), in a study of such programs in three states, found that most programs had very limited capacity to teach subject matter. That is, the programs studied did not have enough faculty to cover a range of fields and levels of schooling, and the limited instructional time in the programs did not allow for significant attention to subject-matter preparation.

Despite a great deal of enthusiasm about content knowledge, recent reviews of the literature suggest that there is very little research on teachers' content knowledge and that what does exist focuses primarily on mathematics and science (Wilson, Floden, and Ferrini Mundy, 2001; Allen, 2003; Floden and Meniketti, 2005). The variability in what is mandated by states and taught under the umbrella of required subject-matter courses within and across states, pathways, and programs might account in part for the confusing results of research in this area (see Chapters 5-8 for further discussion).

### Requirements for Pedagogical and Other Professional Knowledge

Scholars of education have identified other kinds of knowledge they believe all teachers need, regardless of the subject or age group they teach. A report by the National Academy of Education (Darling-Hammond and Bransford, 2005) draws on professional and scholarly consensus in asserting that there is a body of research that ought to influence the preparation of every new teacher. It identifies the core knowledge and skills that beginning teachers need in eight domains, including learning, development, social contexts and purposes of education, and classroom management. Despite the existence of this sort of guidance, programs appear to vary in terms of how they conceptualize teachers' professional knowledge, as distinct from subject-matter knowledge, as well as in the emphasis they place on different kinds of professional knowledge.

For example, some programs offer a generic methods class, for teachers preparing for all grade levels and subject matters. Other programs treat pedagogical knowledge as content specific and offer subject-specific courses in both content and pedagogy, taking their cue from the concept of "pedagogical content knowledge" as a specific kind of knowledge of how to make subject-matter knowledge accessible to students (see Shulman, 1986). (Pedagogical content knowledge is discussed in subsequent chapters.)

Professional preparation typically involves a range of other kinds of study as well, such as history of education, educational psychology, measurement and assessment, educational foundations, multiculturalism and diversity, theories of learning, classroom management, special education, and reading. Some programs offer extensive coursework in these domains; others offer condensed approaches. While "alternative" programs are often seen as requiring less coursework than "traditional" ones, there has been little systematic study of what is and is not actually offered in different programs.

To consider one alternative program, TFA has developed a summer preparation program that includes courses in educational theory, classroom management, literacy, and instructional planning and delivery. After the summer training, TFA corps members may take classes at local universities, where the content of their programs might be very similar to courses taken by prospective teachers who are entering teaching through a college-recommending pathway. Case studies of programs in other pathways reveal a high degree of variability in the focus of coursework, including courses on pedagogy, classroom management, educational theory, and child development (Humphrey and Wechsler, 2005).

There are many other topics that teacher preparation programs cover, including formative and summative assessment, the use of education data, teacher research, and the like. In the rest of this section we consider what is known about three aspects of professional knowledge: classroom management and methods, teaching diverse students, and foundations of education.

## Classroom Management and Methods

Preparing teachers to take charge of a classroom and to guide and manage their students is a basic responsibility for programs. As LePage and colleagues (2005) noted in an overview of the subject, classroom management "encompasses many practices integral to teaching," including "developing relationships; structuring respectful classroom communities where students can work productively; . . . making decisions about timing and other aspects of instructional planning; successfully motivating children to learn; and encouraging parent involvement" (p. 327). The authors further note that, based on surveys of teachers about their preparation, programs seem to have become more likely to offer formal instruction in classroom management over the past few decades, rather than leaving it for on-the-job learning. The authors suggest that there are three components to learning this skill: practical experience with students (see section on Field and Clinical Experiences), coursework on the links between theory and practice, and study with teacher educators who effectively model good classroom management.

Research on the effectiveness of approaches to teaching classroom management is, however, scant. In a review of studies related to classroom management published over several decades, Clift and Brady (2005) found that the majority were short-term case studies, classroom observations, and other qualitative snapshots of changes in teachers' attitudes and behaviors. They identified a few empirical studies, but they were not able to find answers to basic questions about the effects of methods courses or whether it makes a difference how methods courses are structured and presented within the curriculum. They concluded that although methods courses do seem to affect teachers' beliefs, "it is difficult to predict what effect a specific course or experience may have" (p. 331). They also found that the value of methods courses seems to be linked to opportunities to apply what is learned in the classroom, and they suggested that ongoing professional development, as well as field experience that reinforces the concepts learned in the classroom, foster the learning of methods.

## Teaching Diverse Students

We note in Chapter 1 that teachers of all subjects and age groups can expect to be responsible, in the course of a career, for the learning of students with any of a wide range of disabilities, students who need language support, students whose formal education has been disrupted, and students from diverse cultural backgrounds with values and customs different from those of the majorities in their communities.

Aspiring teachers now have the option of choosing special education or English as a second language (ESL) as a specialty and pursuing concentrated studies in those areas (although becoming a specialist is not the only way to develop this expertise). However, the more general challenge of preparing all teachers to be effective with diverse student populations is increasingly recognized as an important goal of teacher preparation, which cuts across academic disciplines. We are not the first to recognize that this situation presents a conundrum. The sometimes stark achievement gaps among various groups have called attention to the urgent need for greater attention to the educational needs of underserved groups, as well as the importance of preparing teachers with the knowledge and skills to work effectively with these students. At the same time, however, separately addressing the needs of particular groups, such as students with disabilities and English-language learners, can have the paradoxical effect of further marginalizing them. That is, some would argue that it is not enough for a school to hire special education or ESL teachers or for a teacher preparation program to offer those subjects as specialties because all teachers ought to be prepared to work with the variety of students they will encounter.

In response to growing concern that teachers have not been adequately prepared to address the needs of diverse students, teacher preparation programs have begun to adapt their curricula to include this type of preparation, and researchers have begun to examine these programs and their effects (see, e.g., Banks et al., 2005; Hollins and Guzman, 2005; Pugach, 2005; Rothstein-Fisch and Trumbull, 2008).

Hollins and Guzman (2005) summarized the research on preparing teachers to work with diverse student populations. Their principal finding was that despite growing recognition of the importance of this aspect of preparation, research on it has been thinly funded, and methodological challenges have not been overcome. Most of the available studies are small in scale and cannot provide answers to questions about how teachers might best be prepared. The authors found that while models for providing this kind of training are available, it appears that they have not been consistently used and that measuring outcomes has proved difficult. Much of the research examines teachers' attitudes and predispositions regarding people who are different from themselves and changes in their attitudes that take place in response to educational experiences. Research on how preparation can improve teachers' effectiveness in this domain is almost nonexistent.

As part of the National Academy of Education research summary (Darling-Hammond and Bransford, 2005), Banks and colleagues (2005) developed recommendations for preparing teachers to be effective with diverse populations, based on their synthesis of relevant information from research in several areas: development, learning, and learning differences; content pedagogy, assessment, and classroom management; and culture and its influences on learning. They identify a range of knowledge and skills that are valuable: self-knowledge, cultural and linguistic knowledge, culturally informed pedagogical knowledge, knowledge about the nature of learning differences, knowledge of teaching methods and materials suitable for different kinds of learning needs, and knowledge of home-school relationships. They offer a variety of suggestions and models for how these goals might be pursued, grounded primarily in the findings of small-scale studies, but few of these have been adopted on a wide scale, and we do not know of any systematic research that has tested the proposed models.

## Foundations of Education

Teacher preparation programs usually offer a range of courses that can be loosely categorized as covering the foundations of education, which include educational psychology, history of education, and sociology or philosophy of education (Floden and Meniketti, 2005). In a search for studies of the effects of these kinds of courses, the authors found just five small-scale studies. They note that these small-scale studies would be useful in evaluating the value of individual courses and for demonstrating the kinds of benefits such courses may have, but they cannot be used to support any broad conclusions.

In a study of alternative programs in three states, Johnson and colleagues (2005) found that the programs tended to focus on the most practical sorts of training, rather than theoretical coursework. They also found that the emphasis in these programs varied in part depending on whether they were district-based: if so they were focused on preparing teachers to fill vacancies in that district; if not, they were more likely to be designed to prepare teachers to work in a variety of settings. The locally based programs tended to provide targeted preparation for particular teaching circumstances, such as reaching underserved students.

## Field and Clinical Experiences

Ensuring that novices will be able to apply the knowledge they have gained in a classroom to real situations is a key challenge in any field. Whether for a doctor learning how to insert a needle or make an incision or for a teacher learning what to say to a disruptive student or how to encourage student participation in class discussions, professional preparation must provide opportunities to practice new skills and apply new knowledge. Like every other element of teacher preparation, field experiences vary. Some university-based programs place students in classrooms as early as their freshman year. These early opportunities often involve observing or tutoring students, watching teacher or parent conferences, reading to children, and observing instruction (Clift and Brady, 2005).

Although the student teaching experience is viewed as a hallmark of many programs, and states generally require some kind of student teaching for all certification programs, little systematic information is available about how much time aspiring teachers spend in field experiences or how those experiences are structured, or about differences across pathways in what is available or required. In a recent survey of alumni of university-based teacher education programs, 60 percent of teachers reported that their student teaching experience lasted for a semester, roughly 20 percent reported having had a longer one, and another 20 percent reported having spent less than a semester (Levine, 2006).

Even less is known about field experiences in "alternative" pathways. In the most high profile of these, the Teaching Fellows Program and TFA, prospective teachers become teachers of record after one summer's training, and they teach a full load of courses while simultaneously completing their coursework for certification. Similarly, in some district-based internship programs, new teachers receive a temporary license, are assigned to their own courses, and complete credentialing requirements through district-sponsored courses or at local universities. A more recent option is the urban teacher residency program, in which prospective teachers are placed with mentors who support them while they gradually take on teaching responsibilities and complete relevant coursework. Johnson and colleagues (2005) found that the alternative programs in three states had difficulty meeting their goals for providing students with clinical experiences. Local districts were not uniformly welcoming to aspiring teachers from these programs, and it was often difficult to match teacher candidates with placements and mentors that matched their schedules, credentials, and goals. The researchers found that locally based programs had an easier time finding suitable matches.

Some programs also require teacher candidates to complete a capstone, or final project, which can take many forms. Some New York City teacher preparation programs require the development of portfolios that track prospective teachers' coursework and field experience over time. Other capstone projects require action research, in which new teachers collect and analyze data from their field experiences related to a particular question about their practice, or teacher may complete a thesis (Boyd et al., 2009).

The research on the effects of field experiences with different attributes, such as their length, quality, or organizational structure, or accompanying assignments, is slim and tends to focus narrowly on specific types of experiences, such as student teaching. Even simple descriptive information about the nature of clinical experiences is scarce. However, data from the 31 programs included in the New York City analysis provide a detailed look at the field experiences required of prospective elementary school teachers in the college-recommending programs in the study sample (Grossman et al., 2008). Program-level data show that the duration of fieldwork and student teaching typically far exceeded the state-mandated 100 hours and 40 days, respectively. In this study, the length of experience was not what stood out. Rather, the differences across and within programs in the specific attributes of the fieldwork were striking. For example, the programs varied in terms of the qualifications of the fieldwork supervisors and the frequency with which supervisors met with program participants.

Research on the effects of various kinds of clinical experiences is limited. Clift and Brady (2005) found a small number of studies that examined the effects of field experience on teachers' beliefs and attitudes. The available research suggests that aspiring teachers find that field experiences reinforce the material they have learned in the classroom, and that the experiences provide useful opportunities to put it into practice. In more recent work, researchers on the Teacher Pathways Project used a composite measure of ways in which field experiences are linked to preparation in courses (e.g., assessing student reading ability/achievement, studying student work in math, planning lessons) to examine the possible effects of this sort of preparation on the effectiveness of teachers once they complete their training and work in the classroom (Boyd et al., 2009). The study showed that a range of practice-related teacher education experiences seem to improve the effectiveness of beginning teachers.

The study we commissioned in New York City found that both program oversight of student teaching and a required capstone project—two types of practice-based preparation that the researchers isolated in their analysis—were associated with gains for the students of new elementary teachers in both English/language arts and mathematics. These two program features had the strongest and most consistent effect in the models estimated for this analysis, showing statistically and substantively significant effects for both first- and second-year teachers and for both subject areas (Grossman et al., 2008). These findings are suggestive, but more systematic study of field experience is needed.

## Faculty and Staff Qualifications

The characteristics of the instructional staff in teacher preparation programs are likely to play a role in outcomes for aspiring teachers. We found that a wide range of professionals—including tenure-track faculty, adjunct faculty, doctoral students, and practicing and retired K-12 teachers—serve as instructors in preparation programs. Again, however, as with other areas we studied, it is not possible to draw any conclusions from the available information.

It is difficult to ascertain the qualifications of the people who staff teacher preparation programs. According to Levine (2006), more than half of prospective teachers are educated in institutions identified as less selective (i.e., where faculty are not expected to be active scholars themselves). But many education faculty members do not work in teacher preparation programs—the work of colleges and schools of education includes school psychology, counseling psychology, and other fields—and faculty may be housed in different units across university and college campuses.

Faculty members in university-based teacher education programs are predominantly white women, with a median age of 51 years. This demographic profile is similar to that of faculty in other university departments, though women are far more common on education faculties than elsewhere on campus, according to 2004 data from the National Study of Postsecondary Faculty (NSOPF) (http://nces.ed.gov/pubs2005/2005172.pdf [November 2009]). Fifty-one percent of education faculty members are full time, and of those, 36 percent are tenure-track faculty (only in the health sciences is there are a smaller proportion of full-time faculty having tenure). On average, 56 percent of college faculty are employed full time, and no program area has a lower proportion of its faculty working full time than does education. (Programs with the highest percentages of full-time faculty include engineering and agriculture/home economics, both with 78 percent; natural sciences, with 76 percent; and social sciences, with 70 percent.) The average annual base salary for full-time education faculty was $58,000 in 2003, compared with $70,500 for all full-time faculty.

About one-quarter of full-time education faculty members hold the rank of full professor; education faculty are more likely than their peers in other program areas to be assistant professors (28 percent) or have ranks other than professor or lecturer (15 percent). Nearly 75 percent of full-time education faculty members have doctoral degrees. Less than 5 percent of full-time education faculty report research as their principal activity, compared with 15 percent across all program areas surveyed. More than 67 percent of full-time education faculty report teaching as their principal activity, and another 20 percent focus on administration, the highest among all program areas and nearly double the percentage across academic areas.

Very little is known about the demographic characteristics and qualifications of clinical faculty (who are typically practitioners) or the doctoral students who serve crucial roles as supervisors for student teachers. And next to nothing is known about the instructors who staff programs that are not university based. Since much of the coursework for participants in alternative program candidates is housed in schools of education, it may well be that in large measure the same instructional faculty teach in the two pathways. In contrast, school district-based programs may be staffed by school district employees, and TFA alumni often serve as staff at the program's summer institute.

The dearth of information on the qualifications of teacher educators is troubling. Ongoing work in New York City has shown limited evidence that specific aspects of faculty qualifications may promote teacher effectiveness: researchers there found that the percent of faculty with tenure is positively related to student achievement in mathematics in the first year of teaching, but does not affect teachers in English/language arts or second-year mathematics teachers (see Boyd et al., 2009). This finding is just one hint of the importance of learning much more about the qualifications of faculty and staff across all pathways and programs.

## UNANSWERED QUESTIONS ABOUT TEACHER PREPARATION

Perhaps because teacher preparation in the United States is a diverse landscape of programs that coexist within and across different pathways, there is little centralized information about how teachers are prepared for their profession. The committee can do little more than describe this variation and observe that in the last 20 years there have been many efforts to explore new ways of preparing teachers. There are a number of elements that are well established as accepted aspects of teacher preparation—including subject-matter knowledge and fieldwork—yet the implementation even of these relatively agreed-on features varies widely.

In terms of evidence about how these features might contribute to teacher effectiveness, the committee found virtually no evidence. The available research does not show stable, significant differences in the effectiveness of teachers who took different pathways into the field (as those pathways are currently defined). Looking at characteristics of the primary features of programs, we found that a significant amount of qualitative and small-scale research suggests promising avenues for further investigation. For example, the research on field experience suggests that programs that link these experiences to theoretical study in the classroom may be more effective than those that do not, at least in teachers' eyes. There is very little empirical evidence, however, to support recommendations that particular features, or ways of implementing them, should be adopted because they are demonstrably better.

New projects and reviews of previous research have refocused policy attention on the need to learn more about teacher education, yet important questions remain unanswered. In our view, a fresh look at research related to teacher preparation is in order, with four goals:

1. to determine the relative effectiveness of different pathways and pathway characteristics;
2. to determine the relative effectiveness of the components of those pathways and programs;
3. to better describe the characteristics of teacher candidates and how those relate to program selection and the quality of the teacher workforce; and
4. to guide both innovation and policy making.

A better understanding of the effects of different kinds of preparation will require a sharpened strategy for identifying meaningful distinctions among pathways and programs. At present, two conflicting basic premises are implicit in policy debates about how to improve teacher quality and preparation. One is that any well-educated person can teach without needing much special preparation: therefore, states should relax barriers to entry (such as degree or coursework requirements) so they can recruit "the best and brightest." The contrary premise is that teachers need particular and extensive preparation, and that therefore, states should increase the requirements for prospective teachers to ensure that they have the necessary skills and knowledge. These conflicting approaches highlight interest in three factors: the selectivity of preparation programs; the timing of teacher training—that is, the relative value of requiring teachers to complete most of their training before becoming a classroom teacher; and the effects of various components and characteristics of teacher preparation programs.

## Selectivity

How academically able are the individuals who become teachers? Questions about selectivity have been around at least since George Bernard Shaw suggested that it is those who can't "do" who end up as teachers. The concept of selectivity is not as straightforward as it sounds, however, since programs may consider a number of factors in selecting students: in addition to grade point average (GPA) or other indicators of academic achievement, programs may consider such subjective factors as demonstrated commitment to educational equity.

Several analyses of changes in academic qualifications have shown that, on average, entering teachers today have substantially lower academic qualifications (in terms of test scores and the selectivity of their undergraduate institutions) than they did a generation ago (Corcoran, Evans, and Schwab, 2004; Bacolod, 2007). Yet a study of candidates who took the Praxis test (see Educational Testing Service, http://www.ets.org [May 2010]) for teachers during two time periods—1994 to 1997 and 2002 to 2005—(a subset of all teachers) showed that the candidates in the more recent group had a stronger academic profile, in terms of SAT[5] scores and undergraduate GPA, than the earlier group had. It also showed that teachers in secondary schools have much stronger profiles than other teachers (Gitomer, 2007). Zumwalt and Craig (2005) examined the literature on indicators of teacher quality and note the difficulty of drawing firm conclusions about the quality of teacher education students, given the lack of comprehensive comparable data. For example, the authors point out that comparing the average SAT and ACT (formerly, American College Testing) scores of teacher candidates entering programs with those successfully completing them reveals that those with the lowest scores tend to drop out in greater numbers at each stage of the process. Thus, the comparison will look somewhat different depending on the stage at which it is made.

What about the selectivity of specific teacher preparation pathways and programs? A recent study found that among first-year teachers participating in the Schools and Staffing Survey conducted by the National Center for Education Statistics, about one-quarter of teachers received baccalaureate degrees from highly competitive postsecondary institutions, and about one-quarter received their degrees from the least competitive colleges or universities (Cohen-Vogel and Smith, 2007). This study included teachers from both university-based and other pathways. The researchers found no significant differences in the overall selectiveness of the programs they identified as traditional or alternative. Similarly, a study by the National Council on Evaluation Education (NCEE) (Constantine et al., 2009) found no significant differences between the two groups of teachers they analyzed in terms of their SAT (college-entry test) scores or the selectivity of the colleges in which they had earned their baccalaureate degrees.

Cohen-Vogel and Smith (2007) did, however, document substantial variation in the degree of selectivity across programs. That is, within so-called alternative pathways, some programs were highly selective, and others were not. A similar variation was documented within traditional programs. This finding is consistent with smaller studies of minimum grade point average and college entrance test score requirements for admissions across teacher preparation programs, which also show that average requirements are comparable across traditional and alternative categories but that there is substantial variation in these measures of selectivity within categories (Leal, 2004; Walsh and Jacobs, 2007). Thus, selectivity is not clearly related to whether a program is labeled traditional or alternative.

For a closer look at the variation in selectivity between and within pathway types, the committee considered state-specific data on four measures of selectivity for the major pathways to teaching in New York and

---

[5]Formerly known as the Scholastic Aptitude Test, it is now, formally, the SAT Reasoning Test.

PATHWAYS TO TEACHING AND TEACHER PREPARATION PROGRAMS 57

**TABLE 3-3** Teacher Selectivity in New York City by Pathways: 2004

| Pathway | Proportion from Most Competitive Colleges[a] | Proportion from Least Competitive Colleges[a] | Proportion Who Passed General Knowledge State Certification Exam on First Try | Average SAT Scores: Math/Verbal |
|---|---|---|---|---|
| "Traditional"[b] | 0.08 | 0.20 | 0.81 | 489/490 |
| (N = 934) | 0.23 | 0.14 | 0.88 | 505/510 |
| University-based "Alternative"[c] (N = 1,632) | 0.33 | 0.15 | 0.98 | 550/557 |
| Transcript Review (N = 256) | 0.17 | 0.29 | 0.79 | 495/490 |
| Temporary License (N = 316) | 0.18 | 0.24 | 0.84 | 512/525 |
| Other (N = 138) | 0.21 | 0.16 | 0.92 | 526/532 |

[a]Ratings from Barron's 2009 Profiles of American Colleges College Division of Barron's Educational Series (Ed.). *Barron's Profiles of American Colleges.*
[b]College-recommending, graduate.
[c]Including Teach for America, Teaching Fellows, etc.
SOURCE: Adapted from Grossman et al. (2008, Table 19).

Florida from our commissioned studies. Grossman et al. (2008) found that New York teachers who entered the profession through alternative pathways were stronger than other teachers in terms of various academic measures. However, the variation within these two categories is great, so the traditional and alternative categories do not provide helpful distinctions in characterizing teacher preparation with respect to selectivity. Table 3-3 shows the comparisons on various indicators among teachers who entered through different pathways.

Sass (2008) conducted a similar analysis for Florida. He noted that unusually high demand for new teachers in Florida may account for his finding that there are a large number of alternative routes, as well as a much greater proportion of teachers who are prepared outside of the state's colleges and universities, than in other states. He found that the state's traditional teacher preparation institutions vary widely in their selectivity, as shown in Table 3-4.

These analyses show that the nature and degree of variability on in-

**TABLE 3-4** Teacher Selectivity in Florida, by Pathway: Teachers with Elementary Certification

| Path of Entry | Proportion from Most Competitive Colleges (Barron's ratings)[a] | Proportion from Least Competitive Colleges (Barron's ratings) | Proportion Who Passed General Knowledge State Certification Exam | Average Total SAT Score |
|---|---|---|---|---|
| Graduate of Florida Teacher Preparation Program ("Traditional") (N = 9,716) | 0.11 | 0.22 | Math 0.57 Reading 0.76 English 0.77 Essay 0.90 | 929 |
| Entry Through Any "Alternative" Route (N = 18,258) | 0.12 | 0.20 | Math 0.59 Reading 0.78 English 0.79 Essay 0.90 | 948 |
| Course Analysis (N = 10,538) | 0.15 | 0.19 | Math 0.60 Reading 0.79 English 0.78 Essay 0.90 | 947 |
| Certified in Another State (N = 5,111) | 0.08 | 0.22 | | |
| Graduate of an Out-of-State Teacher Preparation Program (N = 2,391) | 0.45 | 0.24 | Math 0.53 Reading 0.79 English 0.80 Essay 0.80 | |
| District Alternative Certification Program (N = 196) | 0.26 | 0.12 | Math 0.81 Reading 0.94 English 0.96 Essay 0.96 | 985 |

[a]Ratings from Barron's 2009 Profiles of American Colleges College Division of Barron's Educational Series (Ed.). *Barron's Profiles of American Colleges.*
SOURCE: Sass (2008, Table B2).

dicators of selectivity one finds depends on the specific comparisons one makes. The data from New York and Florida generally show that the variability in selectivity becomes more pronounced when the comparisons are between specific programs rather than across broad categories, reinforcing our concern that research on the role of selectivity needs to probe beyond aggregated "traditional" and "alternative" pathway descriptors.

But the important question is whether differences in selectivity matter in terms of teacher effectiveness. Some scholars have argued that high standards for academic preparation (e.g., college-entrance test scores, quality of undergraduate institutions, enrollment or achievement in undergraduate courses) are essential characteristics of good teacher preparation programs (e.g., Hickock, 1998; Wayne and Youngs, 2003). And some research has shown that there may be value in matching students and teachers by race, suggesting that explicitly recruiting teachers of color may be associated with teacher effectiveness (Hanushek et al., 2005). Furthermore, in a recent study of the relationship between teacher credentials and K-12 student achievement in North Carolina, researchers found that the quality of teachers' undergraduate institution—an indicator of general ability—is predictive of their students' achievement at the high school level, as well as at the elementary level (though for the elementary grades the size of the effect is smaller) (Clotfelter, Ladd, and Vigdor, 2007). Using similar analyses and measures, a study of new teachers in New York City (Boyd et al., 2008) also found support for the idea that measures of academic selectivity are associated with teacher effectiveness in the classroom. Although this research is not conclusive, the evidence points to the potential importance of program selectivity as one of several important factors in the preparation of high-quality teachers.

## Timing of Professional Education

Programs and pathways also vary in the amount of preparation that is required before a candidate becomes a teacher of record (a salaried teacher who has full responsibility for a full schedule of classes). Preparation may begin as early as the freshman year of an undergraduate program or when a teacher candidate leaves another career to enter teaching. Some programs designate new teachers as teachers of record as soon as they enter the program; in other programs teachers take on the full responsibilities of a teacher more gradually. For example, in New York State, all teachers are required to earn a master's degree before full certification, although the amount of preparation they have completed before receiving initial certification may vary. Thus, pathways appear to differ more in how much preparation takes place before full certification than in the total amount of preparation that is required.

Moreover, even programs that focus on preparation that occurs before candidates enter the classroom vary considerably in terms of the number of courses and extent of field experiences offered or required. Data compiled by Editorial Projects in Education (2006) for traditional programs show that for secondary school teachers, 6 states require an undergraduate major in the area of certification and 38 states have some other kind of minimum subject-matter degree or coursework requirements. For middle school certification, 3 states require a major, and 12 states require some other minimum degree or coursework requirement. A total of 35 states require a minimum amount of clinical experiences prior to initial certification.

In contrast, most alternative programs allow prospective teachers who have a bachelor's degree but have not taken any teacher education courses to begin as teachers of record after some abbreviated preparation. Few states have minimum requirements for the quantity of preparation in these programs, but 27 states do have subject-matter degree or coursework requirements for teachers who go through these pathways, and 28 specify a minimum duration of preservice training. These requirements vary considerably: some states require 1 week, and others require 12 credit hours; 16 states require practice teaching (Editorial Projects in Education, 2006).

Disentangling quantity and quality is not easy. One cannot presume that the amount of initial professional preparation is related to the quality of that preparation, though it seems likely that there is an optimal range below which teachers might be significantly unprepared and above which there may be diminishing returns. However, this is another area in which documentation and investigation of the effects of differences would be valuable.

## Content and Characteristics of Teacher Preparation

As noted above, programs and pathways also differ in the quality and quantity of the material that new teachers are expected to master in order to be fully credentialed, regardless of when the preparation takes place. For example, in Florida all of the different initial preparation pathways lead to full certification, and thus there are substantial differences in the intensity of formal preparation teachers have received at the time they earn full certification. The Florida teacher candidates who choose the (relatively new) ABCTE pathway are typically granted their permanent license after 6-10 months of individually paced work, with no formal coursework required. Constantine and her colleagues (2009) examined the content and quantity of coursework for several areas (e.g., mathematics or reading pedagogy and fieldwork) and found no significant relationship between their measures and achievement outcomes for students. We discuss the content of teacher preparation programs in greater detail in Chapters 5-7.

## Tradeoffs Between Selectivity and Intensity

The reason for exploring the issues above is to shed light on questions about how selective programs should be and how they should structure and design their requirements. These are largely empirical questions that have yet to be carefully addressed by research. Yet states are faced with the challenge of filling teacher vacancies each year (producing the quantity of teachers needed) while ensuring that those hired are effective in the classroom (producing the quality of teachers needed). Policy proposals to address these dual concerns are often viewed as working at cross purposes. If states raise the bar for entry into K-12 teaching, with the goal of raising the level of quality (e.g., by requiring specific degrees, majors, minors, or coursework), they may exacerbate teacher shortages. If states are less selective, they may be hiring ineffective teachers.

This tradeoff relates to the classic tension, noted above, about whether teachers are born or made. Raising licensure requirements is a strategy grounded in the assumption that teachers need specific professional preparation prior to teaching. In contrast, opening the profession through the approval of early-entry pathways is a strategy grounded in the assumption that teachers are born: if they are generically academically able, on-the-job professional development can fill in any gaps in preparation.

In economic terms, preparation is a cost to individuals considering teaching as a career.[6] Thus, it is entirely possible that raising entry requirements could dissuade some individuals from entering teaching. If this happens, and the ability of the teacher pool remains unchanged, school districts will have fewer individuals to choose from to fill vacancies and will be forced to hire less qualified candidates.

It is more likely, however, that raising preservice preparation requirements would have two effects: some individuals would choose not to seek a career in teaching, but the effectiveness of those who did would be greater than it would otherwise be. If so, the effect on the average quality of teachers is hard to predict, though it is likely that the quality of teachers would have distributional consequences. In other words, some schools would be able to hire better teachers than they otherwise would have, while other schools (most likely those with less desirable working conditions) would be forced to hire less qualified teachers. Ultimately, the question turns on whether the potential benefits of high-intensity preservice requirements exceed the potential costs of discouraging promising teacher candidates.

As we note in Chapter 1, teaching is one of the nation's largest occupations for college-educated workers, and there are considerable challenges associated with preparing a high-quality workforce of this size. At present, many teachers are not paid well in comparison with workers in comparable fields, and teaching is not a high-status occupation. Given the size of the teaching force, it is likely that there is no one best pathway to high-quality preparation for teachers. What is clear, however, is the importance of developing more comprehensive data on which to base recommendations for the composition of teacher education programs and pathways.

---

[6]Though it is worth noting that the preparation is likely to yield benefits even for individuals who do not become employed as teachers.

## CONCLUSION

Issues concerning teacher preparation and its effectiveness have received a perhaps unprecedented wave of attention for the past 10 years. Several important reports have emerged, including one summarizing the empirical research on various aspect of teacher education (Cochran-Smith and Zeichner, 2005) and one summarizing the relevance of research on teaching and learning to the preparation of teachers (Darling-Hammond and Bransford, 2005). In addition, a growing number of studies have addressed the relative effectiveness of various forms of preparation.

These efforts have certainly helped clarify what is and is not known about teacher education, and they have also made clear that there are no definitive answers to even the most basic questions. More work is needed—to develop a clearer picture both of how teachers are prepared and of which aspects of their preparation have the greatest effects on the quality of the teaching force. Chapter 9 presents the framework we propose for structuring this work.

Until that research is done and its findings known, teacher educators will continue to rely on their best judgment and whatever research is available, and the 200,000 new teachers who enter the field each year will quickly find out what they know and what they would like to know. The absence of clear evidence to answer basic and important questions is not a reason to question every operating assumption that now guides teacher preparation.

The research that has been done generally seems to reinforce what might be described as commonsense thinking. For example, there is some evidence that fieldwork (classroom teaching) that is designed to link to and reinforce the theoretical material aspiring teachers have learned in the classroom is more effective than fieldwork that is not. There is not, however, empirical support for firm recommendations about when the fieldwork should take place in the course of preparation, how long it should last, or what it should encompass. So the recommendation we could safely make would be to design the fieldwork thoughtfully—hardly a momentous contribution to policy discourse.

Nevertheless, while the field awaits further empirical study of the effects of different approaches, we believe that teacher preparation programs can benefit from learning about promising innovations and can look to the available evidence, case studies, and other literature for guidance. And we highlight the importance of research that can provide answers to the many pressing questions about teacher preparation.

**Conclusion 3-1:** There is currently little definitive evidence that particular approaches to teacher preparation yield teachers whose students are more successful than others: such research is badly needed. We believe that the highest priority research would be studies that examine three critical topics in relation to their ultimate effect on student learning:

1. comparisons of programs and pathways in terms of their *selectivity*; their *timing* (whether teachers complete most of their training before or after becoming a classroom teacher); and their specific *components and characteristics* (i.e., instruction in subject matter, field experiences);
2. the effectiveness of various approaches to preparing teachers in classroom management and teaching diverse learners; and
3. the influence of aspects of program structure, such as the design and timing of field experiences and the integration of teacher preparation coursework with coursework in other university departments.

# 4

# Preparing Teachers for All Fields

In this and the next three chapters, we turn to the third question in our charge: To what extent are the ways that teachers are currently being prepared in three key subjects—reading, mathematics, and science—consistent with converging scientific evidence about how they should be prepared?

We began with an effort to develop a clear picture of what the converging scientific evidence shows. That is, we hoped to find in the literature on teaching and learning mathematics, reading, and science some guidance as to what sorts of indicators would be most useful in assessing the quality of teacher preparation in each field. To do this, we broke the question into four parts:[1]

1. What do successful students know about the subject?
2. What instructional opportunities are necessary to support successful students?
3. What do successful teachers know about the subject and how to teach it?
4. What instructional opportunities are necessary to prepare successful teachers?

---

[1]Others have used similar frameworks to consider these questions, most recently, Darling-Hammond and Bransford (2005).

We address these questions for each subject in turn, and we also examine what is known about how teachers are currently prepared in each of these fields. Chapters 5 through 7 describe our findings for reading, mathematics, and science, respectively. However, a number of issues apply across these (and other) subjects, and this chapter discusses these first as grounding for the discipline-specific discussions.

The first part of this chapter looks at the research on the role of content knowledge in teaching that is relevant across disciplines. The second part of the chapter discusses several key issues that complicate an examination of preparing teachers in specific subject areas.

## SUBJECT-MATTER PREPARATION

Common sense suggests that one cannot teach what one does not know. Yet even a wonderfully prepared teacher cannot know everything that is relevant to the material he or she teaches in a given year. Given the practical limitations on the amount of preparation any teacher can reasonably acquire before entering the field, we looked for evidence about the knowledge and skills that are most valuable and should be given the highest priority in teacher preparation programs.

### Teaching and Learning

We looked first to research on learning and cognition for insights about how specific material is learned and might best be taught. This field has blossomed in the last few decades as technological advances have expanded researchers' tools for studying the way people think and learn, which in turn have offered valuable resources for the study of education. *How People Learn* (National Research Council, 2000a) summarizes this work and offers several points that are particularly relevant to teacher preparation. The book describes findings that have emerged from the increasingly multidisciplinary approach to investigating thinking and learning. The science of learning has been expanded by new methods for testing hypotheses about mental functioning (including sophisticated brain imaging technology), as well as strategies for integrating insights from anthropology, linguistics, developmental psychology, neuroscience, and other fields in order to develop richer models of the role of social and cultural contexts in learning. Although this field is still evolving, it has provided a detailed picture of aspects of cognition and learning (such as memory and the structure of knowledge), problem solving and reasoning, and metacognition, all of which have implications for education.[2] Much of the research in this field

---

[2]The first chapter of *How People Learn* provides a detailed discussion of the development of the science of learning and the research on which it is based.

is of a different nature from the empirical research on questions about education policy and practice, but it has influenced the research we examined on teaching and learning in the three content areas. Although the connections between this literature and teacher preparation are more logical than empirical, we believe this knowledge base is an important foundation for thinking about the extent to which teacher preparation is "consistent with convergent scientific evidence," as our charge directed.

Most of the cognitive research has focused on student learning, rather than on teaching or teachers' learning. *How People Learn* concludes that "To develop competence in an area of inquiry, students must: (a) have a deep foundation of factual knowledge, (b) understand facts and ideas in the context of a conceptual framework, and (c) organize knowledge in ways that facilitate retrieval and application" (National Research Council, 2000a, p. 16). The small body of work that focuses on teaching helps to support logical inferences about teaching in a manner consistent with this model of learning. First, *How People Learn* describes the critical distinction between novices and experts in any context and how the development of expertise is gradual. With continued learning in any field—chess, auto mechanics, mathematics, or English literature, for example—individuals gradually accumulate "extensive knowledge that affects what they notice and how they organize, represent, and interpret information" and this accumulation, in turn, "affects their ability to remember, reason, and solve problems" (National Research Council, 2000a, p. 19). Thus, teachers do not have to be experts in every field of knowledge they teach, in the sense that it is not necessary, for example, to have a Ph.D. in physics to teach secondary-level physics effectively or to have spent decades studying Shakespeare's plays to teach them effectively to middle school students. The report summarizes the implications for teachers of its conclusions about learning this way (p. 20):

> Teachers must come to teaching with the experience of in-depth study of the subject area themselves. Before a teacher can develop powerful pedagogical tools, he or she must be familiar with the progress of inquiry and the terms of discourse in the discipline, as well as understand the relationship between information and the concepts that help organize that information in the discipline. But equally important, the teacher must have a grasp of the growth and development of students' thinking about these concepts.

*How Students Learn* (National Research Council, 2005) applies the findings in *How People Learn* to strategies for science, mathematics, and history classrooms. This report was designed to provide examples to illustrate the practical implications of the science of learning in particular contexts, and relies on both research and practice. Experts do not just know more facts in a given area than nonexperts know (in any specific field), they also have a framework for understanding and applying what they know. *How Students Learn* describes the essential linkage between factual knowledge and conceptual frameworks, termed learning with understanding, in this way: "competent performance is built on neither factual nor conceptual understanding alone; the concepts take on meaning in the knowledge-rich contexts in which they are applied" (p. 6). Learning with understanding takes time, and is a cumulative process.

This work suggests that content knowledge, defined as a body of conceptual and factual knowledge, is an essential basis for effective teaching in a given field. But, as *How People Learn* points out, having expertise, or deep content knowledge, is not a sufficient foundation by itself for effective teaching. To foster learning, teachers draw on understanding of how knowledge develops in a particular domain. They also rely on understanding of the kinds of difficulties students typically have as their learning progresses and of how to build on students' gradually accumulating knowledge and understanding. This kind of knowledge is called pedagogical content knowledge. Teachers constantly weave this kind of knowledge with their regular content knowledge in making countless judgments about how to proceed in the classroom (see, e.g., Shulman, 1987; Grossman, 1990).

There is a critical distinction between pedagogical content knowledge and the advanced content knowledge that one would develop by taking upper-level courses in a subject, and thus it is important to be clear that aspiring teachers cannot develop pedagogical content knowledge simply by taking additional courses in their field, even though a thorough grounding in university-level study for a particular field of learning is an important prerequisite. Much recent research has attempted to disentangle the different kinds of knowledge that teachers have. Particularly in the context of mathematics and science, researchers have paid considerable attention to content knowledge for teachers, including pedagogical content knowledge, and we discuss this research in Chapters 6 and 7.

## Coursework

Another body of research has examined the effects of different kinds of coursework offered in preparation programs on teachers' practice and outcomes for students. Darling-Hammond and her colleagues (2005) report a basic relationship between "teacher effectiveness and the quantity of training teachers have received in subject matter and content-specific teaching methods" (p. 395). However, these studies did not examine the nature of the preparation and thus offer little guidance as to what aspects of it have value or precisely how they increase teachers' effectiveness. They also do not provide clear answers to questions about how much coursework would be valuable in particular areas. The authors describe other, smaller-scale studies that suggest that teacher preparation that focuses on how students learn particular content and ways of helping them develop deeper conceptual understanding have concrete benefits.

Wilson, Floden, and Ferrini-Mundy (2001) also reviewed the literature on content preparation—focusing only on studies that had been published in peer-reviewed journals—and provided detailed descriptions of their methods. They concluded that although it is clear that subject matter is important, the limited research base does not permit more specific conclusions. Some research on elementary teachers has documented gaps in elementary teachers' understanding of mathematics. Other research (which consisted of small-scale descriptive studies and correlational studies using larger datasets) did not distinguish precisely what makes some kinds of coursework more effective than others. The authors also concluded that proxies for teacher knowledge, such as grade point averages or completion of a major or minor in a subject, are not precise enough to capture the potentially important differences in teachers' preparation. The authors thus stress that simply requiring that prospective teachers major in a subject or take a certain number of courses is not likely to result in material improvements in teacher quality, partly because they found little evidence of correlation between pedagogical content knowledge and, for example, the number of mathematics courses taken.

Constantine and colleagues (2009) examined course-taking patterns for aspiring teachers in both alternative and traditional pathways and confirmed that the amount of coursework in all subjects taken varies dramatically between pathways and also that that there is considerable variation within both pathways.

Similarly, Wilson and her colleagues (2001) found that although there is support for the assertion that preparation in pedagogy (e.g., courses in instructional methods, learning theories, foundations of education, and classroom management) improves both teachers' practice and outcomes for students, the research has not yet made clear what specific elements yield results. The authors also examined questions about field experiences, which, though very different from coursework, can play a role in content preparation. Most of what they found was research on teachers' attitudes, showing that teachers view them as very valuable aspects of their preparation. Field experiences are planned with a variety of goals, which include shaping teachers' attitudes and expectations of their students, helping them to build classroom management skills, and providing opportunities to apply what they have learned in their courses (the goal most relevant to content preparation). As we discuss in Chapter 3, research has not shown that particular sorts of fieldwork are essential aspects of subject-matter preparation.

Floden and Meniketti (2005) summarize empirical research published in peer-reviewed journals since 1990 that focuses on the effects of coursework in particular content areas, in general arts and sciences, and in the foundations of education. They caution that the empirical base is surprisingly thin and that the bulk of the available research addresses secondary school mathematics. Empirical support is only clear for the general proposition that prospective mathematics teachers should take at least enough undergraduate mathematics to develop a sound (more than mechanical) grounding in the field. Moreover, some research supports the counterintuitive finding that there may be diminishing returns to study that goes beyond a certain number of courses, at least for elementary mathematics teachers (e.g., Monk, 1994).

Floden and Meniketti (2005) call attention to the many questions raised by this body of work, describing the limitations in the amount of empirical research as "sobering" (p. 282). They note for example, that studies that evaluated the effects of particular coursework did not take into account the differences among prospective teachers as they began the preparation programs and that few could control for selection bias in the way teachers were distributed among different programs. Similarly, the few available studies of the effects of general undergraduate arts and sciences coursework seem to support only general conclusions about the value of developing subject-matter knowledge and general cognitive skills. An even scantier body of work on coursework in the foundations of education suggests promising practices rather than providing the basis for broad conclusions. We discuss below reasons why research has not provided firmer answers to questions about subject-matter preparation.

Grossman, Schoenfeld, and Lee (2005) examined the pedagogical content knowledge of teachers of mathematics and English/language arts, drawing on research and professional consensus. They provide examples to illustrate the ways teachers use pedagogical content knowledge in lessons and discuss the implications of the available research for the curricula of teacher education programs. They particularly emphasize that prospective teachers should develop the tools to continue their own learning in the discipline they will teach and that they should be prepared to learn from experience as they progress in their careers. The authors argue that a foundational understanding of the ways student learn the subject matter is a key tool for doing both.

## EVALUATION AND RESEARCH CHALLENGES

The research on learning provides not only support for the basic proposition that teachers benefit from substantial study in their fields, but also a sophisticated model for thinking about what it takes to teach subject matter well. This research, coupled with the more limited findings from research on the effects of particular types of coursework, however, provides only broad guidance to those who plan or oversee the curricula of teacher preparation programs. It is likely to be difficult to translate what is known into indicators that could readily be used in evaluating teacher preparation programs or in a large-scale effort to collect data about how well such programs are putting research findings into practice.

One challenge for those responsible for teacher preparation curricula is that reasonable people may disagree about what it means to be proficient in a subject. Scholars in each discipline make this sort of decision when they design courses of study, but the variation across institutions regarding requirements for majoring in a particular subject, for example, demonstrate wide diversity of opinion. States' content and performance standards for K-12 students are often the starting point for discussions of what teachers ought to know, yet to ground expectations for teachers in student standards would mean accepting a limiting and limited view of what teachers do.

Establishing research-based recommendations for the quantity of coursework would pose a challenge as well. The number of courses a prospective teacher has taken in, say, mathematics is a very crude proxy for the amount of mathematical knowledge he or she has; moreover, as noted above, it has no clear relationship to the development of pedagogical content knowledge. In addition, teachers often have multiple areas of teaching responsibility and may not know what assignments they will have in the future. Science teachers, in particular, may be expected to teach biology, physics, earth science, or general science—and many aspiring teachers may consider it prudent to try to become qualified in a range of fields.

Grossman, Schoenfeld, and Lee (2005) discuss the complications of determining what sorts of content knowledge and pedagogical content knowledge elementary teachers need. They argue that prospective elementary teachers have just as great a need for both strong liberal arts preparation and the opportunity to develop expertise and pedagogical content knowledge in a particular subject matter, as do teachers of older students. Acknowledging that prescriptions in this area are based on logical inference and experience rather than empirical research, the authors assert that although all prospective elementary teachers should be well prepared for both mathematics and reading instruction, if they also have the option of specializing in other areas, such as science, social studies, or art, there would be benefits for teachers, students, and schools.

Another challenge for anyone wishing to make firm recommendations about teacher preparation is that, as we discuss in Chapter 3, the people who enter teacher preparation programs are highly varied in terms of their academic skills and preparation, as well as their goals. They include very bright and highly motivated students with strong academic preparation, and they also include students who are unsure about how interested they are in teaching and students with weaknesses in their academic preparation. Students with interest and capacity in some subject areas, particularly mathematics and science, are in relatively short supply. Because the demand for new teachers is so great, it is difficult for teacher preparation programs to exclude candidates whom they recognize have weaknesses in their academic preparation. The presence of these students, however, creates an extra burden for programs because the programs must address whatever deficiencies these students have while also preparing them to succeed as teachers. The necessary remediation is also costly in terms of both time and financial resources.

As detailed above, the empirical support for the proposition that strong subject-matter preparation is crucial for teachers is limited and inconsistent. Two factors account for this limitation: the inadequacy of available proxy measures of the subject-matter knowledge needed for teaching and the very limited resources that have been invested in high-quality, large-scale research.

We discuss the need for more large-scale research in Chapter 9. On the question of how one might measure teachers' knowledge and skills for research purposes, we offer several observations. A number of studies have shown weak relationships between the number of courses taken or the degree earned by a prospective teacher and the value that teacher adds to his or her students' achievement on standardized tests. We believe that this sort of research provides only very provisional answers to questions about the value of courses or degrees because standardized tests of student achievement were not designed to support inferences about teachers' effectiveness.

Many assessments of students' knowledge and skills place the most emphasis on the kinds of outcomes that are relatively easy to measure at the expense of other, perhaps more important, content. The challenge of accurately assessing both complex subject matter and skills and variations in how students progress make it difficult for researchers to measure links between teachers' preparation and the performance of their students (see Chapter 2).

One issue with studies that assess teacher effectiveness using student achievement scores is that the relationship they examine is what statisticians call distal—that is, a significant amount of time lapses between undergraduate course-taking and the teaching that might be expected to influence students' test performance. Numerous intervening influences may affect a teacher as he or she progresses through a program and into a classroom, which makes it exceedingly difficult to identify the effect of a single influence, such as subject-matter coursework. Another issue is that the available research generally does not distinguish among teachers' preparation that may vary dramatically. Considering these difficulties, the positive links that have been found are remarkable—and offer hope that better data will yield insights into what makes a difference and how best to prepare teachers.

Several recent studies of the effects of teachers' subject-matter knowledge on student achievement gains and other outcomes have identified new measures in reading (Phelps and Schilling, 2004) and mathematics (Hill, Schilling, and Ball, 2004). A study using the new mathematics measures found a positive relationship between teachers' mathematical knowledge and students' achievement (Hill, Rowan, and Ball, 2005). (This work is discussed in Chapter 6.) These and other studies may help the field develop more explicit ideas of what it means to acquire strong subject-matter knowledge, how to measure that knowledge, and how to design teacher preparation experiences to promote acquisition of that knowledge.[3]

## CONCLUSION

On the basis of the limited available research related to content preparation, there are the beginnings of answers to our four questions regarding what students and teachers need to know and what learning opportunities they need. The research on thinking and learning has identified two elements as key to the capacity to teach in a way that fosters the kind of learning described above:

- subject-matter expertise that encompasses a deep foundation of factual knowledge, understanding of how that knowledge fits in the conceptual framework of the field of study, and an internal organization of that knowledge that facilitates retrieval and application of his or her knowledge; and
- pedagogical content knowledge in a given subject-matter field, that is, an understanding of how students' learning develops in that field, the kinds of misconceptions students may develop, and strategies for addressing students' evolving needs.

The specific type and degree of knowledge and skills will likely vary both by subject and by the age group a teacher is preparing to teach, as we discuss in Chapters 5-7. For example, elementary school teachers would likely focus less on developing expertise and pedagogical content knowledge in a single field than would teachers who will specialize in a one field. Nevertheless, these three types of knowledge are important for all teachers.

---

[3]These ideas have important implications for the way states certify teachers. Certification requirements often focus on counts of course credits in particular subject areas, without regard for the actual content of the courses. Most states have abandoned a generic science certification, for example, recognizing that certification by field (e.g., biology or chemistry) would be more useful. Some states (such as Pennsylvania) have also begun to rethink elementary certification to allow more specialization.

# 5

# Preparing Reading Teachers

Teaching reading well is far more complicated than it might seem to a casual observer. Reading is a skill that can be developed by some learners regardless of the quality of instruction they receive, and an able and well-prepared child can make the experience of learning to read look fairly effortless. What casual observers may miss is the extent of knowledge and preparation a skillful teacher brings to a classroom that may include students with a range of impediments to learning to read. Successful reading teachers—and we include both teachers of elementary students in the early stages of reading, and teachers of older students who are struggling with reading—understand how students learn to read and how to provide the support they need.

Yet this description hardly captures the complexity of preparing students to flourish in the workplace and in a society that requires high-level uses of text. Teachers of reading are called on to prepare students to interpret complex ideas, critically analyze arguments, synthesize information from multiple sources, and use reading to build their knowledge. When literacy is measured by these criteria, the literacy crisis in the United States is evident.

According to the most recent "reading report card" for the nation (Lee, Grigg, and Donahue, 2007), 67 percent of 4th graders and 74 percent of 8th graders are scoring at minimal levels of reading competency. There has been no significant improvement in reading achievement at grades 8 and 12 since 1992, and the achievement gaps for historically underperforming subgroups have not been reduced (Grigg, Donahue, and Dion, 2007; Lee,

Grigg, and Donahue, 2007). Furthermore, 4th- and 8th-grade students who are English-language learners scored 36 and 42 standard-scale points, respectively, below the performance of native speakers of English in 2007 (Lee, Grigg, and Donahue, 2007).

In this chapter we first briefly discuss the general state of research on reading. The next four sections address the four questions presented in Chapter 4 as applied to reading:

1. What are students expected to know and be able to do to be successful readers?
2. What instructional opportunities are necessary to support successful students?
3. What do successful teachers know about reading and how to teach reading?
4. What instructional opportunities are necessary to prepare successful teachers?

We then turn to what is known about how teachers are currently being prepared to teach reading, and we close with our conclusions.

## THE RESEARCH BASE

The available research that relates specifically to the preparation of reading teachers is relatively sparse, but we identified a range of materials that shed light on our questions about what preparation for reading teachers ought to entail and on what reading programs currently require. The overwhelming majority of the research we found on reading education concerns two topics: the process of learning to read and strategies for teaching the elements of fluent, accurate reading, and for addressing problems that can delay the development of reading skills.

The study of reading has followed a variety of pathways in the course of a long history (Venezky, 1984). As the practical necessity and prevalence of literacy have grown, scholars from a range of fields—including linguistics, neuroscience, and cognitive and developmental psychology, as well as sociology and history—have explored questions about how people learn to read, reading difficulties, and other questions pertaining to literacy. Yet there are now so many publications on teaching reading, from so many sources, that there is a certain amount of fog around the question of how much of the guidance is based on research.

The National Reading Panel identified approximately 100,000 research studies published between 1966 and the late 1990s (National Institute of Child Health and Human Development, 2000). These publications include summary documents that synthesize many research threads, consensus documents, position papers, and standards documents, as well as published research articles. The research itself draws on a variety of methodological approaches, including correlational studies that identify connections between particular practices and student outcomes as well as experimental and quasi-experimental studies that use controls to assess the effects of instruction. The "reading wars," which were based on differences between proponents of the whole-language and phonics-based approaches to teaching reading to young children, illustrate how easily questions about literacy and reading have been politicized (Lemann, 1997). Thus, sorting through all of the research and other publications about reading is a major task.

For our work, we were fortunate to have three influential publications that have summarized this work, by the National Research Council (NRC) (1998), the National Reading Panel (NRP) of the National Institute of Child Health and Human Development (2000), and the International Reading Association (2007). We have relied particularly on these documents because their authors are groups that represent the leading scholars in the field and because the authors established rigorous criteria for their reviews of the literature. However, we also consulted a number of other documents that summarize and reflect prominent theoretical stances and positions in the field.

There is a strong, empirically based consensus about our first two questions: what students are expected to know and be able to do to be successful readers at different stages and what kinds of instructional opportunities support the development of successful readers. For our third question, what successful teachers know about reading, there is a growing consensus, though one less well supported by empirical evidence. And for our fourth question, what preparation helps teachers become successful at teaching reading, we found very little evidence. We also found comparatively little evidence on the current preparation of reading teachers, though studies of specific jurisdictions and a small number of other studies provide some insights.

## QUESTION 1: WHAT ARE STUDENTS EXPECTED TO KNOW AND BE ABLE TO DO TO BE SUCCESSFUL READERS?

Reading, a skill relevant and necessary in every field of academic study and in most other aspects of life, is somewhat different from other school subjects. Theories—such as cognitive theories about text comprehension or sociocultural theories about the role of context in shaping literacy learning opportunities—have made important contributions to the understanding of reading. However, the "big ideas"[1] of reading are not theories and con-

---

[1] The concept of big ideas is a rhetorical device first used in discussions of science education.

cepts that are central to any field of academic inquiry. Rather, the principal elements of the knowledge of how students develop as readers, and how successful readers navigate texts, have emerged from many disciplines, from the study of a range of questions using a range of methods.

Research on reading has produced a portrait of successful readers at various stages of their development and has characterized the principal difficulties that impede progress in learning to read fluently. We summarize here the main findings from the three summary documents that relate to the question of what successful readers know.

### Preventing Reading Difficulties in Young Children

The committee that developed *Preventing Reading Difficulties in Young Children* (National Research Council, 1998) was asked to consider the effectiveness of interventions for young children who are at risk of having problems learning to read. The committee examined a range of evidence, including case studies, correlational studies, experimental and quasi-experimental studies, epidemiological studies, ethnographies, and other work. The committee looked for converging evidence from a range of sources to support their conclusions. The report's introduction contains a detailed discussion of the complex issues associated with evidence in the field of reading (pp. 34-40).

The committee found that children who are successfully learning to read have

- a working understanding of how sounds are represented alphabetically,
- sufficient practice in reading to achieve fluency with different kinds of texts,
- sufficient background knowledge and vocabulary to render written texts meaningful and interesting,
- control over procedures for monitoring comprehension and repairing misunderstandings, and
- continued interest and motivation to read for a variety of purposes.

There are three potential stumbling blocks that may impede children's progress toward skilled reading. The first obstacle, which arises at the outset of reading acquisition, is difficulty understanding and using the alphabetic principle—the idea that written spellings systematically represent spoken words. It is hard to comprehend connected text if word recognition is inaccurate or laborious. The second obstacle is a failure to transfer the comprehension skills of spoken language to reading and to acquire new strategies that may be specifically needed for reading. The third obstacle to reading will magnify the first two: the absence or loss of an initial motivation to read or failure to develop an appreciation of the rewards of reading.

## National Reading Panel

In response to a congressional charge, the National Institute of Child Health and Human Development, a division of the National Institutes of Health, formed the NRP to "assess the status of research-based knowledge, including the effectiveness of various approaches to teaching children to read" (National Institute of Child Health and Human Development, 2000, p. 1). The report was designed to build on the 1998 NRC report.

The NRP's process included public hearings that involved teachers, parents, university scholars, educational policy experts, and others in wide-ranging discussions of learning and teaching reading, as well as a systematic review of a voluminous literature. The NRP used specific criteria to identify findings that were supported by high-quality experimental studies. It selected for consideration studies that measured reading as an outcome, were published in English in a refereed journal, focused on children's reading development from prekindergarten through 12th grade, and used an experimental or quasi-experimental design with a control group or a multiple baseline method. The NRP also coded the selected studies for certain qualities, such as sample characteristics, degree of detail of description of interventions, methods, and outcome measures (National Institute of Child Health and Human Development, 2000).

The NRP's findings confirmed the definition of the components of successful reading offered in the 1998 NRC report. In terms of what enables students to become successful readers, the NRP organized its findings around three foundational elements—alphabetics, fluency, and comprehension—that encompass the basic skills all readers need to master.

Alphabetics includes both phonemic awareness and phonics, which the report describes as the "two best school-entry predictors of how well children will learn to read during the first two years of instruction" (p. 7). Phonemes are defined as "the smallest units composing spoken language." The two sounds that make up the word "go," for example, are two phonemes. A phoneme can be identified by a single letter, but phonemes are not synonymous with either letters or syllables. Thus, phonemic awareness, the ability to recognize and use spoken phonemes, precedes understanding of phonics, the way "letters are linked to sounds (phonemes) to form letter-sound correspondences." The NRP found that "systematic phonics instruction produces significant benefits for children in kindergarten through 6th grade and for children having difficulty learning to read" (National Institute of Child Health and Human Development, 2000, p. 9).

Students must also develop fluency, or the capacity to "read orally with speed, accuracy, and proper expression" (p. 11). Fluency increases with practice in oral and silent reading.

Both alphabetic skill and fluency are essential for students to achieve the purpose of reading, comprehension. Viewed as "essential not only to academic learning in all subject areas but to lifelong learning as well" (p. 13), comprehension is described by the NRP a "complex cognitive process" that requires an adequate vocabulary, purposeful "interaction with the text," and the capacity to relate ideas in the text to personal knowledge and experiences (National Institute of Child Health and Human Development, 2000, p. 13).

Because they overlap, the underlying skills may be grouped in various ways (e.g., phonemic awareness and phonics may be treated as one skill or two) than the one used by the NRP report. However, the field has achieved consensus on the basic components of what a successful reader "knows." These elements—phonemic awareness, phonics, fluency, vocabulary, and comprehension—are increasingly identified as the most important content for teacher preparation courses (August and Shanahan, 2006).

### International Reading Association

The International Reading Association (IRA) has synthesized the literature on reading with the goal of offering guidance on preparation for reading teachers. Its findings are presented in the form of a multipart study of effective practices (2003a), standards for reading professionals (2003b), and a research synthesis (2007). The study on practices (2003a) included a survey of reading teacher educators, an in-depth look at several programs identified as exemplary, and analysis of the effectiveness of the graduates of those programs. The IRA standards (2003b) are used by the faculties of teacher preparation programs and state departments of education in planning for the training of classroom reading teachers, paraprofessionals, reading specialists and coaches, reading teacher educators, and administrators. They are also used for evaluating both candidates and programs. A revised version (which will incorporate new comments from panels of experts and reviewers) is scheduled for publication in 2010.

The IRA's 2007 report synthesized findings from the 2003 study, as well as a review of empirical research by Risko and colleagues (2008) (discussed below). Many of its findings are more pertinent to the committee's questions 2, 3, and 4, than to question 1, but with regard to what successful readers know, it essentially follows the NRP in identifying what it refers to as the major components of reading. The IRA's purpose in these three documents is to guide instruction and teacher preparation, so it discusses the skills in the context of strategies for teachers.

From these summary reports it is clear that there is a consensus among leaders in the field of reading that successful beginning readers possess six foundational skills:

1. oral language as a base for learning,
2. phonemic awareness,
3. a grasp of phonics,
4. fluency,
5. vocabulary knowledge, and
6. comprehension strategies.

### Adolescent Readers and English-Language Learners

The basic picture of what successful readers know begins with young children whose first language is English. The picture is somewhat different for adolescent readers and English-language learners. The still-developing literacy of adolescents has been less thoroughly studied than that of young children, though some recent work has expanded thinking on this topic (International Reading Association and the National Middle School Association 2002; Kamil et al., 2008). Successful adolescent readers have mastered phonemic awareness, phonics, and fluency by the middle school years, but they face higher demands for vocabulary and comprehension than do younger students. Once they reach middle school, students must rely on academic vocabulary and comprehension to learn other subjects (though they begin "reading to learn" during the primary grades). Development of vocabulary and comprehension continues throughout life—unlike phonemic awareness, phonics, and fluency, which become automatic once they are mastered.

Adolescents who are reading successfully expand and broaden their comprehension skills and strategies across a range of texts. The texts they read present complex ideas, technical vocabulary, an array of graphical representations that have to be interpreted, and underlying structures that mirror the discipline in which they are reading (e.g., scientific argumentation) (Greenleaf et al., 2001). These skills and strategies include predicting the content of upcoming texts, summarizing to get the gist of a document, and monitoring their own comprehension (Dole et al., 1991). Adolescents are still building stores of word knowledge that will help them in adult life and in studying new or greatly expanded knowledge domains, such as science and history (Beck, McKeown, and Kucan, 2002). Many of these skills are reflected in the proficiency standards for 8th- and 12th-grade readers established for the National Assessment of Educational Progress (NAEP) (National Center for Education Statistics, 2005). Thus, adolescent readers build on the skills established in the elementary years by solidifying their comprehension skills and accelerating their acquisition of the vocabulary necessary to read effectively in variety of fields.

The foundational reading skills that successful native English speakers develop apply to English-language learners as well, according to the National Literacy Panel on Language Minority Children and Youth (August and Shanahan, 2006, 2008). This panel of experts (in a range of fields relevant to language acquisition and literacy for non-native English speakers) reviewed research studies published in peer-reviewed journals, most of which used experimental or quasi-experimental designs.

The panel found that reading development for English-language learners presents several distinct challenges. Transferring conceptual knowledge and intellectual skills from students' native language to English is not automatic, and progress with English depends in part on both the stage of development the student has reached before beginning to learn English and the strength of the skills he or she has developed in the first language. We address instructional strategies for both struggling adolescent readers and English-language learners in the discussion of question 3, below.

## QUESTION 2: WHAT INSTRUCTIONAL OPPORTUNITIES ARE NECESSARY TO SUPPORT SUCCESSFUL READERS?

Instructional opportunities encompass more than teaching—curriculum, instructional materials, and other elements are also important—but the opportunities that teachers can provide are our focus. We again begin with the consensus reports. *Preventing Reading Difficulties in Young Children* describes the kinds of instruction that help students become successful readers (National Research Council, 1998). They include instruction in the various uses and functions of written language and an appreciation and command of them; the use of the alphabetic principle in reading and writing; and language and metacognitive skills to meet the demands of understanding printed texts. Specifically, the report finds that adequate reading instruction for young children provides them with opportunities to:

- use reading to obtain meaning from print,
- have frequent and intensive opportunities to read,
- be exposed to frequent, regular spelling-sound relationships,
- learn about the nature of the alphabetic writing system, and
- understand the structure of spoken words.

As noted above, the NRP report (National Institute of Child Health and Human Development, 2000) builds on NRC's conclusions, and it identifies instruction in the five foundational skills as the learning experiences with the strongest basis in empirical research. The report addresses alphabetics (including phonemic awareness and phonics), fluency, and comprehension (including vocabulary and comprehension).

The NRP panel subgroups who examined those three topics were charged with identifying effective instructional practices for each topic. The NRP found that the research base is strongest and most explicit for skills related to alphabetics. For example, instruction in phonemic awareness and phonics has been found to improve students' reading, decoding, spelling, and comprehension skills. In particular, an approach called systematic phonics instruction is identified as a key means of building essential skills, though the authors caution that it is a means to an end, and that overemphasis on phonics instruction, at the expense of other kinds of instruction, is "unlikely to be very effective" (p. 10).

The NRP found less to say about fluency, noting only that both guided oral reading and independent silent reading are the strategies typically used to boost fluency, but that this kind of instruction is not emphasized as much as it should be. The report also identifies "guided repeated oral reading" as an important experience for all students—those who are developing in the typical way and those who are struggling, even though methodologically strong evidence linking these experiences to fluency is not available. Both direct and indirect vocabulary instruction also appear to be valuable: the NRP found that students benefit from exposure to multiple methods of vocabulary instruction, though there is no firm basis for identifying specific methods or combinations as optimal or even essential.

With regard to comprehension, the NRP report identified a solid research basis for seven types of strategies for instruction. These include, for example, teaching readers to summarize what they have read, generate questions about a text, and use graphic organizers. The NRP found that exposure to multiple methods of comprehension instruction yields the best outcomes. It did not find evidence to support specific recommendations about which strategies are best at different stages of development.

Opportunities for teachers and students to discuss the material students are reading have also been identified as a valuable tool for developing comprehension (Applebee et al., 2003). Discussions that are largely directed by the teacher—reflecting goals the teacher has identified or challenges the teacher anticipates (such as complex or unfamiliar ideas or vocabulary or support features such as maps and graphs that require interpretation)—build specific comprehension skills. Discussion-based approaches are most successful when teachers are knowledgeable about the content of the text, thoughtful about the kinds of questions that are likely to lead the students to deep understanding of the ideas, and capable of adjusting to students' needs and challenges as the discussion unfolds.

We note that there are several approaches to instruction that are designed to build comprehension and that a debate has developed between those who favor strategy instruction and those who favor content instruction. Strategy instruction, which entails explicitly teaching the processes used in reading for understanding, has been prominent in the literature, including the National Reading Panel Report (National Institute of Child Health and Human Development, 2000). This model of instruction is principally based on theories regarding self-regulation. The alternative approach focuses on the way readers continuously build a mental representation of a text, and it calls for a focus on content, rather than processes.

The two approaches have been studied independently, but it is only recently that researchers have investigated their comparative advantages. McKeown, Beck, and Blake (2009) compared the effects of each approach and also compared them with the effects of a control approach, instruction guided by a basal reading program. This quasi-experimental study was conducted over 2 years with 5th-grade students in an urban setting. The "strategies" group received explicit teaching in specific procedures for interacting with text (i.e., summarizing, predicting, drawing inferences, generating questions, and monitoring comprehension). The "content" group responded to general questions about the meaning of the text (e.g., "What's going on here?" "How does all this connect with what we read earlier?"). For the control group, the researchers extracted comprehension-related questions from the teachers' edition of a basal reading program. Measures used to assess the effectiveness of instruction included assessments of the understanding of the texts taught and assessments that asked students to go beyond what they had been explicitly taught. The results of this study were mixed: they showed no difference across the approaches on one measure but more positive results for the content-based approach on others.

## QUESTION 3: WHAT DO SUCCESSFUL TEACHERS KNOW ABOUT READING AND HOW TO TEACH IT?

The volume of available guidance to reading teachers shows that many practitioners and researchers have strong views about the knowledge and skills that are most important for teachers of reading; however, the research has less to offer on this question than on the question of what successful students know. The three summary reports from the National Research Council (1998), the International Reading Association (2007), and the National Reading Panel (National Institute of Child Health and Human Development, 2000) have put forward summary descriptions of what excellent reading teachers know and can do. The next section summarizes those three reports on this question; the following two sections cover two special groups, adolescents and English-language learners.

## Overview

*Preparing Our Teachers,* a report designed to distill from the 1998 NRC report practical suggestions for teachers and teacher preparation programs, stresses the importance of a well-rounded education for prospective teachers (Strickland et al., 2002): "Because reading touches all content areas—from sciences and social studies to literature and philosophy, . . . good teachers benefit from being well read themselves and knowledgeable in many disciplines" (p. 17). The report advocates that teachers develop knowledge across a range of fields and topics—including the behavioral and cognitive sciences, the social sciences, and language and literature—as well as a detailed understanding of the content of relevant academic standards.

The NRP's vision of what teachers need to know is grounded in their framing of what students need to know. Thus, they posit that teachers need to understand and know how to teach the foundational reading skills (National Institute of Child Health and Human Development, 2000).[2] However, the NRP notes that there are numerous ways to teach these skills and that the evidence does not provide completely clear indications of which approaches are best, which are most suitable for particular groups of students, or how best to apply evidence-based techniques. Thus, the NRP asserts that prospective teachers should learn how to apply emerging empirical evidence in making their own judgments about instructional programs or developing instructional approaches for themselves, based on the needs of their students.

For example, only a handful of studies that met the NRP criteria addressed specific approaches for teaching comprehension—one of the foundational skills. The few studies that were available (related to the specific strategies known as the direct explanation approach and the transactional strategy approach) support the conclusion that formal instruction is necessary for teachers to implement them effectively. The panel also found that research on the development of reading comprehension skills provided important guidance for effective instruction (National Institute of Child Health and Human Development, 2000, p. 13):

> First, reading comprehension is a complex process that cannot be understood without a clear description of the role that vocabulary development and vocabulary instruction play in the understanding of what has been read. Second, comprehension is an active process that requires an intentional and thoughtful interaction between the reader and the text. Third, the preparation of teachers to better equip students to develop and apply reading comprehension strategies is intimately linked to students' achievement in this area.

---

[2]Reading researchers tend not to use the term pedagogical content knowledge, but teachers' knowledge of how to teach reading could be understood as a form of it.

The panel conducted similar analyses for the elements of alphabetics and fluency and found empirical support for the effectiveness of a number of instructional strategies, such as teaching children to manipulate phonemes in words and guided oral reading, in helping students develop as readers. Nevertheless, the NRP report notes that many specific questions about instructional approaches remain unanswered.

The IRA identifies an array of knowledge that is important for teachers to have. Based on professional judgment and on a review of the literature on reading and reading instruction, the IRA concluded that any preparation program for reading teachers should include six elements (International Reading Association, 2007):[3]

1.  A foundation in research and theory: Teachers must develop a thorough understanding of language and reading development as well as an understanding of learning theory and motivation in order to ground their instructional decision making effectively.

2.  Word-level instructional strategies: Teachers must be prepared to use multiple strategies for developing students' knowledge of word meanings and strategies for word identification. This includes the study of the phonemic basis for oral language, phonics instruction, and attention to syntax and semantics as support for word recognition and self-monitoring.

3.  Text-level comprehension strategies: Teachers must be prepared to teach multiple strategies that readers can use to construct meaning from text and to monitor their comprehension. They must understand the ways in which vocabulary (word meaning) and fluency instruction can support comprehension and develop the capacity for critical analysis of texts that considers multiple perspectives.

4.  Reading-writing connections: Teachers must be prepared to teach strategies that connect writing to the reading of literary and information texts as a support for comprehension. This includes attention to teaching conventions of writing.

5.  Instructional approaches and materials: Teachers must be prepared to use a variety of instructional strategies and materials selectively, appropriately, and flexibly.

6.  Assessment: Teachers must be prepared to use appropriate assessment techniques to support responsive instructional decision making and reflection.

---

[3]These six elements are described on pages 2 through 6 of International Reading Association (2007); we have paraphrased the descriptions.

The IRA's standards for reading professionals address five areas: foundational knowledge; instructional strategies and curriculum materials; assessment, diagnosis, and evaluation; creating a literate environment; and professional development (International Reading Association, 2003b).[4] The standards in each area provide further detail about the knowledge and skills they believe teachers should have. For example, a reading specialist should be able to "refer to major theories in the foundational areas as they relate to reading [and to] explain, compare, and contrast the theories" (see http://www.reading.org/downloads/resources/545standards2003/index. html [February 2010]).

There is little empirical evidence that directly links particular knowledge and skills that teachers have to outcomes for students. However, experts have drawn logical conclusions about what teachers should know and be able to do from research concerning the attributes of successful readers and instructional strategies that have been successful, as well as normative views of the professional knowledge necessary to teach reading. The current working hypothesis is not that teachers need to master particular instructional strategies, but that there is an arsenal of strategies they can use to meet the needs of diverse students. Experts believe that teachers draw on both a macrolevel understanding of instructional goals (such as assessing and diagnosing readers' strengths and weaknesses, adapting available strategies and materials to students' needs, creating a rich literary environment with numerous and varied opportunities to practice reading skills, etc.), as well as a microlevel understanding of the foundational skills and challenges students face in mastering them, building vocabulary and comprehension (including, for example, a detailed picture of developmental stages and knowledge of how to effectively group diverse students).

In short, reading teachers rely on a broad-based understanding of:

- the foundational elements of reading and the theory on which they are based;
- the range of instructional strategies they can use to develop each of these skills in diverse students; and
- the materials and technological resources they can use to support student learning.

---

[4] Instructional strategies and curriculum materials assessment, diagnosis, and evaluation, and creating a literate environment could all be understood to be part of a teacher's pedagogical content knowledge.

## Teaching Adolescent Readers

Common sense suggests that the teaching of reading is different in elementary schools than it is in middle and high schools. Elementary schools have a built-in support system for the development of successful reading. That system includes a period of time devoted each day to instruction by a teacher who has special training in reading, and elementary schools often have reading specialists and interventions for struggling readers. Middle and secondary schools, however, less frequently have systems in place to support struggling readers. English/language arts classes may offer instruction aimed at building reading and writing skills, but students who are not yet reading well are at a disadvantage, not only in those classes, but also in other classes that draw on reading skills, such as history, science, and mathematics.

Recent research has identified instructional strategies that seem to be effective with struggling adolescent readers (Kamil, 2003; Biancarosa and Snow, 2006; see also Graham and Perin, 2007; Haynes, 2007; Heller and Greenleaf, 2007; Short and Fitzsimmons, 2007).[5] For example, in a recent report that was based on an expert panel's review of current research that would be useful in identifying the most promising approaches to supporting struggling adolescent readers, Biancarosa and Snow (2006) identified nine key instructional components of effective adolescent literacy programs that have yielded improvement in reading and writing abilities:

1. direct, explicit comprehension instruction;
2. effective instructional principles embedded in content;
3. motivation and self-directed reading;
4. text-based collaborative learning;
5. strategic tutoring;
6. diverse texts;
7. intensive writing;
8. technology component; and
9. ongoing formative assessment of students.

A report from the What Works Clearinghouse (a project of the Department of Education's Institute of Education Sciences that assesses the research support for education programs and practices) has examined class-

---

[5]The IRA collaborated with the National Middle School Association to produce a joint position statement summarizing the key elements of reading instruction for this age group, which draws on the association's own publications. The statement recommends that schools provide: ongoing reading instruction across the curriculum for all students; assessment that informs instruction; and ample opportunities to read and discuss reading with others (International Reading Association and National Middle School Association, 2002).

room practices and interventions that target the needs of adolescent readers (Kamil et al., 2008). The authors recommend five specific practices, with different levels of evidentiary support: for 1, 2, and 5, the evidence is strong; for 3 and 4, it is moderate.[6] Their recommendations are that teachers (p. 7):

1. provide explicit vocabulary instruction,
2. provide direct and explicit comprehension strategy instruction,
3. provide opportunities for extended discussion of text meaning and interpretations,
4. increase student motivation and engagement in literacy learning, and
5. make available intensive and individualized interventions for struggling readers that can be provided by trained specialists.

There is ample evidence that many students have not become successful readers by the time they leave elementary school (see, e.g., Lee, Grigg, and Donahue, 2007). Thus, it is important that teachers of middle and high school students understand the importance of helping students continue to build on the foundational reading skills established in elementary school and know how to identify students who are still struggling. Although researchers are now focusing greater attention than previously on the distinct needs of struggling adolescent readers, the literature supplies more promising ideas than settled research on the most effective ways to reach these students. Those who have studied the issue believe that teachers who work with adolescents draw on strategies for fostering motivation to read, building vocabulary, and expanding students' capacity to comprehend a variety of information and literary texts.

## Teaching English-Language Learners

Although there are teaching specialists trained to work with English-language learners (see Chapter 3), most of those students do not have enough access to specialists, either because they are moved out of language support classes before they are proficient or because they are expected to function in mainstream classes with teachers who have not been prepared to address their needs while extra language support is provided separately (Lucas and Grinberg, 2008). These students would be best served if their teachers understood the factors that affect their reading development and

---

[6]The authors describe strong evidence as including "both studies with high internal validity and studies with strong external validity." They offer a detailed discussion of their criteria (Kamil et al., 2008,Table 1, p. 2).

were prepared to address them. Unfortunately the empirical evidence on what this preparation should consist of is limited.

## Preparation for All Teachers

The National Literacy Panel for Language Minority Children and Youth prepared a report similar to that of the National Reading Panel, which summarized the evidence on the development of literacy among English-language learners using similar criteria in identifying high-quality empirical research (August and Shanahan, 2006). The panel reviewed studies on the development of literacy through five domains: the differences between the development of literacy in language-minority students and mainstream students; cross-linguistic relationships between oral language development and literacy in students' first and second languages; sociocultural contexts and literacy development; instruction and professional development; and student assessment. The panel identified the knowledge it views as important for teachers who will work with English-language learners:

- understanding of the complexity of the reading process for English-language learners;
- competence at explicit instruction in vocabulary, the development of oral proficiency;
- content instruction that focuses on learning from text, understanding and producing academic language, genre differentiation, and academic writing;
- understanding of home-school differences in interaction patterns or styles and individual differences among the wide range of English-language learners; and
- understanding of the ways language and reading interact, the skills that transfer into English, and how to facilitate that transfer; and understanding of the context in which second-language learners develop as readers.

Lucas and Grinberg (2008) also summarized the literature available, including the limited number of empirical studies and other materials. They found that it is valuable for teachers of English-language learners, regardless of the subject they are teaching, to have knowledge of (p. 614):

- the language backgrounds, experiences, and proficiencies of their students;
- second-language development;
- the connection between language, culture, and identity; and
- language forms, mechanics, and uses.

It is valuable for teachers to understand their students' linguistic backgrounds for several reasons. A strong teacher-student relationship has benefits for students' academic development, for example, and teaching that draws on students' linguistic traditions facilitates their learning. In terms of second-language development, Lucas and Grinberg (2008) cite a range of empirical and other work that indicates that the development of literacy is much smoother for English-language learners if they have already developed strong skills in their native language and that teachers should help students draw on their original language as a support in improving their English.

Lucas and Grinberg also report that it is important that teachers recognize the difference between conversational and academic language. Students cannot succeed at studying academic subjects in a second language until they have sufficient proficiency in listening, speaking, reading, and writing. Moreover, anxiety, which is more likely if their skills in any of these areas are limited, can impede learning. The authors note that teaching of grammar has fallen out of favor in the English curriculum and that many teachers have not studied a second language; however, they also note that educational linguists have argued that teachers need specific knowledge of language mechanics and usage in order to facilitate their students' language development.

Calderón (2007) has also summarized key aspects of second-language learning in a teaching framework that is based on a set of longitudinal studies in which strategies were field-tested around the country. Calderón notes that English-language learners who already have strong literacy skills in their own language have a significant advantage, but that transferring knowledge and skills from one language to another may not be automatic. English language learners may need to be explicitly taught to transfer these skills.

Furthermore, Calderón notes, building vocabulary depth (the degree of knowledge of a word) and breadth (the number of words) is more challenging for English-language learners than for native English speakers. More than a third of subject-specific vocabulary words in English are cognates with Spanish, for example, but many other words that seem to be cognates actually have different meanings in English and have to be learned (Calderón, 2007). All readers comprehend texts on familiar topics more readily than unfamiliar ones, and English-language learners may have difficulty comprehending texts, even if they are proficient readers in terms of their decoding and fluency, if they are unfamiliar with the vocabulary and content of a text. Adolescent English-language learners who have opportunities to apply comprehension skills to content texts in their native language acquire these skills much faster because they understand the text.

Once these skills are acquired in their native languages, they can be transferred to English reading (August and Shanahan, 2006).

## Middle and High School Teachers

English-language learners of middle or high school age present a particular challenge. The integration of second-language and reading development requires specific teacher preparation, particularly for those who teach English-language learners in content areas such as mathematics, science, and social studies (August et al., 2005a; Valdés et al., 2005; August and Calderón, 2006; Calderón, 2007; Short and Fitzsimmons, 2007; August, 2008). The challenge is particularly hard for English-language learners who are newcomers or "students with interrupted formal education," who may be reading at a 1st- to 3rd-grade level. These students are at a significant disadvantage because they are not generally offered the literacy instruction provided to students in elementary school (August et al., 2005b; Carnegie Corporation of New York, 2010).

Not only are middle and high school English-language learners expected to master complex course content, often with minimal background knowledge or preparation, but they also have fewer years to master the English language. English-language learners can be fluent readers even when they do not fully understand the meaning of the words they read (Stahl, 2003; Calderón et al., 2005). When English-language learners are promoted from grade to grade on the basis of fluency assessments, they may not receive appropriate instruction on vocabulary and reading comprehension (August et al., 2005c). Thus, these students benefit if their teachers of mathematics, science, and social studies can integrate explicit vocabulary and reading comprehension instruction that focuses on their subject-matter instruction (Short and Fitzsimmons, 2007). However, according to a report from the National Center for Education Statistics (2002), in 1999-2000 only 12.5 percent of teachers who taught English-language learners had received 8 or more hours of training in teaching these students during the preceding 3 years.

## Reading Teachers

Teachers of any subject or grade may be called on to address the needs of English-language learners, but reading teachers have a particular responsibility to understand the challenges of second-language acquisition. The literature we reviewed indicates the value for elementary reading teachers, reading specialists for all levels, and middle and high school English/language arts teachers of a clear theoretical understanding of the process of learning to read for English-language learners, strategies for assessing the literacy skills of these students, and a range of strategies for targeting their needs, as well as resources for additional support (Fillmore and Snow, 2000; Valdéz et al., 2005). There is little empirical research to demonstrate that teachers who have been taught particular knowledge and skills have students who learn better than others. However, there is a consensus on the skills and knowledge most useful to teachers of reading, which provides the best available guidance for the preparation of teachers of reading:

- the foundational elements of reading and the theory on which they are based;
- the range of instructional strategies they can use to develop each of these skills in diverse students;
- the materials and technological resources they need to support student learning;
- a clear theoretical understanding of the process of learning to read for English-language learners, strategies for assessing the literacy skills of these students, and the range of available strategies for targeting their needs, as well as resources for additional support; and
- strategies for helping struggling older readers build foundational skills, foster motivation to read, build vocabulary, and improve comprehension of a variety of information and literary texts.

## QUESTION 4: WHAT INSTRUCTIONAL OPPORTUNITIES ARE NECESSARY TO PREPARE SUCCESSFUL READING TEACHERS?

Relatively few empirical studies have been focused on the question of how teachers ought to be prepared to teach reading. The NRP examined this question and identified just 11 studies that addressed preservice education and also met the selection criteria for their report (National Institute of Child Health and Human Development, 2000). These studies did not address long-term outcomes or outcomes for students, and there were too few of them for the NRP to draw specific conclusions about what should happen in teacher preparation programs. The NRP report noted that many questions—regarding the content, length, and effectiveness of preservice education, and other issues—deserve further research.

In its synthesis of empirical and theoretical work on teacher preparation, the IRA's Teacher Education Task Force identified six characteristics as essential to programs that "produce teachers who teach reading well" (International Reading Association, 2007, p. 1). Not all of those characteristics are directly relevant to the experiences prospective teachers should have, and they are derived less from empirical research than from an analysis of programs selected as examples of a diverse range of program types. We include them here because the programs were reviewed in unusual depth, and the IRA's exploratory work has been influential in the field:

- Content: The programs draw on an integrated body of research focusing on how students become successful readers and how teachers support students with instruction.
- Faculty and teaching: The faculty is committed to effective instruction that delivers appropriate content and models successful instructional techniques for students.
- Apprenticeships, field experiences, and practice: The programs move teachers through systematically arrayed field experiences that are closely coordinated with their coursework and expose them to excellent modes and mentors.
- Diversity: The programs are saturated with an awareness of diversity, and they produce teachers who know how to teach diverse students in diverse settings.
- Candidate and program assessment: The programs intentionally and regularly assess their students, graduates, faculty, and curriculum to guide instructional decision making and program development.
- Governance, resources, and vision: The programs are centered on a vision of quality teaching that produces a community of future leaders in reading education. The governance gives faculty appropriate control for realizing that vision.

Following the task force's work, the IRA established a new program in 2008 to promote and honor excellence in the preparation of reading teachers, the Certificate of Distinction. The certificate is designed to recognize programs that "consistently prepare well-qualified reading teachers who know about and use evidence-based practices" (see http://www.reading. org [October 2009]).

Risko and her colleagues (2008) also analyzed the research on the education of reading teachers. They identified 82 studies that focused on the preparation of teachers for K-12 classroom reading instruction that met their critieria. They selected for review empirical studies that reflected a variety of methodological stances and were published between 1990 and 2006 in a peer-reviewed journal. The outcomes they examined included both changes in teachers' beliefs and attitudes in the course of their education, as well as gains they made in knowledge and skills. The findings in this paper are primarily suggestive of experiences that may be valuable, depending on the goals one identifies for teacher preparation.

The authors offer a detailed critique of the available literature, as well as several findings about practices that seem to be associated with effectiveness. They observe that evidence shows that "reading teacher preparation programs have been relatively successful in changing prospective teachers' knowledge and beliefs" (Risko et al., 2008, p. 252) and that there is some (but less) evidence that they affect teaching practice. The authors identify a few elements of teacher preparation as likely to be effective:

- explicit examples and explanations of material;
- a "learning and doing approach," in which teacher educators model the pedagogical strategies they are teaching their students to use;
- opportunities for guided practice of teaching strategies in the university classroom and with students;
- extended opportunities for fieldwork and sustained interactions with students; and
- mentoring that includes both feedback on teaching and peer coaching.

Although there is very little empirical basis for claims about precisely how prospective reading teachers should be prepared, two elements stand out from the literature as likely to be valuable and should be examined more rigorously:

1. coursework that provides opportunities to engage substantively with the theoretical foundations of reading research as well as the range of pedagogical approaches currently viewed as having merit; and
2. extensive opportunities for fieldwork that includes supervised practice teaching content and using strategies covered in class work, as well as continuing feedback from faculty, experienced colleagues, and peers.

## HOW READING TEACHERS ARE CURRENTLY PREPARED

As we discuss in Chapter 3, very few national-level data are available on program requirements, coursework, and other features of study for general teacher candidates or for those who specialize in reading or other subjects. However, states' policies and requirements regarding readiness to teach reading provide some indications of the characteristics of reading preparation programs. In addition, we commissioned analyses of New York City and Florida about the preparation of reading teachers in those two jurisdictions. Finally, we reviewed a handful of studies that have focused in various ways on the content of literacy preparation in teacher preparation programs.

### State Policies

In looking at state policies, we turned first to the question of what states require of teacher preparation programs. Information about state policies is available in a database compiled by the Education Commission of the States (which includes the 50 states, American Samoa, Puerto Rico, and the Virgin Islands)[7] and information from our commissioned analyses. The database tracks state policies related to various questions, including whether the state's standards for beginning teachers or requirements for preparation programs include any provisions related to the teaching of reading. The database includes excerpts from state policy documents describing requirements for undergraduate and postgraduate teacher preparation programs, which were reviewed for accuracy by state personnel.

We found that states fall into four rough categories: virtually no guidance (24 states); a specified number of credit hours (10 states); adherence to specific guidelines (4 states); and substantive guidance (15 states). In the first group, the 24 states either have no policy on the preparation of reading teachers or the only policy is an extremely general statement that does not offer any meaningful guidance for programs. In the next group, 10 states specify a certain number of credit hours in reading, but they offer no guidance as to what the credits should cover. In the third group, four states specify that programs should adhere to the guidelines of the National Council for Accreditation in Teacher Education, the Interstate New Teacher Assessment and Support Consortium, or both. Last, 15 states offer some kind of substantive guidance (some in that category also specified a number of credit hours).

Among the 15 states that do offer some type of guidance, however, there is a considerable range in the nature of their guidance. In Alabama, for example, institutions are responsible for producing teacher candidates who demonstrate knowledge of:

- language development and the role of language in learning;
- how to develop a print and language rich classroom that fosters interest and growth in all aspects of literacy;
- classroom environments and instruction that develop and extend students' competence in reading, writing, speaking and listening; and

---

[7]This database is hosted by the National Comprehensive Center for Teacher Quality, which is a collaboration among the Education Commission of the States, the Educational Testing Service, Learning Point Associates, and Vanderbilt University; see http://www.tqsource.org/ [October 2009].

- assessment tools to monitor the acquisition of reading strategies, improve reading instruction and identify students who require additional instruction.

Massachusetts specifies that "All teacher candidates must have the subject-matter knowledge required to teach reading. Elementary teacher candidates complete instruction in reading/language arts, reading theory, and research and practice." North Carolina stipulates that teachers must know the North Carolina and district standards for reading.

Examining the reading content of teacher certification exams provides yet another window into the kinds of reading instructional practices and knowledge beginning teachers are expected to have. Though these examinations vary by state, a recent study of state licensure examinations for prospective elementary school teachers found the focus on literacy across a range of commonly used teacher tests was wanting (Stotsky, 2006). For example, the study concluded that the content of an exam developed by the Educational Testing Service and used by 35 states includes only a tiny fraction of items that address phonemic awareness, phonics, and vocabulary knowledge—three of the foundational reading skills. And only four states—California, Massachusetts, Oklahoma, and Tennessee—require a separate reading test for licensing elementary school teachers. (The study does not provide details on the nature of these tests.) In short, states have very different policies related to teacher preparation in reading.

Our commissioned studies also showed considerable variation within regions. In New York, to obtain a childhood education certificate (to teach grades 1-6) through its traditional route, the state requires a minimum of six credits in language and literacy, which typically translates to roughly two three-credit courses (Grossman et al., 2008). But for the 18 institutions and 31 childhood programs that prepare the majority of teachers for New York City schools (of which 26 are labeled "college-recommending" and 5 as "early-entry"), this state-set minimum requirement did not translate into similar program requirements. In general, the programs required considerably more literacy courses than the state-mandated floor: on average, teacher candidates must take 10.5 credits in English/language arts coursework, substantially more than the 6 credits in English/language arts methods classes required by the state (Grossman et al., 2008).

Though the New York City programs generally require more English/language arts coursework than the state requires, the variation among the programs is striking. One program requires no credits, while another requires 39; the standard deviation in number of credits is 7.7—nearly three-quarters the size of the mean number of credits. A similar pattern emerges from an examination of English/language arts methods credits in particular:

the standard deviation is 3.2, with programs requiring anywhere from zero to 15 credits (Grossman et al., 2008).

We learned more about the content of these courses through surveys of new teachers that probed what kinds of learning opportunities received the most and least emphasis in their preparation programs. New teachers in New York City reported that their programs typically emphasized learning about characteristics of emergent readers, studying or analyzing children's literature, learning ways to build student interest and motivation to read, and learning how to activate students' prior knowledge. By contrast, the topics and opportunities receiving the least emphasis included opportunities to explore New York State standards and assessments for fourth graders or the New York City English/language arts curriculum, and learning how to support older students who are learning to read (Grossman et al., 2008).

## Descriptive Studies

We found a handful of studies that include some kind of description of English/language arts teacher training. One study analyzed secondary English/language arts methods courses across 81 universities and classified them into types, such as survey, workshop, or theoretical. The authors found a great degree of variability in the ways in which these methods courses were taught (Smagorinsky and Whiting, 1995). Research conducted by the National Center for Research on Teacher Learning (1991) at Michigan State University focused in part on opportunities for learning about teaching writing and mathematics to diverse learners at seven teacher preparation programs of different types in the United States. This descriptive study (often called the TELT study, for Teacher Education and Learning to Teach) found considerable variation across the programs with respect to subject-specific teaching of writing. The authors cite fundamental differences in the substantive orientation of the program—either a "traditional management-oriented" program or a "reform" oriented on—as the source of the variation in program content and its effect on teacher practice (Kennedy, 1998).

There are several case studies of "exemplary" or "excellent" literacy teacher preparation programs that discuss various aspects of literacy program components (e.g., International Reading Association, 2005). However, because these studies used different selection methodologies and asked different questions, we could not develop summative statements from them about the kinds of preparation that prospective teachers receive in the area of literacy.

## CONCLUSIONS

Our charge was to examine the extent to which teacher education programs draw on converging scientific evidence regarding the teaching of reading. However, we were able to find very little information about teacher education programs in general—except that they vary greatly—so we cannot answer this question well. The data available regarding the types of instruction and experiences that participants receive in teacher education programs do not provide a sufficient basis for any conclusions about the extent to which teacher preparation programs in reading draw on converging scientific evidence regarding the teaching of reading or other relevant aspects of literacy education.

Although our four-question framework had the effect of highlighting the relative dearth of empirical evidence about what teachers should know and how they should be prepared, we did find useful research. There is a reasonable body of empirical research concerning the question of what effective readers know and can do, though more information about English-language learners and adolescent readers is needed. There is also empirical evidence about the instructional strategies that help students learn to read, but there is no definitive guidance that points to particular effective strategies. The literature on what teachers need to know is extremely limited, and the empirical evidence on effective teacher preparation nearly nonexistent.

We did find considerable conceptual overlap across the four questions, and there have been concerted efforts by experts to provide guidance about both how to teach reading and how to prepare teachers to teach reading given those conceptual connections. Researchers who have immersed themselves in these questions and expert panels that have sifted through various kinds of evidence have concluded that teachers of reading rely on a sophisticated understanding of the development of literacy, the many factors that influence it, and the array of strategies they can use, along with the capacity to keep collecting evidence as they refine their practice. Box 5-1 highlights the way in which the foundational skills anchor thinking about each facet of teaching and learning reading by drawing together examples from the discussions of the four questions. These examples illustrate themes in the research on reading, but they do not offer a detailed picture of the knowledge and skills that would be most important to an individual teacher candidate, nor of how teachers ought to be taught. The work does support logical arguments about the kinds of educational experiences likely to be beneficial; see Appendix B for examples.

The preparation of future reading teachers should be grounded in the best available scientific literature related to literacy teaching and learning. Although there is a voluminous literature on reading, it does not provide

**BOX 5-1**
**Teaching and Learning Reading—The Foundational Skills**

*The Foundational Skills:*
*Phonemic awareness, phonics, fluency, vocabulary, comprehension*

**Examples of Student Opportunities to Learn**
Small-group instruction focused on, e.g., recognizing and manipulating phonemes

Explicit instruction in, e.g., the systematic relationships between spoken sounds and letters

Guided oral reading

Independent reading

**Examples of Teacher Knowledge and Skills**
Understanding of the way the five foundational skills are integrated in fluent reading

Understanding of developmental benchmarks

Strategies for assessing and monitoring student progress

Strategies for systematic phonics instruction, e.g., synthetic phonics (children learn to convert letters or letter combinations into sounds and how to blend them into words)

Familiarity with literature appropriate to developmental levels

**Examples of Teacher Opportunities to Learn**
Coursework in the theoretical basis for the foundational reading skills

Guided practice in the university classroom

Extended fieldwork

Mentoring and peer feedback

Practice applying student data to classroom challenges

an empirical basis for complete answers to all of our questions. We close the chapter with what we conclude can be drawn from this literature now and the areas in which further investigation is needed.

We found the strongest basis for conclusions about what students need to know and be able to do to be successful readers.

> **Conclusion 5-1:** Successful beginning readers possess a set of foundational skills that enable them not only to continue growing as readers but also to progress in all academic subjects. A variety of instructional approaches that address these foundational skills can be effective when used by teachers who have a grounding in the foundational elements and the theory on which they are based.

The importance of those foundational skills supports conclusions about what is most important in the preparation of teachers of reading:

> **Conclusion 5-2:** It is plausible that preparation in the nature of the foundational reading skills and research-based instructional approaches would improve teachers' practice to a degree that would be evident in learning outcomes for their students. However, there is currently no clear evidence that such preparation does indeed improve teacher effectiveness or about how such preparation should be carried out.

> **Conclusion 5-3:** There are very few systematic data about the nature of the preparation in reading that prospective teachers receive across the nation. The limited information that exists suggests that the nature of preparation of prospective teachers for reading instruction is widely variable both across and within states.

> **Conclusion 5-4:** Little is known about the best ways to prepare prospective teachers to teach reading. Systematic data are needed on the nature and content of the coursework and other experiences that constitute teacher preparation in reading.

Systematic data would make it possible to monitor and evaluate teacher preparation in reading and to conduct research on the relative effectiveness of different preparation approaches. The kind of data collection and effectiveness research we envision would be focused in particular on preparation related to the foundational reading skills and the instructional approaches that have been shown to be effective in teaching reading. Examples of the sorts of research that are most needed include

- investigations of the development of teachers' knowledge and skills as they progress from novices to accomplished reading teachers;
- expansion of the array of tools for investigating the relationship between features of teacher education and teachers' preparedness to teach;
- efficacy studies and scale-up studies that use experimental or quasi-experimental methods and measures; and
- investigations of outcomes for teachers exposed to particular coursework and fieldwork.

We discuss the need for research more fully in Chapter 9.

# 6

# Preparing Mathematics Teachers

The preparation of mathematics teachers in the United States has been a topic of increasingly impassioned discussion in the last 20 years. There is deep concern about the numeracy of the nation's high school graduates, as well as concern about perceived shortages of highly qualified mathematics teachers. The organization of U.S. schooling as three stages—elementary (kindergarten through grade 4 or 5), middle (grade 5 or 6 through 8), and secondary or high (grades 9 through 12)—presents particular challenges for mathematics education. Mathematics learning at each of these levels has a distinct character, reflecting the developmental and educational needs of different age groups. For teachers, this structure has meant that different sorts of preparation are required to teach each level. Most elementary teachers are prepared to teach all subjects, while teachers at the secondary level are prepared as specialists in a particular content area. Preparation for middle grades mathematics teachers varies from place to place, and certification requirements reflect the ambiguous status of middle school. For example, many states offer grade K-8 certification to teachers prepared as generalists, as well as grade 7-12 certification to those specifically prepared to teach mathematics.

Though the preparation of elementary, middle, and secondary level teachers may differ, expectations for all mathematics teachers have increased steadily and dramatically over the last few decades. In particular, schools now try to teach more mathematics earlier than was the case even a decade ago. The most visible evidence of this change has been the push to encourage all high school students to take both 2 years of algebra and

1 year of geometry. Many districts and even some states have made it a goal that all students take algebra I by the 8th grade.

U.S. students are not yet, as a group, meeting the higher expectations of recent years. Trends in student achievement in mathematics, as measured by the National Assessment of Educational Progress (NAEP), have shown considerable improvement since 1990, but the 2009 results showed that just 39 percent of 4th graders and 34 percent of 8th graders are performing at or above the proficient level (National Center for Education Statistics, 2009). In the mathematics portion of the Third International Mathematics and Science Study (TIMSS), U.S. 4th and 8th graders scored above the median, but the nation was not among the top-performing nations (Gonzales et al., 2008). A 1998 comparison of the performance of older students showed that U.S. students were among the lowest performing group of the 21 nations in the study (National Center for Education Statistics, 1998).

At the same time, considerable evidence indicates that many teachers, especially in grades K-8, are not well prepared to teach challenging mathematics. The time allotted for mathematics content in the preparation of many elementary and middle school teachers is unlikely to be adequate, and many secondary school mathematics teachers (including those in the middle grades who are prepared as specialists) may also be receiving training that does not prepare them to teach advanced-level mathematics (e.g., algebra, geometry, and trigonometry). Mathematics teachers may also need specific preparation for the challenge of teaching mathematics in ways that engage *all* students and gives them a chance to succeed. Moreover, many of those who teach mathematics in U.S. secondary schools, especially in poor and underserved communities, lack appropriate certification and adequate content preparation. These concerns have been evident for a long time, and their persistence underscores the importance of assessing the status of the preparation of mathematics teachers.[1]

This chapter is organized as was the preceding one, beginning with a brief overview of the research base and then turning to our four key questions:

1. What do successful students know about mathematics?
2. What instructional opportunities are necessary to support successful students?
3. What do successful teachers know about mathematics and how to teach it?

---

[1]When possible, we have addressed the differing needs of K-8 teachers of mathematics and secondary mathematics teachers, but we note that much of the literature focuses on the teachers of younger students.

4. What instructional opportunities are necessary to prepare success-ful teachers?

We continue with what is known about how mathematics teachers are currently prepared, and we end the chapter with our conclusions.

## THE RESEARCH BASE

The literature on which we could rely for this chapter was an amal-gam of empirical research and other kinds of work. The community of mathematics educators and mathematicians has synthesized the intellectual principles of mathematics with insights from other fields (e.g., cognitive and developmental psychology), the practice-based wisdom of classroom teachers, and the available empirical research to develop guidelines for mathematics teaching and learning. The National Council of Teachers of Mathematics (NCTM), the National Research Council (NRC), the Confer-ence Board of the Mathematical Sciences, and, most recently, the National Mathematics Advisory Panel have published some of the most widely known documents. Each of those documents is the product of extensive efforts to collaborate, develop consensus, and distill practical guidance from theoretical models as well as research, and we have relied heavily on them. The influence of the research in learning and cognition that we dis-cuss in Chapter 4 is evident in the reports of those groups and the field of mathematics education generally. State standards and curricula have also provided outlines of the content and skills students are expected to master. Thus, we had an array of resources on which to draw, although the empiri-cal base is less direct than that for reading. We have attempted to describe the research base on which the points we highlight rests.

## QUESTION 1: WHAT DO SUCCESSFUL STUDENTS KNOW ABOUT MATHEMATICS?

Looking first at what students ought to learn, we found numerous sources. As part of the standards movement that began in the 1980s, states developed mathematics standards, and, along with professional societies and other interest groups, have used a variety of approaches to arrive at descriptions of the fundamental mathematical skills and knowledge that the states believe students should be taught. Although these descriptions might seem similar to most people, they reflect important differences among mathematics educators, differences that have at times been contentious. Indeed, the phrase "math wars" has been used to describe the debate over what mathematics should be taught to K-12 students and how it should be taught. In particular, much debate has centered on the relative emphasis that should be given to the mastery of basic skills and the development of conceptual understanding, though most state and other standards documents now acknowledge the importance of both.

In 1989, the NCTM became the first professional society to respond to the call for subject-matter standards when they released *Curriculum and Evaluation Standards for School Mathematics*. These standards were developed through a multiyear consensus process led by committees of NCTM members. This document was followed by companion documents on teaching and assessment in mathematics, and the NCTM standards had a strong influence on the standards adopted by many states. A series of more recent publications have also been important.

*Principles and Standards for School Mathematics* (National Council of Teachers of Mathematics, 2000), which offered an update of the group's earlier documents and was based on a more detailed review of the theory, research, and practice literature, has been particularly influential (also see Kilpatrick, Martin, and Schifter, 2003). *Principles* offers five content standards (number and operations, algebra, geometry, measurement, and data analysis and probability) and five process standards (problem solving, reasoning and proof, communication, connections, and representation). In this volume, the NCTM discusses its vision for achieving the 10 standards in four grade bands (pre-K through grade 2, grades 3-5, grades 6-8, and grades 9-12) and identifies six principles for school mathematics (equity, curriculum, teaching, learning, assessment, and technology). The high visibility of the NCTM standards is evident in the fact that nearly 85 percent of U.S. teachers surveyed as part of the Third International Mathematics and Science Study reported that they were familiar with them (though there is no hard evidence about whether the standards have changed teachers' practice or even whether teachers have read them) (National Center for Education Statistics, 2003b).

In 2006, the NCTM released *Curriculum Focal Points for Pre-Kindergarten Through Grade 8 Mathematics: A Quest for Coherence*. This document provides explicit guidance as to the most important mathematics topics that should be taught at each grade level, identifying the "ideas, concepts, skills, and procedures that form the foundation for understanding and using mathematics" (see http://www.nctm.org/standards/content.aspx?id=270 [November 2009]). The document is designed to guide states and school districts as they revise their standards, curricula, and assessment programs. As this report is being prepared, the NCTM has another task force at work on a companion document addressing high school mathematics. The NCTM documents stress that their standards are for all students, regardless of their interests or career aspirations. In general, the NCTM documents reflect an effort to achieve consensus among mathematics teachers, mathematics educators, mathematicians, and education researchers, and they drew on the available research.

Another report, *Adding it Up* (National Research Council, 2001a), has also synthesized the available literature on mathematics learning. It used the topic of number as taught in grades pre-K through 8 as a focus in addressing the question of what constitutes mathematical proficiency. The report was based on a review of empirical research that met the committee's standards for relevance, soundness, and generalizability, as well as other literature. The report notes that choices about the mathematics children should be taught are both reflections of "what society wants educated adults to know" and "value judgments based on previous experience and convictions [which] fall outside the domain of research" (p. 21). The report describes mathematical proficiency as having five intertwined strands: conceptual understanding, procedural fluency, strategic competence, adaptive reasoning, and productive disposition.

Efforts to address high school preparation include the American Diploma Project sponsored by Achieve, Inc., which produced benchmarks for college readiness (see http://www.achieve.org/ [February 2010]), the College Board Standards for Success, and the Common Core Project sponsored by the National Governors Association and Council of Chief State School Officers, now under way.

In *Foundations for Success,* the National Mathematics Advisory Panel (2008) synthesized empirical research related to students' readiness to succeed in algebra. The panel focused on studies that used a randomized control design or statistical procedures to compensate for deviations from that model. However, because there were not enough studies of that type to address all of the panel's questions, other research was considered as well. We note that this was a different criterion than was used by the developers of the NCTM standards or the National Research Council panel, and these differences have contributed to differences among the various reports. Some have criticized *Foundations for Success* for relying on a base that was excessively thin (excluding descriptive studies, for example) and thus excluding valuable findings. Others have supported the panel's strict definition of research utility.[2] The panel addressed many aspects of mathematics education, and among its findings and recommendations are several regarding what students should learn. The panel focused on what was needed for students to be successful in learning algebra (National Mathematics Advisory Panel, 2008, p. xix):

> To prepare students for Algebra, the curriculum must simultaneously develop conceptual understanding, computational fluency, and problem-

---

[2]For a discussion of this controversy, see the December 2008 issue of *Educational Researcher*, which was a special issue devoted to the report of the National Mathematics Advisory Panel.

solving skills. Debates regarding the relative importance of these aspects of mathematical knowledge are misguided. These capabilities are mutually supportive, each facilitating learning of the other.

To identify the essential concepts and skills that prepare students for algebra coursework, the panel drew on a range of sources, including: the curricula for grades 1 through 8 from the countries that performed best on TIMSS, *Focal Points* (National Council of Teachers of Mathematics, 2000), the six highest-rated state curriculum frameworks in mathematics, a 2007 survey of ACT, Inc., and a survey of algebra I teachers. The panel also reviewed state standards for algebra I and II, current school algebra and integrated mathematics textbooks, the algebra objectives in the 2005 grade 12 assessment of the NAEP, the American Diploma Project standards from Achieve, Inc., and Singapore's algebra standards. Based on all the information gathered and professional judgment, the panel identified what they called the critical foundation of algebra and the major topics of school algebra. The panel also stressed the importance of coherence across the curriculum and the establishment of logical priorities for each year of study.

All of these documents—*Principles and Standards for School Mathematics, Curriculum Focal Points, Adding It Up,* and *Foundations for Success*—attempt to answer questions about what successful mathematics students know. But none of the documents could rely on empirical research that demonstrates that students who have mastered these domains of mathematical knowledge and skill are more productive or successful at their schoolwork or in life. As in any subject, standards for mathematics are collective decisions about which learning goals should take priority over others, not conclusions based on empirical evidence (though evidence of various sorts may influence the standards). Thus, the various descriptions of the mathematics that should be taught in K-12 differ in both their perspective and the degree of detail they provide.

More important, the documents reflect important shifts in the thinking of mathematics education leaders about what students need to learn. Most notably, they show an increasing tendency to provide guidance that is both focused and concrete. They also reflect a growing consensus about the most important aspects of student learning in mathematics, which is based in part on the research on learning and thinking (see Chapter 4). For example, they reflect research that has identified the importance of learning with understanding, as opposed to memorizing isolated facts, and the importance of opportunities to engage in mathematical reasoning and problem solving. Both ideas have important implications for mathematics education, which we discuss below.

Every state has its own standards for mathematics, and there are significant differences among them (Raimi and Braden, 1998; Klein, 2005; National Research Council, 2008).[3] Although a detailed content analysis of the similarities and differences among these standards was beyond the scope of this committee's work, it is clear from our review that a number of important themes are consistently identified as important. Although these themes are not exclusively based on empirical research, and they have evolved through a certain amount of struggle and disagreement, a reasonable consensus has been achieved on the question of what mathematics students should be taught in grades K-8.

Unfortunately, the picture is much less clear for grades 9 through 12 because the base of research on student learning related to secondary school mathematics topics and courses is relatively thin. Thus, the field tends to rely more heavily on professional judgment when deciding on curriculum for high school students. For example, views differ about the place of calculus and statistics. Yet there is consensus that for students to be successful in high school mathematics courses, they need preparation in the basic topic areas—including number, operations, and fractions—and there is little disagreement that students also need to develop conceptual understanding, procedural fluency, and confidence in their capacity to learn mathematics.

In general, successful mathematics learning entails the cumulative development of increasingly sophisticated conceptual understanding, procedural fluency, and capacity for reasoning and problem solving.[4] Moreover, there is broad general agreement about the topics to be included in the curriculum for grades K-8, though the relative emphasis they should receive and their exact placement by grade is not settled.

## QUESTION 2: WHAT INSTRUCTIONAL OPPORTUNITIES ARE NECESSARY TO SUPPORT SUCCESSFUL MATHEMATICS STUDENTS?

Turning to the question of what sorts of instructional opportunities enable students to learn mathematics effectively, we found that useful guidance comes from the research on how students learn. *How Students Learn: History, Mathematics, and Science in the Classroom* (National Research Council, 2005) summarizes the major findings from research on learning and cognition as they pertain to K-12 teaching and learning. This report builds on previous NRC syntheses of research on learning, particularly

---

[3] As this report is being written, an effort to engage states in a collaboration to develop common standards in key academic subjects, sponsored by the National Governors Association and the Council for Chief State School Officers, is in its beginning stages.

[4] Progress in mathematics, as in any subject, is likely to depend in part on students' motivation but this issue has not been a central theme in research related to teacher preparation.

*How People Learn* (National Research Council, 2000a) (discussed in Chapter 4), and both have been influential in mathematics education.

*How Students Learn* begins by applying three broad principles about learning to the teaching of mathematics: that engaging students' prior conceptions is critical to successful learning, that learning with understanding entails an integration of factual knowledge and conceptual frameworks, and that students need to learn how to monitor their learning. Thus, the authors assert that mathematics instruction should

- build on and refine the mathematical understandings, intuitions, and resourcefulness that students bring to the classroom;
- organize the skills and competencies required to do mathematics fluently around a set of core mathematical concepts; and
- help students use metacognitive strategies when solving mathematics problems.

Addressing students' existing ideas is important for two reasons. First, lingering misconceptions about mathematical concepts may interfere with learning. Second, students who believe, for example, that some people have the ability to "do math" and some do not, that mathematics is exclusively a matter of learning and following rules in order to obtain a correct answer, or that mathematics is exclusively a matter of reasoning (and does not also require considerable mastery of factual knowledge) are much more likely to struggle with mathematics, and perhaps give up on it. Thus, it is important that all students participate in activities that make their informal or naïve mathematical ideas and reasoning explicit so that they might examine— along with their teachers—which aspects of their thinking are valid and which are not. More generally, instruction designed to help students bridge gaps between naïve conceptions and the mathematical understanding they need to develop is important.

With regard to organizing skills around mathematical concepts, *How Students Learn* stresses that, in order to succeed as mathematics becomes more complex through the school years, students develop "learning paths from more informal concrete methods to abbreviated, more general, and more abstract methods" (National Research Council, 2005, p. 232). Though mastering mathematical procedures is very important, instruction that emphasizes them at the expense of developing conceptual frameworks leaves students ill equipped for algebra and higher-level mathematics. Likewise, instruction that emphasizes conceptual understanding without corresponding attention to the development of skills may leave students unprepared for the skill-oriented aspects of higher-level mathematics. The report makes clear that there is no need to choose between the two: mathematical proficiency requires both, as well as attention to reasoning and problem solving. In addition, instruction should help students develop the metacognitive skills and confidence to monitor and regulate their own mathematical thinking. For example, instruction that helps students use common errors as a tool for identifying misconceptions may support students' development of problem-solving skills.

*Adding It Up* (National Research Council, 2001a) also addresses instruction, noting that debates about alternative approaches to teaching, such as traditional versus reform, or direct instruction versus inquiry, obscure the broader point that effective instruction is a successful interaction among three elements: teachers' knowledge and use of mathematical content, teachers' attention to and handling of the students, and students' engagement in and use of mathematical tasks. Thus, while the instructional choices teachers make are important, the way they are carried out is equally so.

For example, *Adding It Up* cites research (e.g., Stein, Grover, and Henningsen, 1996; Henningsen and Stein, 1997) that a cognitively demanding task may become routine if the teacher specifies explicit procedures for completing it or takes over the demanding aspects as soon as students appear to struggle. The TIMSS 1999 video study identified the ability to maintain the high-level demands of cognitively challenging tasks during instruction as the central feature that distinguished classroom teaching in countries with high-performing students from teaching in countries with lower performing students (including the United States) (National Center for Education Statistics, 2003c; Stigler and Hiebert, 2004). This research suggests that student engagement is fostered when teachers choose tasks that build on the students' prior knowledge and guide them to the next level, rather than demonstrating exactly how to proceed, and that it is essential that students think through concepts for themselves. Other factors identified as effective include thoughtful lesson planning that tracks students' developing understanding and allocation of sufficient time for students to achieve lesson goals.

The National Mathematics Advisory Panel made similar points, and it found no rigorous research to support claims that instruction that is either exclusively "teacher-centered" or exclusively "student-centered" is better. The panel did, however, find some evidence to support the effectiveness of cooperative learning practices and the regular use of formative assessment in elementary mathematics instruction as a tool for tailoring instruction to students' needs. The panel called attention to the limited amount of rigorous empirical research available to answer questions about mathematics teaching and learning, and it recommended a variety of research to test hypotheses about the most effective approaches.

In sum, there is growing agreement on the specifics of what students should be taught, but there are fewer specific answers as to the best ways to teach that material. Mathematics educators have established a clear consensus, based on research evidence, that the development of mathematical proficiency requires continual instructional opportunities for students to build their understanding of core mathematical concepts, fluency with mathematics procedures, and metacognitive strategies to guide their own mathematical learning. However, there is little empirical evidence to support detailed conclusions about precisely how this is best accomplished.

## QUESTION 3: WHAT DO SUCCESSFUL TEACHERS KNOW ABOUT MATHEMATICS AND HOW TO TEACH IT?

There is strong reason to believe that teachers' knowledge and skills make a difference in their practice (Wenglinsky, 2002; Rockoff, 2004; Rivkin, Hanushek, and Kain, 2005; Clotfelter, Ladd, and Vigdor, 2007). Researchers have tried to disentangle the different kinds of knowledge about mathematics, about students, and about the learning process that teachers use (Ball, Lubienski, and Mewborn, 2001). Research that has searched for connections between straightforward—yet crude—measures of teacher knowledge (such as number of courses taken or degrees earned) and student learning has provided relatively little insight into questions about what skills and knowledge are most valuable for teachers (see Chapter 3). For example, research shows that high school students taught by mathematics majors outperform students taught by teachers who majored in some other field, but that research does not illuminate what it is that the teachers who majored in mathematics do in the classroom (Monk and King, 1994; Goldhaber and Brewer, 1997; Rowan, Chiang, and Miller, 1997; Wilson, Floden, and Ferrini-Mundy, 2001; Floden and Maniketti, 2005).

Beginning in the 1980s, a growing number of scholars looked to more qualitative research—largely based on interviews and classroom observations—to provide richer pictures of the mathematical thinking teachers do when teaching. These studies supported the development of more nuanced descriptions of teachers' knowledge and skills by illuminating the ways that the mathematical knowledge needed for teaching differs from the mathematical knowledge needed to succeed in advanced courses. The concept of pedagogical content knowledge gave a name to the knowledge of content as it applies to and can be used in teaching (see, e.g., Shulman, 1986; Ball, Lubienski, and Mewborn, 2001).

Mathematicians have always played a critical role in defining the kinds of knowledge and skills that are most useful to mathematics teachers. Several recent publications, including textbooks for aspiring elementary mathematics teachers, studies, and analytic essays, have laid out current thinking (e.g., Parker and Baldridge, 2003; Beckmann, 2004; Milgram, 2005; Wu, 2007). For example, Wu (2007) argued that, at a minimum, teachers of grades 5-12 must be knowledgeable about the importance of definitions, the ubiquity of reasoning, the precision and coherence of the discipline, and the fact that the concepts and skills in the curriculum are there for a purpose (how to solve problems). Ideally, he argues, teachers in the primary grades should know all these things, too, but pedagogical knowledge carries more weight for teachers of younger students. An additional obvious difference between the requirements for elementary teachers and high school teachers is that teaching older students carries a greater demand for both technical skills and abstract reasoning.

These developments in the understanding of mathematics teaching provide a critical framework for teacher education, although they do not provide empirical support for a concrete description of precisely how to teach mathematics (Ball, Lubienski, and Mewborn, 2001). However, the sophistication of this sort of analysis of classroom teaching provides a way to understand an exceptionally complex process. The combination of this descriptive work and analyses by mathematicians provides an invaluable component of the research base.

Many of the same sources that have offered visions of what students need to learn have also made recommendations as to what mathematics teachers need to know. These summary documents draw on the range of quantitative and qualitative research available, as well as on the professional judgment of scholars and practitioners.

The NCTM has developed professional standards for mathematics teachers to accompany their content standards (National Council of Teachers of Mathematics, 1991). Similarly, states have developed standards for mathematics teachers, drawing on such resources as the standards from NCTM and the Interstate New Teacher Assessment and Support Consortium (INTASC). The focus of these resources, however, is on ensuring that teachers have studied the material covered in the standards and curricula for students. They do not, for the most part, address others kinds of knowledge and skills that might be important for teachers.

*Adding It Up* (National Research Council, 2001a) also describes the knowledge of mathematics, students, and instructional practices that are important for teachers. The report stresses that, to be effective, teachers not only need to understand mathematical concepts and know how to perform mathematical procedures, but also to understand the conceptual foundations of that knowledge; it is also important that they have strong confidence in their own mathematical competence. The report notes that a substantial body of work has documented the deficiencies in U.S. mathematics teachers' base of knowledge—and that even when teachers understand the mathematics content they are responsible for teaching, they often lack deeper understanding of the way mathematical knowledge is generated and established.

*The Mathematical Education of Teachers,* a report prepared by the

Conference Board of the Mathematical Sciences and published by American Mathematical Society and the Mathematical Association of America (2001), offers guidelines for the preparation of mathematics teachers and is arguably the primary document that guides departments of mathematics regarding the teaching of mathematics to future teachers. The report's recommendations are grounded in the conviction that a central goal of preservice mathematics education is to develop teachers who have excellent problem-solving and mathematical-reasoning skills themselves, and the report describes specific kinds of knowledge teachers at different grade levels need related to the topics they will teach their students. The report emphasizes how important it is that teachers understand links between the material taught in the early grades and more sophisticated concepts that will build on the earlier learning: it is not sufficient for teachers to master only the level of mathematics they will be teaching.

Moreover, the report observes that the challenges of teaching each level are distinct and require different preparation, as current certification requirements reflect. It notes in particular that teachers of middle grades mathematics often "have been prepared to teach elementary school mathematics and lack the broader background needed to teach the more advanced mathematics of the middle grades" (Conference Board of the Mathematical Sciences, 2001, see http://www.cbmsweb.org/MET_Document/chapter_4.htm [November 2009]).

The National Mathematics Advisory Panel also searched for evidence about the connections between teachers' knowledge and instructional practice and student outcomes, and for evidence that particular instructional practices are effective. Citing evidence that variation in teacher quality may account for 12 to 14 percent of the variance in elementary students' mathematics learning, the panel examined evidence of teachers' knowledge that can be gleaned from certification, courses completed, and assessment results. Noting that these are imprecise measures, the panel nevertheless seconds the recommendation in *Adding It Up*, asserting that "teachers must know in detail the mathematical content they are responsible for teaching and its connections to other important mathematics" (National Mathematics Advisory Panel, 2008, p. xxi).

Thus, despite the lack of substantial and consistent empirical evidence, there is a growing consensus about the kinds of mathematical knowledge effective teachers have. Current research and professional consensus correspond in suggesting that all mathematics teachers, even elementary teachers, rely on a combination of mathematics knowledge and pedagogical knowledge:

- mathematical knowledge for teaching, that is, knowledge not just of the content they are responsible for teaching, but also of the broader mathematical context for that knowledge and the connections between the material they teach and other important mathematics content;

- understanding of the way mathematics learning develops and of the variation in cognitive approaches to mathematical thinking; and
- command of an array of instructional strategies designed to develop students' mathematical learning that are grounded in both practice and research.

## QUESTION 4: WHAT INSTRUCTIONAL OPPORTUNITIES ARE NECESSARY TO PREPARE SUCCESSFUL MATHEMATICS TEACHERS?

How might teachers best acquire the knowledge and skills they need? The work of Deborah Ball (1990, 1991, 1993) on the knowledge of elementary school teachers, as well as Liping Ma's (1999) influential comparison of Chinese and American teachers, which built on Ball's work, have sparked a renewal of interest among mathematicians and mathematics teacher educators in the preparation of mathematics teachers. Other resources include guidelines for preparation programs, as well as research regarding elements of preparation that can be linked to positive outcomes for students. Nevertheless, there is relatively little empirical evidence to support guidelines for teacher preparation.

The report prepared by the Conference Board of the Mathematical Sciences (2001) offers guidelines for teachers' mathematics preparation.[5] The board's guidance is based on available scholarship on mathematics education and the judgment of professional mathematicians. The board's report offered three specific recommendations:

1. Prospective elementary grade teachers should be required to take at least 9 semester-hours on fundamental ideas of elementary school mathematics.
2. Prospective middle grades teachers of mathematics should be required to take at least 21 semester-hours of mathematics, [including] at least 12 semester-hours on fundamental ideas of school mathematics appropriate for middle grades teachers.

---

[5]The National Council on Teacher Quality (Greenberg and Walsh, 2008) also developed recommendations to guide programs, which address the content knowledge teachers should acquire, the need for higher admissions standards, the need for an assessment suitable for establishing that graduating teachers have mastered the requisite knowledge, the importance of linkage between content and methods courses as well as fieldwork, and the qualifications of mathematics teacher educators. The guidelines are based primarily on studies of course syllabi used in preparation programs.

3. Prospective high school teachers of mathematics should be required to complete the equivalent of an undergraduate major in mathematics, [including] a 6-hour capstone course connecting their college mathematics courses with high school mathematics.

David Monk (1994) also examined the effects of course taking on teacher effectiveness, using data from the Longitudinal Survey of American Youth. He found that students whose teachers had taken more mathematics courses performed better on achievement tests than their peers whose teachers had taken fewer such courses. He also found that courses that addressed teaching methods showed an even stronger benefit. Floden and Meniketti (2005) summarized the findings of this and other research on the effects of undergraduate coursework on teachers' knowledge. They identified studies that examined correlations between coursework and teacher performance and correlations between coursework and student achievement and those that examined the content knowledge of prospective teachers and studies that examined what teachers learn from particular courses. Many studies focused on mathematics, and they provided support for the claim that studying college-level mathematics has benefits for prospective secondary level teachers. However, the research provides little clear guidance as to what the content of the coursework should be and even less guidance about content preparation for teachers of lower grades. Floden and Meniketti also note that currently available measures of teacher knowledge and of student outcomes are imprecise tools for assessing the impact of teacher education (see also Wilson, Floden, and Ferrini-Mundy, 2001).

Ball, Hill, and Bass (2005) conducted an analysis of the role of mathematical knowledge and skills in elementary teaching in order to develop a "practice-based portrait of . . . mathematical knowledge for teaching" (p. 17). They then developed measures of this knowledge to use in linking it to student achievement. The researchers argue that teachers need to have "a specialized fluency with mathematical language, with what counts as a mathematical explanation, and with how to use symbols with care" (p. 21). They found that teachers need not only to be able do the mathematics they are teaching, but to "think from the learner's perspective and to consider what it takes to understand a mathematical idea for someone seeing it for the first time" (p. 21) (see also Hill, Rowan, and Ball, 2005). Through a longitudinal study of schools engaged in reform efforts, Ball and her colleagues were able to link 1st- and 3rd-grade teachers' responses to the measure of professional knowledge with their students' scores on the TerraNova assessment (Ball, Lubienski, and Mewborn, 2001). The results showed a significant relationship between students' gains and their teachers' degree of professional knowledge.

This body of work clearly supports the intuitive belief that content knowledge is important. The research on student learning described above also supports the proposition that prospective mathematics teachers should study mathematics learning and teaching methods.[6]

Finally, a study of the preparation of middle school mathematics teachers in six nations (Schmidt et al., 2007) follows up on findings from the 1987 TIMSS study. That study had shown that, in general, middle school students in the United States were not exposed to mathematics curricula that were as focused, coherent, and rigorous as those in countries (including Korea and Taiwan) whose students scored higher on TIMSS. Schmidt and his colleagues examined teacher preparation in those countries and found that training in the high-performing countries includes extensive educational opportunities in mathematics and in the practical aspects of teaching students in the middle grades.

The relevant body of work on what instructional opportunities are most valuable for mathematics teachers is growing but thus far is largely descriptive, and it has not identified causal relationships between specific aspects of preparation programs and measures of prospective teachers' subsequent effectiveness. Nevertheless, the field of mathematics education has established a firm consensus that to prepare effective K-12 mathematics teachers, a program should provide prospective teachers with the knowledge and skills described by the Conference Board of the Mathematical Sciences:

- a deep understanding of the mathematics they will teach,
- courses that focus on a thorough development of basic mathematical ideas, and
- courses that develop careful reasoning and mathematical "common sense" in analyzing conceptual relationships and solving problems, and courses that develop the habits of mind of a mathematical thinker.

---

[6]Ongoing research offers the prospect of further insights. For instance, McCrory and her colleagues are investigating the link between what is taught in college-level mathematics classes designed for elementary teachers and what prospective teachers understand about the mathematics they are taught (see McCrory and Cannata, 2007; see also http://meet.educ. msu.edu/research.htm [February 2010]). Having surveyed 56 mathematics departments and 79 instructors, she has found that, on average, elementary teachers are expected to take two mathematics classes, although this is increasing, especially for middle school certification. Her research also indicates that instructors are committed and enthusiastic, but not necessarily knowledgeable, about mathematics education.

## HOW MATHEMATICS TEACHERS ARE CURRENTLY PREPARED

Concern about the adequacy of current teacher preparation in mathematics is unmistakable, and it is particularly sharp with regard to K-8 teachers. Evidence from many sources suggests that many teachers do not have sufficient mathematical knowledge (see, e.g., Ball, 1991; Ma, 1999). Specifically, as Wu (2002) has observed, "we have not done nearly enough to help teachers understand the essential characteristics of mathematics: its precision, the ubiquity of logical reasoning, and its coherence as a discipline" (p. 2). Furthermore, there is reason to believe that teachers lack other relevant professional knowledge as well, including mathematics-specific pedagogical knowledge.

We had two major sources of information about how teacher preparation in mathematics is currently being conducted—state requirements and coursework—although much of the information is somewhat indirect.

### State Requirements

We begin with the requirements states have established for licensing mathematics teachers, which influence the goals teacher preparation programs set for themselves. According to data collected by Editorial Projects in Education, 33 of the 50 states and the District of Columbia require that high school teachers have majored in the subject they plan to teach in order to be certified, but only 3 states have that requirement for middle school teachers (data from 2006 and 2008; see http://www.edcounts.org/ [February 2010]). Forty-two states require prospective teachers to pass a written test in the subject in which they want to be certified, and six require passage of a written test in subject-specific pedagogy.

Limited information is available on the content of teacher certification tests. A study of certification and licensure examinations in mathematics by the Education Trust (1999) reviewed the level of mathematics knowledge necessary to succeed on the tests required of secondary mathematics teachers. The authors found that the tests rarely assessed content that exceeded knowledge that an 11th or 12th grader would be expected to have and did not reflect the deep knowledge of the subject one would expect of a college-educated mathematics major or someone who had done advanced study of school mathematics. Moreover, the Education Trust found that the cut scores (for passing or failing) for most state licensure examinations are so low that prospective teachers do not even need to have a working knowledge of high school mathematics in order to pass. Although this study is modest, its results align with the general perception that state tests for teacher certification do not reflect ambitious conceptions of content knowledge.

The prevalence of so-called out-of-field teachers, those who are not certified in the subject they are teaching, is another indication that states sometimes find it difficult to ensure that mathematics teachers are well prepared. We discuss this issue below.

## Coursework

The Conference Board of the Mathematical Sciences (CBMS) conducts a survey every 5 years of undergraduate education in mathematics in the United States, and it includes some questions about the preparation of K-12 mathematics teachers (Lutzer, Maxwell, and Rodi, 2007). The most recent report describes the complexity of developing a statistical profile of undergraduate mathematics preparation programs because of their variation. However, Lutzer and colleagues report that 56 percent of programs have the same requirements for mathematics certification for all K-8 teachers of mathematics, regardless of the level (e.g., kindergarten or 8th grade) those candidates intended to teach. They also found that the average number of mathematics courses required for K-8 teachers was 2.1.

For teachers seeking K-8 mathematics certification, 4 percent of programs do not require any mathematics courses, 63 percent require one or two courses, 33 percent require three or four courses, and none requires five or more courses. In contrast, 58 percent of programs require five or more courses for teachers of the upper elementary grades.[7] Thus, most programs fall well short of the recommendations of *The Mathematical Education of Teachers* (Conference Board of the Mathematical Sciences, 2001), and some members of the mathematics community believe the subject-knowledge requirements should be even more demanding than those recommendations.

With the analyses of Florida commissioned for our study, we were able to look in more detail at the average number of mathematics credits earned by Florida teachers by certification area: see Table 6-1. Although these data do not provide information about the content or nature of the coursework, they do suggest significant overall exposure to mathematics, corresponding roughly to 4 three-credit courses for elementary teachers, 15 courses for teachers certified for middle school mathematics, and 19 courses for teachers certified for high school mathematics.[8]

---

[7]These results correspond to McCrory's emerging results as well as the self-reports of new teachers surveyed as part of the Teacher Pathways Project being conducted by the University at Albany and Stanford University (see http://www.teacherpolicyresearch.org/ TeacherPathwaysProject/tabid/81/Default.aspx [February 2010]).

[8]One possible explanation for this relatively high number of courses—in comparison with those typical in other states and programs—is that if many of Florida's courses are remedial or elementary in nature, they would be likely to meet frequently each week, thus yielding a high number of credit hours.

**TABLE 6-1** Mean Mathematics Credit Hours, Florida Mathematics
Teachers

| Certification Area | Math Education | Noneducation Math Credit Hours | Noneducation Statistics Credit Hours |
|---|---|---|---|
| Elementary School [N = 3,684] | 4.43 | 5.56 | 1.90 |
| Middle School [N = 244] | 14.42 | 27.27 | 3.84 |
| High School [N = 216] | 17.72 | 34.88 | 4.58 |

NOTE: Samples include only teachers with 100 or more known credit hours in university-designated courses taken in Florida public community colleges and universities prior to their first year of teaching in Florida public schools.
SOURCE: Data from Sass (2008, Tables B10a, B10b, B10c).

In terms of the actual content of the coursework to which aspiring mathematics teachers are exposed, there are few sources.[9] The Education Commission of the States has assembled information about whether or not states require that teacher preparation programs align their curricula with the state's K-12 curriculum standards or their standards for teachers (or both), which offers an indirect indicator (see http://www.ecs.org/). Of the 50 states and American Samoa, the District of Columbia, Guam, Puerto Rico, and the Virgin Islands, 25 require alignment with both, and 16 have no policy for either (as of 2006); another 8 require only alignment with the K-12 curriculum, and 6 require only alignment with standards for teachers.

A survey of first-year teachers in New York City that was part of our commissioned analysis included questions about their preparation and provides some additional hints about content (Grossman et al., 2008). Current elementary teachers and middle and secondary level mathematics teachers were asked about the extent to which their teacher preparation program gave them the opportunity to do and learn a variety of things, such as learning about the typical difficulties students have with aspects of mathematics. The new teachers rated their opportunities on a 5-point scale, with 1 being no opportunity and 5 being extensive opportunity. The teaching activities covered in the survey were described in short phrases, so few conclusions

[9]Greenberg and Walsh conducted a study (National Council on Teacher Quality, 2007) in which they analyzed course syllabi and textbook content to gain a sense of the mathematics preparation provided to elementary teachers, but syllabi and textbook content are very inexact measures of course content.

can be drawn about the extent to which they track with the kinds of approaches we describe above. Nevertheless, the teachers' responses to several of the questions that seem most congruent with the kinds of teaching advocated by the mathematics education community are suggestive: see Table 6-2. Elementary teachers reported taking an average of 1.81 courses in mathematics; they also reported having a modest exposure to learning about the difficulties their students might have with place value or algebra. Although the survey was small in scale, it does suggest that New York City teachers who graduated recently from a teacher education program do not receive extensive exposure to these elements.

Other evidence comes from a study in which the preparation of U.S. middle school mathematics teachers was compared with that of their counterparts in other countries (Schmidt et al., 2007). The study, which compared teachers' knowledge and skills in mathematics and mathematical pedagogy, found that U.S. teachers scored in the middle or close to the bottom in comparison with teachers in the countries whose students performed well on the TIMSS study. The results suggested possible differences in preparation across countries, and the study's authors concluded that the

**TABLE 6-2** New York City Teachers' Reported Exposure to Mathematics Preparation

| Opportunity to Learn Mathematics Education Approach or Strategy | Mean Response on 1-5 Scale[a] |
|---|---|
| Elementary Teachers | |
| Learn typical difficulties students have with place value. | 2.71 |
| Practice what you learned about teaching math in your field experience. | 3.26 |
| How many courses did you take in the teaching of math at the college level? | 1.81 [not on 5-point scale] |
| Secondary Teachers | |
| Learn different ways that students solve particular problems. | 3.34 |
| Learn theoretical concepts and ideas underlying mathematical applications. | 3.36 |
| Learn about typical difficulties students have with algebra. | 2.5 |

NOTE: Results are for teachers who attended an undergraduate teacher preparation program. Data are also available for teachers who followed other pathways.

[a]A respondent who rated his or her exposure as a 3 would be indicating that it was roughly halfway between none at all and extensive.

SOURCE: Data from Matt Ronfeldt, University of Michigan (personal communication, 2008).

preparation available to U.S. teachers provided less "extensive educational opportunities in mathematics and in the practical aspects of teaching mathematics to students in the middle grades" (Schmidt et al., 2007, p. 2). The researchers were not able to use representative samples of teachers in each country; they relied on convenience samples. A comparative study of mathematics teachers' preparation and mathematical knowledge using national probability samples is currently being conducted by the International Association for the Evaluation of Educational Achievement (see http://www.iea.nl/teds-m.html [November 2009]).

Many students, particularly at the secondary level, are taught mathematics by teachers who are not certified in that subject (because of a dearth of certified teachers), and these teachers are likely to have taken even fewer courses in mathematics than certified mathematics teachers. The problem is more acute in mathematics than in other subjects. The National Center for Education Statistics (2003a) reports that in the 1999-2000 school year, 23.0 percent of middle school students and 10.1 percent of secondary students were taught mathematics by a teacher who was not certified to teach mathematics and had not majored in it. (Note that the grades encompassed by middle school, as well as the requirements to teach at that level, vary.) Using data from the Schools and Staffing Survey, Richard Ingersoll (2008) found that 38 percent of the teachers who taught mathematics to grades 7 through 12 did not have either a major or a minor in mathematics, mathematics education, or a related field. The problem is greatest in high-poverty schools, where students are approximately twice as likely to have a mathematics teacher who is not certified in the subject. A study of the effects of teachers' credentials on student achievement (Clotfelter, Ladd, and Vigdor, 2007) provides evidence that students whose teachers are certified in the subject they teach achieve at higher levels than students whose teachers are not, particularly in algebra and geometry.

At the state level, there is other evidence of out-of-field teaching. The California Council on Science and Technology (2007) conducted an analysis of career pathways for that state's mathematics and science teachers. They found that 10 percent of middle school and 12 percent of high school mathematics teachers were teaching out of field, and that 40 percent of novice high school mathematics teachers were not well prepared (defined as lacking a preliminary credential). The percentages are highest in low-performing and high-minority schools. They also found that California lacks the capacity to meet the growing demand for fully prepared mathematics (and science) teachers and that the state is not collecting the data necessary to monitor teacher supply and demand.

Our review of these disparate sources of information leaves us with a reasonably firm basis for concluding that many, perhaps most, K-8 mathematics teachers are not adequately prepared, either because they have not received enough mathematics and pedagogical preparation or because they have not received the right sort of preparation; the picture is somewhat less clear for middle and high school teachers. There is relatively scant specific information about precisely what it is that teacher preparation programs do, or fail to do, but there is relatively good evidence that mathematics preparation for prospective teachers provides insufficient coursework in mathematics as a discipline and mathematical pedagogy. Some might suggest that, given the prevalence of out-of-field mathematics teachers, raising standards for aspiring teachers may exacerbate shortages, particularly in high-poverty areas. The committee's view is that the more relevant question is whether there are shortages of adequately prepared teachers.

## CONCLUSIONS

From our review of what mathematics teacher preparation programs ought to be doing, and the information we could find about what they are doing, three key points seem clear. First, there is a strong basis for defining clear expectations for teacher preparation programs for mathematics content and pedagogy, on the basis of some research and the considered judgments of mathematicians and mathematics educators. Second, the limited information available suggests that most programs would probably not currently meet those expectations. Third, systematic data about the content of mathematics teacher preparation are sorely lacking.

Regarding what students need to know, mathematicians and mathematics educators are in accord that successful mathematics learning is most likely when core topics in school mathematics and the five strands of mathematical proficiency identified in *Adding It Up* (conceptual understanding, procedural fluency, strategic competence, adaptive reasoning, and productive disposition) are interwoven at each level of schooling, and students are provided with a coherent curriculum in which clear objectives, based on a logical conception of the mathematics learning trajectory, guide each year of mathematics study. This proposition has logical implications for teacher preparation.

**Conclusion 6-1:** It is plausible that to provide students with the instructional opportunities they need to develop successfully in mathematics, teachers need preparation that covers knowledge of mathematics, of how students learn mathematics, and of mathematical pedagogy, and that is aligned with the recommendations of professional societies.

We particularly note the importance of the knowledge and skills described in Chapter 2 of *The Mathematical Education of Teachers* (Conference Board of the Mathematical Sciences, 2001). However, there is currently no clear evidence that particular approaches to preparation do indeed improve teacher effectiveness, nor clear evidence about how such preparation should be carried out.

Because strong preparation in both mathematics content and mathematics pedagogy are important, it seems logical that the preparation of mathematics teachers should be the joint responsibility of faculties of education and mathematics and statistics. We recognize that this is not a simple matter because of the many competing demands that face faculty in these fields, but we believe that close collaboration among mathematics faculty and mathematics education faculty is the only realistic means of providing the necessary preparation. Such collaboration could both promote research designed to improve the education of teacher candidates and provide teacher candidates with an education that seamlessly integrates mathematics learning and pedagogical learning.

The data regarding what is currently happening in teacher preparation for mathematics is extremely limited, but the information that is available clearly indicates that such preparation is not sufficient. That is, because it appears that many preparation programs fall short of guidelines such as *The Mathematical Education of Teachers* recommendations, it is likely that:

> **Conclusion 6-2:** Many, perhaps most, mathematics teachers lack the level of preparation in mathematics and teaching that the professional community deems adequate to teach mathematics. In addition, there are unacceptably high numbers of teachers of middle and high school mathematics courses who are teaching out of field.

Given the limited evidence base about the effectiveness of different approaches to preparing teachers of mathematics and about the nature of current preparation approaches, additional research is needed:

> **Conclusion 6-3:** Both quantitative and qualitative data about the programs of study in mathematics offered and required at teacher preparation institutions are needed, as is research to improve understanding of what sorts of preparation approaches are most effective at developing effective teachers.

# 7

# Preparing Science Teachers

Much is expected of U.S. science teachers. Student achievement in science, engineering, and technology is directly linked in public discourse with the nation's economic prospects. Moreover, the landscape of what science teachers might be expected to know and be able to do is very large. Depending on the grades they teach, science teachers may be expected to be knowledgeable about basic ideas and content from at least five academic disciplines: biology, chemistry, earth science, mathematics, and physics. They are expected to have a facility with different kinds of scientific inquiry and also, like any teacher, to possess pedagogical content knowledge—that is, to understand how students learn particular content and how to teach it.

Fortunately, there is a large body of scholarship on teaching and learning science, although it is largely descriptive and only a small portion of it is directly relevant to the committee's charge, which was to consider the extent to which the coursework and experiences required of prospective science teachers are consistent with converging scientific evidence. As with the other two subjects, we first describe the research base and then present the evidence using four questions:

1. What do successful students know about science?
2. What instructional opportunities are necessary to support successful students?
3. What do successful teachers know about science and science teaching?

4.  What instructional opportunities are necessary to prepare success-
    ful teachers?

## THE RESEARCH BASE

Although there is a wealth of material on science learning and teaching,
a recent committee that considered science learning and teaching described
this work as mostly "short in duration and limited in scope, focusing on a
few students or a few classrooms, [examining] some small part of the vast
domain of science" (National Research Council, 2007, p. 212). The report
adds that science learning is complex and that "the research on learning
cannot be reduced to a few 'what works' bullets without losing much of
its value" (p. 212). We are greatly indebted to the work of this and several
past National Research Council (NRC) committees that have produced a
number of reports that were extremely useful to us.

First, *National Science Education Standards* (National Research
Council, 1996) provided a definitive resource for the question of what
students need to learn about science. These standards were designed as a
way to coordinate and update previous science standards that had been
developed by the National Science Teachers Association (NSTA) and the
American Association for the Advancement of Science (AAAS).

Another key resource for our committee was *Taking Science to School*
(National Research Council, 2007). This report summarized the evidence
and drew conclusions from the research on science learning and on how science should be taught in K-8 classrooms. The report drew on many sources
of evidence about science and learning and built on findings from previous
NRC reports on learning in young children as well as older children and
adults, mathematics learning, and assessment. The report synthesizes disparate sources of insights related to science education, such as work that
describes the building blocks of science learning in young children, and that
maps the development of proficiency in different aspects of science.[1]

These and other reports, as well as meta-analyses conducted by Davis,
Petish, and Smithey (2006) and by Shroeder and colleagues (2007), were
particularly useful to us in meeting our charge of identifying consensus in
the field and considering the extent to which teacher preparation programs
in science reflect that consensus.[2] In general, however, we note that the
literature on science education includes more professional judgments and

---

[1]The opening chapter of *Taking Science to School* provides a detailed discussion of trends
in scholarship on science learning.

[2]A report from the Carnegie Corporation of New York and the Institute for Advanced Study
(2009) draws on a variety of sources to make recommendations regarding teacher quality and
preparation, standards for student achievement, and other issues.

reasoning about what students and teachers should know than empirical research. Interestingly, less empirical research is available in this field than in the other two we examined. In general, the field of science education is currently dominated by discussions and plausible recommendations regarding what students and teachers should know, but our confidence in those recommendations is tempered by the limited descriptive and experimental empirical evidence that supports them. This circumstance positions the field well for important research on teaching and teacher education in the future.

## QUESTION 1: WHAT DO SUCCESSFUL STUDENTS KNOW ABOUT SCIENCE?

There is no research that directly addresses the question of what students should know. Instead, as in other fields, educators rely on the judgments of experts to determine what should be taught. Although the value of studying science for those who do not intend to pursue a career that requires scientific knowledge and skills is not widely appreciated, considerable attention has been paid to the question of what science proficiency for all students should mean. This attention is especially important in the context of evidence that U.S. students' performance in science on international comparative studies has remained stagnant and is below that of many of the nation's economic competitors.

The 2007 results of the Third Trends in International Mathematics and Science Study (TIMSS) show no improvement in the overall performance of U.S. 4th or 8th graders since the 1995 TIMSS. Looking only at the percentages of U.S. students who performed at or above the advanced level in science, performance has declined for both grades since 1995 (National Center for Education Statistics, 2007). Results from the Programme for International Student Assessment (PISA) for 2006 show that, overall, U.S. students performed below the average for the 57 participating countries, though the percentage of U.S. students performing at the highest level was comparable to that of countries with much higher overall scores. The PISA results indicated that socioeconomic differences accounted for much of the disparity in U.S. students' science performance (Organisation for Economic Co-operation and Development, 2007). Thus, we look first at the arguments for viewing proficiency in science as important for all students. We then look at science standards more generally.

### Science for All Students

*Taking Science to School* (National Research Council, 2007) addresses the question of what science all children should be expected to learn. The report, which focuses on K-8 science education, argues that educators underestimate what young children are capable of as students of science and calls for extensive rethinking of how teachers are prepared. *Taking Science to School* argues that science is an essential component of K-8 education for several reasons:

- Science is a significant part of human culture and represents one of the pinnacles of human thinking capacity.
- It provides a laboratory of common experience for development of language, logic, and problem-solving skills in the classroom.
- A democracy demands that its citizens make personal and community decisions about issues in which scientific information plays a fundamental role, and they hence need knowledge of science as well as an understanding of scientific methodology.
- For some students, it will become a life-long vocation or avocation.
- The nation is dependent on the technical and scientific abilities of its citizens for its economic competitiveness and national needs.

Thus, the report makes clear that science education is important for all students, regardless of their interests and aspirations, because it prepares them to understand and evaluate information and to use evidence when making decisions. AAAS makes a very similar argument in *Science for All Americans* (American Association for the Advancement of Science, 1991), a consensus-based report that reflects the judgments of a broad array of scientists and science educators. The report asserts that a "science-literate person is one who is aware that science, mathematics, and technology are interdependent human enterprises with strengths and limitations; understands key concepts and principles of science; is familiar with the natural world and recognizes both its diversity and unity; and uses scientific knowledge and scientific ways of thinking for individual and social purposes."

In considering what students need to learn about science, *Taking Science to School* hoped to move beyond the dichotomy between content knowledge and skills, arguing that these two elements are completely intertwined in the study and practice of science. To develop science proficiency is to acquire a body of knowledge while also learning how knowledge is "extended, refined, and revised" (National Research Council, 2007, p. 26). The report stresses the value of science literacy even for those who do not ultimately enter a science-related career because students need to understand science as a process and to recognize the precise scientific meanings of words that have different meanings in everyday usage, such as theory, hypothesis, data, evidence, and argument (National Research Council, 2007).

The report identifies four strands of scientific proficiency as important for all students, arguing that successful students (National Research Council, 2007, p. 2):

1. "Know, use, and interpret scientific explanations of the natural world"—they acquire facts and conceptual structures that incorporate those structures, and use them to understand many phenomena in the natural world.
2. "Generate and evaluate scientific evidence and explanation"—they have the knowledge and skills to build and refine models based on evidence, including designing and analyzing empirical investigations and using empirical evidence to construct and defend arguments.
3. "Understand the nature and development of scientific knowledge"—they recognize that science is a particular kind of knowledge with its own sources, justifications, and uncertainties; and that predictions or explanations can be revised on the basis of new evidence or a new conceptual model.
4. "Participate productively in scientific practices and discourse"—they understand the norms of the practice of science and how to participate in scientific debates or adopt a critical stance, and are willing to ask questions.

A National Academies report, *Rising Above the Gathering Storm* (National Academy of Sciences, National Academy of Engineering, and Institute of Medicine, 2007), also addressed the importance of science, technology, engineering, and mathematics (STEM) education in the United States, with a particular focus on high school preparation. The report grounds its argument in the need for skilled workers to fuel economic growth, asserting that the nation needs to prepare a large pool of students to enter STEM majors in college. The report concludes that all students should have access to a solid foundation of science coursework in high school. Without a doubt, the proposition that a strong science, or STEM, education is fundamental for all students has been widely embraced by policy makers, as a recent issue of *Technology Counts* demonstrates (Editorial Projects in Education, 2008).

## Science Standards

The report describing the *National Science Education Standards,* was developed through a multiyear consensus process with input from scientists and science educators, organizations, and the public (National Research Council, 1996). The report provides content standards for students, integrated into a broader vision encompassing teaching, teacher preparation, and other elements.[3] The standards have been widely accepted as the model for the standards used in many states, though other science standards are also available, such as the online "compendium of content standards and benchmarks" developed by McREL (see http://www.mcrel.org/compendium/SubjectTopics.asp?SubjectID=2 [November 2009]).

The standards are grounded in a set of overarching principles that permeate all of the specific standards, including the premise that "science is for all students [and] that learning science is an active process, and that school science [should] reflect the intellectual and cultural traditions that characterize the practice of contemporary science" (National Research Council, 1996, p. 19). The document offers standards for teachers, professional development, and high-quality science programs, for science assessment, and for the content that students should know. The standards follow the lead of the earlier AAAS benchmarks (American Association for the Advancement of Science, 1993) in making scientific inquiry an organizing theme in the expectations for learning (see also the 2004 NSTA position statement, http://www.nsta.org/about/positions/inquiry.aspx [October 2009]). All three documents note that inquiry takes different forms in different contexts, but that it encompasses the ways scientists make observations and collect evidence, use findings to explain and predict, and engage in critical thinking. All three documents also emphasize that students must learn both the concepts and principles of science and the abilities associated with inquiry.

*National Science Education Standards* begins with a unifying standard that applies across grades K-12, concerning the "understanding and abilities associated with major conceptual and procedural schemes [that] need to be developed over an entire education, [and that] transcend disciplinary boundaries" (National Research Council, 1996, p. 104). The other standards are organized by age bands covering grades K-4, 5-8, and 9-12, and cover "inquiry; the traditional subject areas of physical, life, and earth and space sciences; connections between science and technology; science in personal and social perspectives; and the history and nature of science" (p. 104).

The document stresses that the standards were developed as a coherent framework and that all of their elements should be included in any curriculum that is based on them. For each content goal, the report describes fundamental abilities and concepts that underlie each standard. For example, one standard for earth and space science for grades 5-8 is that students should develop an understanding of the structure of the earth system. One of 11 fundamental concepts identified as part of that understanding is that

---

[3]A detailed description of integrated, coherent systems for science education can be found in *Systems for State Science Assessment* (National Research Council, 2006).

"The solid earth is layered with a lithosphere; hot convecting metal; and dense, metallic core" (National Research Council, 1996, p. 159).

The states also have their own standards, which, along with curriculum and assessment documents, make the performance expectations for students at particular grade levels more precise. States have also felt pressure to revise their science standards in response to the requirement in the No Child Left Behind Act, which mandated that by the 2007-2008 school year they establish assessments for grades 3-5, 6-9, and 10-12 that are linked to rigorous content and performance standards.

An assessment of states' standards was outside the scope of our charge, but we note that they vary dramatically, and that, in general, they do not align well to national standards (Porter, 2009). States' science standards have been the subject of various critiques that argue either that some states emphasize factual knowledge at the expense of intellectual rigor or, alternatively, that some have focused on inquiry at the expense of content (Gross et al., 2005; National Research Council, 2006). For example, according to Editorial Projects in Education (2006), 27 states had "clear, specific" standards that were "grounded in content" for the elementary grades in 2007, 32 had such standards for the middle grades, and 27 had such standards for high school. Critics have also suggested that few state science assessments address the kinds of deep understanding that science educators emphasize and have therefore had a negative impact on instruction.

Overall, there is a growing consensus that all students should be provided with a rigorous science education, in the sense advocated by the AAAS and others—that is, one that develops in-depth understanding of the most important topics (American Association for the Advancement of Science, 1991). The consensus from the *National Science Education Standards* and the other documents cited above is that science education should encompass:

- content in the physical, life, and earth and space sciences, organized around the big conceptual ideas of the discipline;
- the intellectual processes essential to science, such as inquiry, hands-on empirical investigation, use of evidence, and interpretation and analysis; and
- familiarity with the nature and history of science and its applications outside the classroom and laboratory.

The NSTA, NRC, AAAS, and Achieve, Inc., are currently collaborating to develop "science anchors" to build on the existing national standards in science. The anchors will establish top priorities for science education and they are now being used as part of the Common National Standards Project (see http://scienceanchors.nsta.org/ [November 2009]).

The *National Science Education Standards* were developed through a consensus process that considered the views of hundreds of people—including nationally known researchers and educators, college faculty, K-12 teachers and administrators, and scientists and engineers. State standards are developed in a similar way. These documents are not the product of empirical testing of hypotheses about outcomes for students exposed to different kinds of science learning: rather, they draw on research, accounts of exemplary practice, and the contributors' own experiences. Thus, standards are a detailed description of what the field of science education has identified as the foundation of science proficiency for K-12 students.

## Learning Progressions and the Big Ideas of Science

The concept of learning progressions—descriptions of the stages of student learning—has had a significant influence on thinking about successful science learning (National Research Council, 2006, 2007; Smith et al., 2006; Corcoran, Mosher, and Rogat, 2009). This idea draws on the cognitive research (discussed in Chapter 4) that has characterized learning as entailing not just the accumulation of facts but also the developing capacity to integrate knowledge and skills for use in solving problems and responding to new situations and information. Scientific knowledge is highly structured, and there are important links among different branches of science. Thus, a critical aspect of science learning is the development of an increasingly sophisticated understanding of how one's growing knowledge base is structured.

Primary scientific concepts—such as that the natural world is composed of a number of interrelated systems—are one of the most important organizing structures in science. They "have broad explanatory scope . . . and are the source of coherence among the various concepts, theories, principles, and explanatory schemes within a discipline" (National Research Council, 2006, p. 40). These primary concepts, or "big ideas," as they have come to be called, provide a fruitful way to organize curriculum and instruction. Researchers have examined the way students' understanding builds sequentially in a number of specific topic areas and have begun developing explicit descriptions of the stages through which understanding grows—"learning progressions." To use an example in *Systems for State Science Assessment* (National Research Council, 2006, p. 45), "before students can understand that organisms get energy from oxidizing their food, they must understand that energy can change from one form to another." These ideas allow educators to map their instruction to this empirically based model of learning. Researchers have traced learning progressions for a small number of domains; many more remain to be mapped.

## QUESTION 2: WHAT INSTRUCTIONAL OPPORTUNITIES ARE NECESSARY TO SUPPORT SUCCESSFUL SCIENCE STUDENTS?

What sorts of instructional experiences can help students meet the ambitious goals described in the national science education standards? Relatively little research is available to provide definitive answers to this question. Indeed, it might be said that far more is known about the kinds of instructional opportunities that are not necessary—because the results of numerous large- and small-scale studies of science achievement suggest that they are not effective. In an overview of research on science learning, (Anderson, 2007, p. 5) noted: "researchers in science education . . . generally agree on one central finding about current school practice: *our institutions of formal education do not help most students to learn science with understanding*" [emphasis in original].

In this section we review what we found about the sorts of experiences that researchers and practitioners have identified as important to successful science learning. We look first at the guides to teaching practice included in standards documents and at other sources.

### Standards

The *National Science Education Standards* (National Research Council, 1996) does not explicitly address the question in the way that we have framed it, but, in support of its focus on conducting scientific inquiry, the document offers many examples and details that demonstrate how students can be taught. Also useful is a supplement to the standards, a practical guide for teaching and learning that focuses on inquiry and highlights key relevant issues and research findings (National Research Council, 2000b). It identifies some relevant general findings about learning, such as that understanding science is more than knowing facts and that students build new knowledge and understanding on what they already know and believe. This report identifies several features of science inquiry in the classroom as essential (National Research Council, 2000b, p. 29):

- The "learner engages in scientifically oriented questions," for example, by posing questions for investigation, rather than answering questions generated by the teacher.
- The "learner gives priority to evidence in responding to questions," for example, by determining what constitutes evidence and collecting it, rather than being given data and instructions as to how to analyze it.
- The "learner formulates explanations for the evidence," for example, by summarizing and considering it, rather than being provided with evidence and guided in how to explain it.

- The "learner connects explanations to scientific knowledge," for example, by independently examining other knowledge resources and forming links, rather than having possible connections explained.
- The "learner communicates and justifies explanations," for example, by developing logical arguments, rather than by being given steps.

The standards also describe standards for teaching and for science programs, from which we infer that, to meet the standards, students need, in addition to exposure to all of the content standards, opportunities to (National Research Council, 1996, pp. 31, 43):

- participate in a community of science learners and engage in discourse about scientific ideas; and
- engage in extended scientific investigations, with access to science materials, media, and other technological resources.

The standards for new science teachers developed by the Interstate New Teacher Assessment and Support Consortium (INTASC) (2002), which are based on the national standards, provide some additional insights into the experiences science students need to have, again grounded in expert judgment rather than empirical research. For example, one core standard for beginning teachers identified by INTASC is that "the teacher of science understands and uses a variety of instructional strategies to encourage students' development of critical thinking, problem solving, and performance skills" (Interstate New Teacher Assessment and Support Consortium, 2002, p. 4). By design, these standards echo the national standards in asserting that "multiple modes of instruction" are needed to be sure that students have the opportunity to "collect, organize and recall information, design and conduct investigations, examine assumptions, make inferences, make generalizations, present structured arguments, and apply new information to existing natural and technological phenomena" (p. 28).

## Other Sources

The question of what sorts of instructional opportunities are necessary to foster science learning is also taken up in *Taking Science to School*, and this report also draws on the *National Science Education Standards*. It proposes that "to develop proficiency in science, students must have the opportunity to participate in [a] full range of activities" (National Research Council, 2007, p. 251), including

- conducting investigations;
- sharing ideas with peers;
- specialized ways of talking and writing;
- mechanical, mathematical, and computer-based modeling; and
- development of representations of phenomena.

Because children bring sometimes naïve understanding of the natural world and scientific concepts to the classroom, the report explains, "instruction needs to build incrementally toward more sophisticated understanding and practices . . . prior knowledge should be evoked and linked to experiences with experiments, data, and phenomena" (National Research Council, 2007, p. 251). (This issue is discussed further below in the context of teachers' knowledge.)

Some research that examines outcomes for students exposed to particular instructional practices and opportunities is also available. In a meta-analysis of research on the effects of teaching strategies[4] on student achievement in science, Shroeder and colleagues (2007) offer limited confirmation of the consensus-based recommendations noted above. The researchers identified mostly quasi-experimental studies that included information about effect sizes or the statistics necessary to calculate effect sizes.[5] Eight instructional strategies were found to have positive effects and significant (that is, unlikely to be attributable to chance) effect sizes: see Box 7-1. However, there were almost no experimental studies, and the quasi-experimental studies were limited in number: the authors found only 15 studies about information technology, 12 studies about inquiry, and 3 studies about questioning. Thus, the studies do not necessarily establish causal links between these strategies and student achievement. Shroeder and colleagues (2007, p. 1438) concluded that multiple studies have shown "that teachers have a profound effect on student learning," but that identifying the specific factors that influence outcomes "is problematic." For example, although there is widespread agreement that pedagogical content knowledge is a very important component of an effective teacher's approaches, there is little research that directly links it to particular student outcomes. In part, this is because the measures of such concepts as teacher knowledge are imprecise and limited in their reliability. Moreover, research on effective science instruction tends to be small in scale and descriptive;

---

[4]"Strategies" refers to actions or approaches that teachers take in interacting with students, such as asking them questions designed to elicit certain kinds of thinking. In the context of reading/language arts education, "strategies" is generally used to refer to actions or thinking that educators encourage students to engage in, such as articulating the questions they have about a text.

[5]In Shroeder et al. (2007), the quasi-experimental category included both studies with no randomization and studies with partial randomization.

---

**BOX 7-1**
**Science Teaching Strategies with Positive Effect Sizes**

Manipulation strategies. Teachers provide students with opportunities to work or practice with physical objects (e.g., developing skills using manipulatives or apparatus, drawing or constructing something).

Enhanced materials strategies. Teachers modify instructional materials (e.g., rewriting or annotating text materials, tape recording directions, simplifying laboratory apparatus).

Assessment strategies. Teachers change the frequency, purpose, or cognitive levels of testing/evaluation (e.g., providing immediate or explanatory feedback, using diagnostic testing, formative testing, retesting, testing for mastery).

Inquiry strategies. Teachers use student-centered instruction that is less step-by-step and teacher-directed than traditional instruction; students answer scientific research questions by analyzing data (e.g., using guided or facilitated inquiry activities, laboratory inquiries).

Enhanced context strategies. Teachers relate learning to students' previous experiences or knowledge or engage students' interest through relating learning to the students'/school's environment or setting (e.g., using problem-based learning, taking field trips, using the schoolyard for lessons, encouraging reflection).

Instructional technology strategies. Teachers use technology to enhance instruction (e.g., using computers, etc., for simulations; modeling abstract concepts and collecting data; showing videos to emphasize a concept; using pictures, photographs, or diagrams).

Collaborative learning strategies. Teachers arrange students in flexible groups to work on various tasks (e.g., conducting lab exercises, inquiry projects, discussions).

---

SOURCE: Information from Shroeder and colleagues (2007, pp. 1445-1446).

---

there have been very few large-scale attempts to systematically compare the effects of different instructional approaches on student achievement (Cohen, Raudenbush, and Ball, 2003).

Shroeder and colleagues also describe findings that support the general approach described in the national science education standards and elsewhere, noting that "no one strategy is as powerful as utilizing a combined strategies approach," and that "in an environment in which [students] can actively connect the instruction to their interests and present understandings and . . . experience collaborative scientific inquiry . . . achievement will be accelerated" (p. 1452). They also found that teaching strategies identified as innovative (as opposed to traditional), such as enhanced context, collaborative learning, and questioning strategies, had more positive influences on achievement than traditional approaches (though the researchers found no studies on direct instruction).

Other studies have examined factors that may affect science learning, such as students' attitudes and motivation, the role of language and scientific discourse, gender and diversity, and classroom learning environments (see, e.g., Gabel, 1994; Abell and Lederman, 2007). This body of work offers intriguing suggestions about factors that may have significant effects on students' science learning, but little that one could point to as necessary instructional opportunities.

In short, there is relatively little empirical evidence that connects the content of science standards to essential instructional opportunities or that establishes the benefits of particular types of instruction for student learning. However, there is a clear inferential link between the nature of what is in the standards and the nature of classroom instruction. Instruction throughout K-12 education is likely to develop science proficiency if it provides students with opportunities for a range of scientific activities and scientific thinking, including, but not limited to: inquiry and investigation, collection and analysis of evidence, logical reasoning, and accumulation and application of information. The opportunity for students' learning to progress logically over time and to build the capacity to link new information to existing conceptual frameworks is also very important.

## QUESTION 3: WHAT DO SUCCESSFUL TEACHERS KNOW ABOUT SCIENCE AND HOW TO TEACH IT?

The knowledge and skills students need to develop in order to be proficient in science encompass material from several academic disciplines and should be accumulated through the entire K-12 progression. Thus, an individual science teacher would not be expected to develop mastery of all of the content described in the national science education standards, but would focus on the standards for the age groups and subjects he or she intends to teach. Yet logic suggests that even teachers of elementary students need a basic familiarity with the big picture of science. Grossman, Schoenfeld, and Lee (2005) note the commonsense proposition that, "teachers should possess deep knowledge of the subjects they teach" (p. 201). It seems probable that in order to foster understanding of connections, address students' questions and misconceptions, and so on, teachers would need to have the confidence and competence that come with mastery of some college-level science. However, we are cautious in drawing this conclusion because no direct empirical evidence is available on this point. Nevertheless, a variety of sources offer perspectives on what effective science teachers know. We begin with standards documents published by national organizations and then consider other sources.

### Professional Standards for Beginning Science Teachers

The *National Science Education Standards* document stresses the central importance of what teachers bring to the classroom; thus, the document actually begins with standards for teachers. The standards for teachers are framed as descriptions of what effective teachers do: see Box 7-2 (National Research Council, 1996). These standards are consistent with the kinds of objectives that have been identified as important for any teacher (discussed in Chapter 3), but they also reflect specific objectives for science learning.

The standards pay particular attention to the role of assessment as a tool for teachers to use in improving their own practice, providing critical feedback to their students, and planning their lessons. The report (National Research Council, 1996) includes standards for the use of both formative and summative assessments.[6]

The National Science Teachers Association (2003) has published standards for science teacher preparation that are based on, and designed to be consistent with, the *National Science Education Standards*. This document describes detailed standards for new teachers in science content, the nature of science, inquiry, science- and technology-related issues, general teaching skills, capacity to plan and implement a science curriculum, capacity to relate science to the community, assessment, capacity to promote safety and welfare (including proper handling of animals and materials), and capacity to sustain their own professional growth.

The *Model Standards in Science for Beginning Teacher Licensing and Development*, standards for beginning science teachers developed by INTASC (Interstate New Teacher Assessment and Support Consortium, 2002), are in line with the teacher preparation standards of both *National Science Education Standards* and the NSTA standards—and all are the product of the general professional consensus within the field of science education. INTASC's 10 principles are listed in Box 7-3.

The three standards documents overlap and provide differing levels of detail about what new teachers need to have mastered. Davis, Petish, and Smithey (2006) conducted a content analysis of the national and INTASC

---

[6]Other NRC reports (National Research Council, 2001b, 2006) provide further detail about the role of assessment in science education systems.

---

**BOX 7-2**
**National Science Education Standards for Teachers**

- Plan an inquiry-based science program—e.g., identify goals, adapt content and curriculum to meet students' needs; select teaching and assessment strategies that support understanding.
- Guide and facilitate learning—e.g., focus, support, and model scientific inquiries, orchestrate classroom discourse following scientific traditions of reasoning and application of evidence.
- Engage in ongoing assessment of their own teaching and of student learning—e.g., use multiple methods to collect data and accurately analyze, apply, and report data.
- Design and manage learning environments that provide students with the time, space, and resources they need—e.g., allow time for extended investigations, ensure a safe working environment, and identify and use available resources in and out of school.
- Develop communities of science learners that reflect the intellectual rigor of scientific inquiry and the attitudes and values conducive to science learning—e.g., display and demand respect for diverse ideas and skills, nurture collaboration, structure and facilitate formal and informal discussion based on shared understanding of science discourse.
- Participate actively in ongoing planning and development of the school science program.

---

SOURCE: National Research Council (1996, p. 4).

---

standards and also reviewed 112 articles related to expectations for new science teachers. They identified five main areas in which the standards agree that teachers must have competence in order to be effective in the classroom: the content and disciplines of science, the characteristics and needs of science learners, instruction, learning environments, and professionalism (the capacity to foster their own development and be contributing members of a learning community).

These standards for science teachers are based on professional consensus and limited evidence about science teaching practices and how children learn scientific concepts and processes. They are not based on evidence that if teacher preparation programs are guided by or meet these standards, K-12 students will have higher achievement. We note, as we have elsewhere, that this approach to identifying standards for professional education is an accepted method of identifying the goals to which programs should aspire, though the lack of supporting empirical evidence reduces our confidence in conclusions about this approach.

**BOX 7-3**
**INTASC Principles for Beginning Science Teachers**

*Principle 1*: The teacher of science understands the central ideas, tools of inquiry, applications, structure of science and of the science disciplines he or she teaches and can create learning activities that make these aspects of content meaningful to students.

*Principle 2*: The teacher of science understands how students learn and develop and can provide learning opportunities that support students' intellectual, social, and personal development.

*Principle 3*: The teacher of science understands how students differ in their approaches to learning and creates instructional opportunities that are adapted to diverse learners.

*Principle 4*: The teacher of science understands and uses a variety of instructional strategies to encourage students' development of critical thinking, problem solving, and performance skills.

*Principle 5*: The teacher of science uses an understanding of individual and group motivation and behavior to create a learning environment that encourages positive social interaction, active engagement in learning, and self-motivation.

*Principle 6*: The teacher of science uses knowledge of effective verbal, nonverbal and media communication techniques to foster active inquiry, collaboration, and supportive interaction in the classroom.

*Principle 7*: The teacher of science plans instruction based upon knowledge of subject matter, students, the community, and curriculum goals.

*Principle 8*: The teacher of science understands and uses formal and informal assessment strategies to evaluate and ensure the continuous intellectual, social and physical development of the student.

*Principle 9*: The teacher of science is a reflective practitioner who continually evaluates the effects of his/her choices and actions on others (students, parents, and other professionals in the learning community) and who actively seeks out opportunities to grow professionally.

*Principle 10*: The teacher of science fosters relationships with school colleagues, parents, and agencies in the larger community to support students' learning and well-being.

SOURCE: Information from Interstate New Teacher Assessment and Support Consortium (2002, pp. 14-33).

## Other Sources

Some researchers have examined links between teacher characteristics and student learning in science. Davis, Petish, and Smithey (2006) reviewed 112 studies that examined new teachers' practices and understandings. For the most part, the reviewed articles were descriptive in nature (most were qualitative), with discussion limited to what the teachers know and do in their classrooms. However, a few studies suggest that three areas have demonstrated effects on teacher practice or student learning.[7] For example, teachers with greater content knowledge may ask more demanding questions and be "more likely to engage in sophisticated teaching practices" (Davis, Petish, and Smithey, 2006, p. 622). By contrast, those with less secure content knowledge "tended not to engage in conceptual-change teaching that accounted for and tried to address students' initial ideas . . ." (p. 626).

A small number of studies also indicate that teachers who are particularly concerned about classroom management tend to be less likely to use reform-oriented teaching practices. Studies that examined the relationship between teachers' self-efficacy and classroom practices showed that "teachers with higher self-efficacy engage students in more student-centered lessons, believe that students are capable of learning through cooperation and experiences, and develop more as science teachers" (Davis, Petish, and Smithey, 2006, p. 631).

The knowledge and practices necessary to successfully teach science are also discussed in *Taking Science to School* (National Research Council, 2007). The report grounds its discussion of what teachers need to know in findings from research on learning and development that elucidate the progressive nature of science learning. The authors found that students' thinking about a given topic grows in sophistication over time and that instruction (and curricula) have generally not accounted for the ways students gradually accumulate both knowledge and understanding. In order for the concepts and reasoning with which students enter school to evolve into the science knowledge described in standards, the authors argue, teachers must understand the levels of intermediate understanding through which students need to pass.

*Taking Science to School* also describes a range of instructional practices that support students in developing proficiency in the four strands of science proficiency (described above), and it offers strategies for applying them with students of different ages. These strategies include, for example, designing experiments, applying theories to make sense of data,

---

[7]We caution that these findings are based on a relatively small number of studies; see Davis, Petish, and Smithey (2006) for details about their methodology.

and constructing scientific explanations and models. But the larger point the report makes is that both learning theory and small-scale studies of science instruction support the conclusion that instructional approaches that involve learners in scientific practice will naturally engage students in the specific elements of learning content and learning to think scientifically that are described in the national science education standards.

*Taking Science to School* also cites the limited evidence that postsecondary study of science is associated with student achievement. A 1983 meta-analysis (Druva and Anderson, 1983) found a positive relationship between student achievement and the number of science courses their teachers had taken. Monk (1994) presents data from a longitudinal survey that addressed this issue for both science and mathematics and also identified positive effects. *Taking Science to School* notes that it is difficult to pinpoint an "optimal" amount of coursework in science content but that the effects of teachers' subject-matter knowledge seem to be greater for older students than younger ones. The report also notes that if college coursework were better aligned with school curricula, the effects might be more pronounced. The report presents findings from case studies that teachers with less content knowledge are less confident and effective at particular skills, such as sustaining an in-depth discussion or addressing student questions accurately and effectively (see, e.g., Hashweh, 1987; Carlsen, 1992, 1998; Sanders, Borko, and Lockard, 1993).

*Taking Science to School* also addresses the importance of understanding learners and learning, suggesting that teachers need to understand what students do when they learn, as well as the types of experiences that produce engagement and conceptual understanding. A variety of studies indicate that it is important for teachers to have accurate mental models of the way students learn and to understand social and other factors that may influence learning. Unfortunately, this research has yet to provide clear guidance that specific knowledge and skills in these areas are associated with benefits for students.[8] Similarly, the report discusses the importance of pedagogical content knowledge, but it acknowledges that "while the logic of subject matter knowledge for teaching is persuasive, there is almost no empirical link between specialized teacher subject matter knowledge and student learning" (National Research Council, 2007, p. 305). We return to the question of pedagogical content knowledge below.

Our review of the literature uncovered very little in the way of empiri-

---

[8]Another NRC report provides further elaboration of the ways students learn science and how understanding of their conceptual development is critical to effective science teaching. *How Students Learn: History, Mathematics, and Science in the Classroom* (National Research Council, 2005) applied to specific academic subjects the findings from an earlier report, *How People Learn* (National Research Council, 2000a), that synthesized recent developments in cognitive science regarding learning (described in Chapter 5).

cal evidence that particular knowledge and skills are essential for science teachers to be effective, although we note that existing research has not been designed to answer this question authoritatively. Yet, as with the instructional opportunities students need, we see a clear logical justification for the largely inference-based arguments made in standards for science teachers and other consensus documents: that to teach students the knowledge and skills required for science proficiency, teachers need knowledge and skills that are congruent with them. The field of science education has established a logical case, bolstered by some empirical evidence, that the following attributes help teachers provide students with the instructional opportunities they need to develop science proficiency:

- grounding in college-level study of the science disciplines suitable to the age groups and subjects they intend to teach, which develops understanding of the big conceptual ideas in science;
- understanding of multifaceted objectives for students' science learning;
- understanding of the ways students develop science proficiency; and
- command of an array of instructional strategies designed to develop students' learn the content, intellectual conventions, and other attributes essential to science proficiency, also known as pedagogical content knowledge.

## QUESTION 4: WHAT INSTRUCTIONAL OPPORTUNITIES ARE NECESSARY TO PREPARE SUCCESSFUL SCIENCE TEACHERS?

With regard to our final question, how teachers might be prepared to teach in the ways we have described, there is very little empirical evidence and less in the way of consensus recommendations from the field than for our other questions.

Looking first at the limited available research, Davis, Petish, and Smithey (2006) found aspects of preparation that may support the development of effective science teachers. They found, for example, that either simple exposure to a greater number of undergraduate science courses or exposure to methods courses can build teachers' sense of self-efficacy (confidence and sense of themselves as effective practitioners). Other studies suggest that courses that use the same general strategies advocated for K-12 classrooms—such as eliciting preconceptions, fostering inquiry—yielded teachers better equipped to use these same approaches, and that "simply requiring more science content courses is not enough to enable teachers to develop improved understanding of science content and inquiry and the nature of science" (p. 633).

With regard to teaching methods, Davis and colleagues also found some studies that suggest that for elementary teachers, training in planning, organizing instruction around important scientific ideas, and coteaching all appear to help teachers improve their attitudes toward science, boost their expectations of their students, and provide effective learning environments. They found indications that fieldwork helps teachers "develop more sophisticated ideas about science instruction and acquire self-efficacy as science teachers" (p. 635).

Lederman and colleagues (2001, p. 139) examined the effectiveness of interventions designed to "make [the nature of science] a pervasive theme throughout" a year of preservice instruction, and "to emphasize the importance of intentionally planning, teaching, and assessing students' conceptions of [the nature of science]." A small group of teacher candidates were followed in their first experience of full-time student teaching. The authors identified four factors as having the greatest influence on these teachers' classroom practice: their initial understanding of the nature of science, knowledge of the subject matter they taught, pedagogical knowledge, and intention to focus on the nature of science.

The *National Science Education Standards* (National Research Council, 1996) offers standards for professional development, which are tightly linked to those we have already discussed for student learning and for teaching. However, the report has little to say about preservice education. The report recommends that preparation for science teachers include the same elements recommended broadly for K-12 students, such as active investigations and strategies to build on teachers' current understanding. *Taking Science to School* (National Research Council, 2007) also addresses teachers' opportunities to learn through both professional development and preservice education. Like the standards, it recommends preparation designed to promote the kind of instruction it describes for K-12 students, grounded in general research on critical features of teacher preparation.

Researchers and faculty concerned with science education for undergraduate students have identified similar goals. For example, faculty from several departments have collaborated through a project at the University of California at Los Angeles to promote science education that includes hands-on research for undergraduates who are not science majors (see http://www.cur.org/publications/AIRE_RAIRE/ucla.asp [October 2009]). Though the program has the goal of promoting science proficiency for all students, it addresses the concern often voiced by the science education community, that K-12 teachers will teach as they have been taught and therefore need improved undergraduate science preparation. Similar concerns for undergraduate faculty are reflected in the goals of another program, Faculty Institutes for Reforming Science Teachers (FIRST), which engages college faculty in professional development designed to promote "active, inquiry-based teaching" that will improve students learning (Lundmark, 2002; see also http://first.ecoinformatics.org/ [October 2009]). The program is designed to help college faculty approach their teaching in the same way they approach their disciplinary research and thus help students learn the way science is practiced (see also Handelsman et al., 2004; Ebert-May and Hodder, 2008). These recommendations and programs build on earlier work, such as reports from the National Center for Improving Science Education (Loucks-Horsley et al., 1989, 1990), which note the importance of both a strong liberal arts preparation and strong undergraduate science instruction for all teachers.

We have little basis on which to offer specific findings about what sorts of instructional experiences teachers need. It seems probable that in order to foster understanding of connections and address students' questions and misconceptions, among other goals, teachers must have the confidence and competence that come with mastery of some college-level science, but the lack of causal evidence tempers our confidence in this conclusion. It also highlights the need for research that explores the causal nature of this relationship.

## HOW SCIENCE TEACHERS ARE CURRENTLY PREPARED

Partly because the advocated approaches for teacher preparation are complex and multifaceted, it is difficult to determine whether current programs are implementing any of the ideas the field has advocated. We could find no systematic information on the content or practices of preparation programs or requirements for science teachers across the states.

We looked for data on states' efforts to guide science teaching through either their certification requirements for science teachers or their licensure requirements for teacher preparation institutions. We found very little information about how states are using their authority to regulate teachers' qualifications or the characteristics of teacher preparation programs, but the hints we could find provided little indication that they are taking full advantage of this authority. According to data collected by Editorial Projects in Education, 33 of the 50 states and the District of Columbia require that high school teachers have majored in the subject they plan to teach in order to be certified, but only 3 have that requirement for middle school teachers (data from 2006 and 2008, see http://www.edcounts.org/ [October 2009]). Forty-two states require prospective teachers to pass a written test in the subject in which they want to be certified, and six require passage of a written test in subject-specific pedagogy.

The Education Commission of the States has assembled information about whether or not states require that teacher preparation programs align their curricula with the state's K-12 curriculum standards or their standards for teachers (see http://www.ecs.org/ [October 2009]). These data (updated to 2006) show that of the 50 states, American Samoa, the District of Columbia, Guam, Puerto Rico, and the Virgin Islands, 25 require both, 6 have no policy for either, 8 require only alignment with the K-12 curriculum, and 6 require only alignment with standards for teachers.

Data on so-called out-of-field teachers, those who are not certified in the subject they are teaching, provide another indication that states are finding it difficult to ensure that all of their science teachers are well prepared. Unfortunately, the only data available are almost a decade old, although there is no reason to believe the situation has improved. The National Center for Education Statistics reports that in the 1999-2000 school year, 17 percent of middle school students and seven percent of secondary students were taught science by a teacher who was not certified to teach science and had not majored in science (see http://nces.ed.gov/programs/coe/2003/pdf/28_2003.pdf [October 2009]). Using data from the Schools and Staffing Survey, Ingersoll (2003) found that 28 percent of the teachers who taught science to grades 7 through 12 "did not have at least a minor in one of the sciences or in science education" (p. 14). Teachers of the physical sciences were significantly more likely to be teaching out of field than were biology teachers. In rural areas there are particular problems with recruiting adequately prepared science teachers, covering all science subjects, and providing adequate professional development and support for teachers in each discipline (Education Development Center, 2003). Because these circumstances are not unusual, many educators have advocated special preparation for this role, such as a degree in natural sciences that covers biology, chemistry, earth sciences, and physics. Some institutions have adopted this policy, including some in the California state university system, particularly for prospective teachers who intend to teach middle school.

These indicators provide only very indirect information about our question, however. For a more detailed look at actual course-taking patterns and other information about preservice science preparation, we had a limited amount of state-specific information. The California Council on Science and Technology (2007) conducted an analysis of career pathways for that state's mathematics and science teachers. The report found that 9 percent of both middle and high school science teachers were teaching out of field and that even larger numbers of novice high school science teachers (35 percent) are not well prepared because the lack a preliminary credential. The percentages were highest in low-performing and high-minority schools. They also found that California lacks the capacity to meet the growing demand for fully prepared science (and mathematics) teachers and that the state is not collecting the data necessary to monitor the supply of and demand for these teachers. However, the analysis did not examine the content of science teacher preparation.

We also commissioned analyses from Florida and New York City (Grossman et al., 2008 Sass, 2008). Table 7-1 below shows the average number of science credits earned by Florida science teachers, by certification area (although the data do not provide information about the content or nature of the coursework). On average, elementary teachers earned about 13 credit hours in science and engineering, corresponding to slightly more than four courses. Secondary teachers certified in chemistry and biology earned an average of 70 and 64 credit hours, respectively, in science and engineering, corresponding to roughly 23 and 21 courses. For both elementary and secondary teachers, more than three-quarters of the science and engineering credit hours came from outside the School of Education.

The analysis of the preparation of teachers in New York City public schools (Grossman et al., 2008) included surveys of teacher preparation program completers and individuals in their first or second year of teaching about various aspects of their preparation. The surveys included items about preparation in science for elementary teachers and middle and high school science teachers.

The survey of first-year teachers in New York City included some questions about their preparation in science. The teachers were asked about the extent to which their teacher preparation program gave them the opportunity to do and learn a variety of things, such as hands-on activities for teaching scientific concepts. They rated their opportunities on a 5-point scale, with 1 being no opportunity and 5 being extensive opportunity. These teachers' responses to several of the questions that seem most congruent with the kinds of teaching advocated by the science education community are suggestive; they are shown in Table 7-2. Although the survey was small in scale, it does suggest that New York City teachers who graduated recently from a teacher education program do not report extensive exposure to the elements advocated by the science education community.

Despite these hints, we do not have the information that would be needed to draw conclusions regarding the types of instruction and experiences that aspiring science teachers receive in teacher education programs. Therefore, we cannot tell how consistently teacher preparation programs in science draw on the converging scientific evidence regarding the teaching of science.

## CONCLUSION

In our review of the literature pertaining to the preparation of science teachers we found some intriguing research, most of it carried out on tightly focused topics and on a small scale, and a compelling logical case for an integrated approach to science education—one that incorporates factual knowledge, scientific inquiry, and the nature of science. The *National*

TABLE 7-1 Mean Science Credit Hours, Florida Science Teachers

| Certification Area | Science Education | Noneducation Science Credit Hours | Noneducation Biology Credit Hours | Noneducation Chemistry Credit Hours | Noneducation Physics Credit Hours | Noneducation Engineering Credit Hours |
|---|---|---|---|---|---|---|
| Elementary [N = 3,684] | 2.72 | 8.78 | 3.81 | 1.11 | 1.76 | 1.40 |
| Chemistry [N = 15] | 11.07 | 57.8 | 22.27 | 23.27 | 6.40 | 1.07 |
| Biology [N = 76] | 11.25 | 51.28 | 29.0 | 13.34 | 5.87 | 1.66 |

NOTES: Samples include only teachers with 100 or more known credit hours in university-designated courses taken in Florida public community colleges and universities prior to their first year of teaching in Florida public schools. No data are available for teachers certified in physics.
SOURCE: Data from Sass (2008).

**TABLE 7-2** New York City Teachers' Reported Exposure to Science Preparation

| Opportunity to Learn Science Education Approach | Mean Response on 1-5 Scale[a] |
|---|---|
| Learn hands-on activities for teaching science concepts | 3.02 |
| Learn how to facilitate student learning in small groups, such as laboratory groups | 3.03 |
| Learn how to use tasks or "discrepant events" to show how preconceptions can be incorrect | 2.39 |
| Learn how to encourage scientific inquiry | 2.81 |
| Practice what you learned about teaching science in your field experience | 2.66 |

NOTES: Results are for teachers who attended an undergraduate teacher preparation program. See Grossman and colleagues (2008) for data on teachers who followed other pathways.

[a]A respondent who rated his or her exposure as a 3 would be indicating that it was roughly half-way between none at all and extensive.

SOURCE: Data from Matt Ronfeldt, University of Michigan (personal communication 2008).

*Science Education Standards,* now more than 10 years old, have been widely accepted and are influential, and they provide a solid grounding for this case that is bolstered by similar documents from the professional societies. The *National Science Education Standards* document was based on a comprehensive effort to establish consensus among a broad-based group of those with expertise and experience in science education, drawing on research wherever possible, and we see no reason to question its content. If one accepts the consensus-based standards from the field, many inferences about the knowledge and skills that will benefit teachers flow logically from its detailed descriptions of the elements of science proficiency.

Despite our concerns about the areas that have not received adequate research attention, we believe that the field has made a strong argument for the approach to science education laid out in the national science education standards. Regarding what students need to know, the field has advocated that all K-12 students receive a science education that encompasses:

- content in the physical, life, and earth and space sciences;
- the intellectual processes essential to science, such as inquiry, hands-on empirical investigation, use of evidence, and interpretation and analysis; and
- familiarity with the nature and history of science and its applications outside the classroom and laboratory.

Regarding the instructional experiences that students need to develop proficiency in science, the consensus in the field is that students need opportunities throughout their K-12 education to engage in a range of scientific activities and scientific thinking, including, but not limited to inquiry and investigation, collection and analysis of evidence, logical reasoning, and accumulation and application of information. They need the opportunity for their learning to develop logically over time and to build the capacity to link new information to existing conceptual frameworks.

If these two propositions about what and how students should learn are true, then it follows that teacher preparation should be aligned with those goals. That is, it is plausible that the following attributes help teachers provide students with the instructional opportunities they need to develop science proficiency:

- grounding in college-level study of the science disciplines suitable to the age groups and subjects they intend to teach;
- understanding of multifaceted objectives for students' science learning;
- understanding of the ways students develop science proficiency; and
- command of an array of instructional strategies designed to develop students' learning of the content, intellectual conventions, and other attributes essential to science proficiency, also known as pedagogical content knowledge.

Logical though this inference is, we recognize that the cost of ensuring that teachers are prepared to meet these ambitious standards would be considerable and that the available guidance as to expectations for individual teachers is very limited. Even less obvious is exactly how teachers might best be prepared to know and do what these standards imply, as we have seen.

This is a significant problem. Current standards specify science education that can only be provided by teachers with a deep engagement in the intellectual processes of science and facility with scientific content, as well as the capacity to provide students with a variety of complex experiences with science. There seems to be a significant disjuncture between this vision and the preparation that aspiring science teachers are currently receiving. A second significant problem is that we could find so little detailed information about that preparation, so we cannot answer the question of how well current practice fits the consensus standards. We began this chapter with the observation that much is expected of science teachers in the United States; it seems to us that the U.S. Department of Education, the states, and the professional societies concerned with the quality of teaching and with science education all share an interest in the way science teachers are prepared.

We also note that much of the available research on science teacher preparation focuses on teachers of grades K-8. Science preparation for secondary students is of equal importance and presents distinct challenges for educators. As we note above, some secondary science teachers have not majored in the science subjects they are teaching or are not certified to teach it. Moreover, it is at this stage that the curriculum for students begins to diverge by scientific discipline. Overall, there are numerous questions about the preparation of science teachers that remain unanswered.

**Conclusion 7-1:** Systematic data are needed on the nature and content of the coursework and other experiences that currently constitute teacher preparation in science. Research is also needed to examine the propositions regarding the teaching and learning of science contained in professional recommendations that have not been adequately examined empirically.

# 8

# Accountability and Quality Control in Teacher Education

Our examination of teacher preparation for reading, mathematics, and science brought out some interesting differences among the three as well as some important similarities. We found a variety of sources to support conclusions relevant to teacher preparation. The support was strongest for conclusions about reading and weakest for conclusions about science. Overall, based on professional consensus in each field about what successful students know and a variety of evidence about the experiences that support student learning, we offer conclusions that can point teacher educators toward the best currently available guidance about preparation in these fields.

The next question to ask, then, is how these conclusions can be useful to policy makers in holding teacher education preparation programs accountable for the quality of the education they provide. Before discussing the utility of our conclusions for this purpose, we consider more broadly the accountability mechanisms in public education and teacher preparation.

## ACCOUNTABILITY: AN OVERVIEW

Accountability—the mechanism by which institutions meet their obligation to report to others about how their resources have been used and to what effect—is a central concept in democratic societies (Trow, 1996). It can function through a variety of structures, including government regulation, private markets, and self-regulation (Graham, Lyman, and Trow, 1995). Accountability has become the cornerstone of K-12 education reform efforts in the United States, as it has in business and other sectors, though there have been disagreements about which sorts of accountability measures are the most useful in the context of public education.

Following decades of state leadership in standards-based accountability, federal policy makers intensified the focus with the No Child Left Behind Act of 2001. That law tied federal funds to measures of student learning, mandating that states assess achievement in core subjects annually with the goal of ensuring that all students reach proficient levels in those subjects by 2014. Educators are expected to draw on a range of performance indicators to diagnose problem areas and sharpen interventions. Though standards-based testing and accountability are not without problems and detractors, most believe that they are here to stay, and that—on balance—they are having a positive effect (Stecher and Naftel, 2006; Massell, 2008).

Two types of accountability bear directly on teacher education, one related to programs and one related to teachers:

1. the direct monitoring of teacher preparation *programs*, by means of program approval and accreditation, and
2. the monitoring of individual *teachers*, through certification and licensure.

States and professional accrediting bodies exert direct influence over the operations and content of teacher education programs. Certification and licensure policies affect teachers directly, but they also affect preparation programs, which have the goal of certifying their graduates in particular areas and preparing them for the tests that states require of prospective teachers. Indeed, in some states the connection is explicit: for example, the subject-matter content standards for Florida teachers are designed to undergird both the state's ongoing approval processes for teacher education programs and the content of the subject-specific certification examinations required for full licensure. In addition, we note that teachers' performance on high-quality state certification and licensure tests could theoretically be an important measure of what graduates of preparation programs have learned.

The charge to this committee does not include reference to accountability or any individual quality control mechanisms. Yet our examination of the quality of teacher education inevitably led us to consider program approval, accreditation, and certification as crucial policy levers. Accountability mechanisms can be viewed as means of protecting the public from educational malpractice, or, more ambitiously, of ensuring that high standards are met. In either view, their functioning is critical to understanding of both the forces that shape teacher preparation and possible opportunities to leverage future improvements. Congress sought this report on the state of teacher preparation because adequate information about key aspects of teacher education is not readily available. Accountability mechanisms are important tools for improving teacher education and could be an excellent ongoing source of the kind of information Congress has requested. For these reasons, we determined that a report on teacher preparation programs would be incomplete if it did not address accountability mechanisms. We look first at accountability mechanisms that affect teachers directly.

## CERTIFICATION, LICENSURE, AND TESTING

### Certification

The quality of individual teachers is addressed by states in various ways. *Certification* is the process by which states assess individuals' qualifications for teaching jobs, and each state develops and enforces certification in its own way. According to data collected by the Education Commission of the States and the National Comprehensive Center for Teacher Quality and made accessible in an interactive website (see http://mb2.ecs.org/reports/reportTQ.aspx?id=1137 [December 2009]), of 54 jurisdictions (states, U.S. Territories, and the District of Columbia), the state board of education authorizes teacher certification in 21, in 16 it is the state education agency, and in 16 it is a board or commission established specifically for that purpose (no policy was found for Guam or Michigan). Requirements may include background checks and fingerprinting; character recommendations; oaths of allegiance; minimum age; state-mandated teacher tests of basic skills, professional knowledge, or content knowledge; the completion of coursework in various domains (e.g., subject-matter majors or minors, the teaching of reading, classroom management, content courses aligned with state level standards for students); and participation in clinical field experiences (National Association of State Directors of Teacher Education and Certification, 2000).

The requirements for teacher certification have evolved over time, reflecting shifting expectations of teachers. In the colonial period, religious elders and important citizens would assess the moral and physical strength of teacher applicants. In the mid-19th century, reformers worked to establish professional standards and examinations. Tests were based on individual authors' views of what constituted professional knowledge, which might include geography or mathematics facts or moral views (Sedlak, 2008). Gradually, the curricula of teacher education programs expanded to include educational foundations (philosophy, psychology, sociology), instructional methods, and subject-matter courses.

Program administrators looked for guidance in designing their curricula from a variety of sources: professional organizations, local and state boards of education, state legislatures, other teacher preparation programs, faculty in the disciplines, state superintendents of schooling, and education research. The content of teacher preparation programs is determined in part by state requirements (which are developed through the political process), but they also reflect the values and views of faculty in both colleges of education and disciplinary departments. There is no centralized source of information about state requirements or the content of teacher preparation programs currently offered in the United States. We could find no evidence that state requirements for teacher certification are based on research findings, and it appears that they vary significantly.

States also vary in the way they classify teaching certifications: teachers can be granted provisional certificates, professional or permanent certificates, or emergency certificates. Most states have a staged licensure process: 31 require an initial license that is valid for 2-5 years, with a permanent license to follow when additional requirements are fulfilled (such as completing advanced degrees or continuing professional development) (National Association of State Directors of Teacher Education and Certification, 2000). To earn a full license, teachers in some states must pass assessments of classroom performance. These assessments include the Interstate New Teacher Assessment and Support Consortium (INTASC) content-specific portfolios and Praxis III, an observation instrument developed by the Educational Testing Service.

## Licensure

The terms certification and licensure are essentially synonymous in education, though that is not the case in all professional contexts. Some states issue teaching certificates and others issue licenses, with both typically serving the same function. The National Board for Professional Teaching Standards also offers certification, available in all states, that identifies successful candidates (among teachers who have been in the classroom for at least 3 years) as accomplished teachers, and the states offer other sorts of specialized certification as well.

## Testing

Forty-two states require some form of teacher testing as part of the certification or licensure process (National Association of State Directors of Teacher Education and Certification, 2000). Teacher tests may cover basic skills, general knowledge, subject-matter knowledge, or pedagogical knowledge. Different tests are used to evaluate candidates in more than 25 credential areas (e.g., elementary education, chemistry, art, special education), and every state sets its own pass rates. There are more than 600 teacher tests currently in use (National Research Council, 2001). Two test development companies, the Educational Testing Service (ETS) and National Evaluation Systems (NES), produce most of these tests, although some states develop their own. The limited information available about the development of these tests suggest that decisions about test content are generally based on either the mapping of K-12 student standards or teacher standards or the consensus views of panels of professionals (teachers, teacher educators, state department staff, faculty from the disciplines) (Wilson and Youngs, 2006).

There is a limited amount of research on the psychometric characteristics of these tests. For example, Wilson and Youngs (2006) located 14 studies of teacher testing, but all were conducted before the National Teachers Examination (NTE) was replaced with PRAXIS. Moreover, variation in the ways these tests are developed and used makes it very difficult to generalize about them. For example, states use different cutoff scores even when using the same test. Moreover, candidates also take these tests at different times in their careers, and thus will have had varying amounts of education and student teaching when they are tested. The available research was not designed to account for these and other sources of variance in performance: consequently, there is very little systematic information about the content or the predictive validity of these tests.

The quality of teacher tests has been a subject of public concern, with critics charging that they are simplistic and calling attention to embarrassingly low cut scores (e.g., Fowler, 2001). ETS has published reports about how their tests are constructed, but most teacher tests are not available to researchers for content analyses or research. One reason for the lack of access is that testing companies invest considerable funds in test development, and they do not want to bear the cost of replacing publicly released items, which they would have to do if the test items were available for study. One report on test content (Mitchell and Barth, 1999) found that most teacher tests in English/language arts, mathematics, and science used a multiple-choice format and covered knowledge at the high school level: they "found no evidence of content at the baccalaureate level" (p. 8).

For tests of professional knowledge to provide valid information on which to base accountability systems, they will need to be aligned with scientifically based research on student learning and instructional practices. However, for this kind of alignment to be possible, the developers of teacher licensing exams would need to make the necessary data available so that qualified researchers can, without breaching test security, study and report on the content of these exams.

## PROGRAM APPROVAL

States also exercise authority over the programs that educate prospective teachers through program approval. An individual teacher can apply directly to the state department of education for certification, but individual teachers can also be recommended for certification by state-approved programs of teacher preparation. That is, program approval allows for graduates of particular programs that meet state criteria to be automatically recommended for individual certification at the program's discretion. State departments of education set program approval requirements and stipulate the review process for program approval, which typically involves an initial registration process and ongoing reviews; this process may or may not be related to national accreditation reviews (National Comprehensive Center for Teacher Quality, 2006). We could find no systematic information on or analysis of how state program approval is carried out or of its effects on quality.

Teacher education programs and state departments of education do have significant experience with managing program approval in their own states. In Michigan, for example, program approval often requires the construction of a matrix that aligns all state requirements to all program content. These analyses can include presentation of annotated course syllabi that highlight and point out where, when, and how particular topics are covered. Reviews may also include materials that demonstrate alignment between a program and state requirements. Some states convene panels of teacher educators from across the state to review these materials.

Teacher education program approval is typically mandatory. However, the effects of state approval on program quality have not been systematically demonstrated. The current mechanisms and standards vary considerably across states, can be inefficient, and can include requirements that have little empirical base.

## STANDARDS

Central to state review and program accreditation processes are the standards against which institutions are judged. Many states have their own standards for teachers, and some have standards for beginning teachers. Others use the standards of the National Council for Accreditation of Teacher Education (NCATE) or the Teacher Education Accreditation Council (TEAC). NCATE's standards are developed through a consensus process and are updated every 7 years (National Council for Accreditation of Teacher Education, 2008). Data from the National Comprehensive Center for Teacher Quality show that 32 states require their programs to align their curricula in some way with K-12 academic standards, and 28 require that programs align their curricula in some way with state standards for K-12 teachers (see http://www2.tqsource.org/mb2dev/reports/reportTQ.aspx?id=946 [December 2009]). However, we were not able to find any comprehensive documentation or analysis of the standards that states used in accrediting teacher preparation institutions. From our examination of materials from TEAC, NCATE, and four states (California, Florida, Michigan, and New York), as well as regional agencies, it seems that states' standards generally incorporate or draw on local requirements and the recommendations of professional associations and that their content and character vary significantly.

The standards that do exist are not based on research that demonstrates links between particular standards and improved outcomes for students taught by teachers who were educated in a particular way because such evidence is not available. Thus, as in other professions, states and accrediting bodies draw on the standards developed by professional associations, other consensus recommendations, widely held commitments, or recognized best practices. We note that teacher education is hardly alone in lacking data that directly link components of professional preparation to the outcomes for those who receive the professionals' services.

## ACCREDITATION

Professional societies associated with other fields, such as architecture, medicine, and law, require preparation programs to obtain national accreditation as a way of assuring the public of the programs' soundness and rigor. This is not a requirement for teacher education programs, though individual states can mandate it, requiring either state program review or accreditation by a national body (National Research Council, 2001). Virtually no research exists that demonstrates the effects of accreditation on teacher quality (Wilson and Youngs, 2006). Again, there is limited centralized information about the specifics of how programs are actually accredited across the states. Data available on the National Comprehensive Center for Teacher Quality website indicates that each state develops its own policy (see http://www2.tqsource.org/prep/policy/index.asp [December 2009]). States may accept the accreditation of one of two national bodies, NCATE and TEAC, or develop their own requirements for program review.

There are also six regional agencies (the Middle States, New England, North Central, Northwest, Southern, and Western Associations of Schools and Colleges) that accredit institutions of higher education—though not teacher education programs specifically—and some states rely on this general accreditation. Many states allow more than one route to program approval, either accepting more than one type of review (national or state) or requiring that programs meet both the standards of a national or regional

**TABLE 8-1** Accreditation for Teacher Preparation Programs

| State | State-Set Requirements | NCATE | TEAC | One or More Regional Bodies | No Policy Found |
|---|---|---|---|---|---|
| AK | | | | * | |
| AL | | | | * | |
| AR | | * | | | |
| AS | | | | | * |
| AZ | | * | * | * | |
| CA | * | | | * | |
| CO | | * | * | * | |
| CT | | * | | * | |
| DC | * | | | | |
| DE | * | * | | | |
| FL | | | | * | |
| GA | | * | * | * | |
| GU | | | | | * |
| HI | | | | | * |
| IA[a] | * | | | | |
| ID | | * | * | * | |
| IL | | * | * | * | |
| IN | | * | | | |
| KS | | * | | | |
| KY | * | * | | | |
| LA | * | * | | | |
| MA | | | | | * |
| MD | | * | | | |
| ME | | * | * | * | |
| MI | * | | | | |
| MN | * | | | | |
| MO | * | * | * | * | |
| MS | | * | | | |
| MT | * | * | | | |
| NC | | * | * | | |

body and additional standards set by the state. Eight states do not appear to have set a formal policy for accreditation. In addition, some states have a policy for intervening with or closing a program that does not meet its criteria. The variation in states' policies regarding accreditation is shown in Table 8-1.

Some states have performance, or competency-based, processes, requiring that programs demonstrate how they ensure that prospective teachers have acquired the necessary knowledge and skill; others examine program outcomes, examining graduation, job placement, and retention rates. See Boxes 8-1 and 8-2 for descriptions of the approval processes for New

**TABLE 8-1** Continued

| State | State-Set Requirements | NCATE | TEAC | One or More Regional Bodies | No Policy Found |
|---|---|---|---|---|---|
| ND | | * | | | |
| NE | * | * | | | |
| NJ | | * | * | | |
| NM | | | | | * |
| NY | * | * | * | * | |
| OH | * | * | | | |
| OK | * | * | | | |
| OR | | | | * | |
| PA | | * | * | * | |
| PR | | * | | | |
| RI | | * | | * | |
| SC | * | * | | | |
| SD | | * | | * | |
| TN | * | | | | |
| TX | * | | | | |
| UT | | * | * | * | |
| VA | | | | | * |
| VI | | | | | * |
| VT | | | | * | |
| WA | | | | * | |
| WI | | | | * | |
| WV | | | | * | |
| WY | | | | | * |
| Total | 17 | 30 | 12 | 22 | 8 |

<sup>a</sup>The database shows no policy for Iowa, but we obtained independent confirmation of the state's policy as well as information for California (Commission on Teacher Credentialing, 2007).
SOURCE: Compiled from data available on the website of the National Comprehensive Center for Teacher Quality, see http://www.ecs.org/html/offsite.asp?document=http%3A%2F%2Fwww%2Etqsource%2Eorg%2Fprep%2Findex%2Easp++ [December 2009]); updated to 2006.

York and Florida, respectively. The accreditation standards for NCATE are shown in Box 8-3.

According to data from NCATE and TEAC, over half of the approximately 1,300 U.S. teacher education programs they examined are accredited by one of the two national bodies: 632 by NCATE (see http://www.ncate.org/public/listofaccredinst.asp [December 2009]) and 59 by TEAC (see http://www.teac.org/index.php/membership/teac-members/ [December 2009]). NCATE, which was established in 1954, draws on the expertise of a variety of professional associations concerned with education in developing its standards; see Box 8-4. (We note that disciplinary organizations, such

## BOX 8-1
## New York State Teacher Education Program Approval Process

The initial process of registering teacher preparation programs in the state involves providing written documentation of such things as program philosophy or mission; faculty cooperation across university departments; efforts to recruit faculty and students from historically underrepresented populations; efforts to educate potential students about labor market conditions for each certification area; use of assessments; and facilities.

In addition to these general requirements, state regulations specify a "content core" and a "pedagogical core" for each certification type. For example, elementary education programs are required to provide study (and specify each by listing the relevant college course numbers) that will permit candidates to obtain an 11-point list of pedagogical knowledge, understanding, and skills (e.g., human development, learning, language acquisition; curriculum planning; technology). The list is different for alternative certification programs. The field experience portion of pedagogical core is further specified, requiring at least 100 hours of field experiences related to coursework prior to student teaching or practica and at least two college-supervised student-teaching experiences of at least 20 school days each. The types of experiences and overseeing faculty are also specified.

Once programs are registered with the state, all programs must be accredited by the state once every 4 years. Accreditation can be obtained through the State Regents Accreditation of Teacher Education (RATE) process or through accreditation by NCATE or TEAC.

RATE includes five standards of quality:

1. commitment and vision
2. philosophy, purposes, and objectives
3. standards for program registration
4. teaching effectiveness of graduates, including evidence their graduates:
   a. promote well-being of all their students
   b. help them learn to their highest levels of achievement and independence
   c. use their knowledge to create nurturing environment for all students
5. assessment of candidate achievement

Additional standards relate to financial resources, support servies, advertising, candidate complaints, public disclosure of accreditation status, and annual reports.

Each program submits a self-study report for review by up to three external reviewers, selected by the New York State Department of Education. The program submits written reports to the state commissioner who makes a recommendation to the Board of Regents, which ultimately decides accreditation action.

as the American Mathematical Society, are not included.) The organization has repeatedly revised the accreditation process. The current process emphasizes the need for institutions to demonstrate that the content of their programs aligns with relevant standards. TEAC was created in 1997 by a group of education school deans and college presidents. TEAC's accreditation model is based on audits in which the organization's quality principles (e.g., evidence of student learning, assessment of student learning) are applied (Murray, 2001). A TEAC audit may be coordinated with state standards and accreditation procedures. As this report is being completed, TEAC and NCATE are discussing possibilities for creating a uniform system of accreditation that would combine their separate efforts.

The accreditation process of the six regional agencies is not comparable to the specialized accreditation offered by NCATE or TEAC. Teacher preparation institutions that are accredited through the regional agencies must demonstrate that they meet the standards of eligibility of the Commission of Higher Education and then go through a process of self-study determined by the regional agency and aligned with that agency's standards. The regional agency procedures may include paper reviews of program curricula; in other cases on-site reviews are conducted by teams of educators and others. Historically, these regional agency reviews have tended to emphasize inputs, asking such questions as whether prospective teachers have the opportunity to learn various knowledge and skills. Only recently has attention turned to accountability for outputs, that is, results.

Accreditation also commonly includes some sort of peer review or audit of programs by teams of peers, which may include teachers, teacher educators, state education department staff, school administrators, and faculty from the disciplines. For example, NCATE has a board of examiners who are trained by NCATE in the accreditation processes (for details, see http://www.ncate.org [October 2009]). TEAC sends a team of auditors to check the accuracy of the materials submitted by an institution. These auditors include TEAC-trained educators, and in some states local practitioners and representatives of the relevant state department of education (for details, see http://www.teac.org [October 2009]). Regional agencies use similar processes, with faculty from peer institutions who make campus visits to check the validity of self-studies. The practices for appointing and educating these visiting peers vary among the accrediting bodies.

We note that the identification of suitable peers for the accreditation of teacher education programs presents some challenges. The criteria for the selection of peers—whether teachers, administrators, or researchers—might have a profound influence on the resulting review because of those individuals' professional views regarding the elements that are important or effective in teacher preparation. Similar concerns would hold for parents, policy makers, or any other participants. Moreover, without a strong empirical

**BOX 8-2**
**Florida State Teacher Education Program Approval Process**

Review and approval of educator preparation programs in Florida consists of two parallel systems—one for initial approval and one for continuing approval—both of which are governed by both law and rules. The focus of the initial review is process oriented; the focus of the continued review is performance based.

In brief, institutions seeking initial approval of their programs submit curriculum folios describing the design, delivery, content, and evaluation of each program for review by statewide teams of peer reviewers. This folio review is followed by an on-site review for institutions that do not currently have approved programs. Initial approval is granted first for all of the programs the institution is seeking approval for; then, the institution transitions to the continued program approval standards and process, for which there are annual reporting requirements and a site visit every 7 years in order to monitor program outcomes, candidate performance, and continuous improvement.

The standards for (performance-based) continued review include three major standards, on content, on the candidate teachers, and continuous improvement. The key elements in each of these standards is shown below.

**Standard 1. Core Curriculum Content**

1. Current mandated state requirements and curricular content are consistently implemented and published in required documents.
2. Field or clinical sites represent diverse cultures and varying exceptionalities and performance levels, in a variety of settings, including high-needs schools.
3. Faculty meet state-mandated requirements for supervision of field or clinical experiences.
4. School district personnel meet state-mandated requirements for supervision of field or clinical experiences.

base on which to make decisions about the quality of teacher preparation, any interested party can claim some reason for participating in accreditation visits and processes.

In sum, teacher education program accreditation traditionally has been voluntary and has been conducted by states and national nongovernmental organizations. More institutions are currently accredited by NCATE than by any other state or national body. The effects of state program reviews and national accreditation on program quality have not been systematically demonstrated. There is no centralized information about how comparable these various modes are. States' accountability practices have relatively little foundation in empirical findings because little such evidence is available. We note that this dilemma is not unique to education.

**Standard 2. Candidate Competency**

1. Each program consistently applies state-mandated admission requirements.
2. Candidate evidence of attainment of uniform core curricular content is assessed and data is collected from coursework, field or clinical experiences, and on the Florida Teacher Certification Examinations.
3. Candidates demonstrate impact on P-12 student learning based on student achievement data in field or clinical experiences and during the first year of teaching.
4. The program documents the assistance and the results of the assistance provided to program completers who do not meet employer satisfaction in their first 2 years of teaching.

**Standard 3. Continuous Improvement**

1. The program remains responsive to the needs of the state and districts served.
2. Employers of program completers indicate satisfaction with the level of preparedness for the first year of teaching, including the rehire rates of program completers and length of stay in the classroom.
3. Program completers indicate satisfaction with the level of preparedness for the first year of teaching.
4. Continuous improvement across and within programs is the result of routine analysis of data collected on Standards 2 and 3; admission, enrollment, and completion status of each candidate; and results of recent faculty experiences.

## COMPARISONS WITH OTHER FIELDS

The challenges of effectively using accountability measures to ensure quality are not unique either to education or to the U.S. system, but the U.S. education system has charted its own course to a considerable extent. A detailed comparative analysis of accountability practices across occupations was not part of the committee's charge and little information was available, but we do note a few general findings. A comparison of preparation and training in seven fields conducted by The Finance Project (Neville, Sherman, and Cohen, 2005) found that the standards for entry are less consistent, across the states, for teaching than for any of the other six fields examined (law, accounting, architecture, nursing, firefighting, and law enforcement).

**BOX 8-3**
**Standards of the National Council of**
**Accreditation in Teacher Education**

Twenty-five states have adopted or adapted NCATE unit standards and administer them. Twenty-five states delegate NCATE to conduct the program review process for purposes of NCATE accreditation and state approval. NCATE has six standards, detailed below.

**Standard 1: Candidate Knowledge, Skills, and Professional Dispositions:** Candidates preparing to work in schools as teachers or other school professionals know and demonstrate the content knowledge, pedagogical content knowledge and skills, pedagogical and professional knowledge and skills, and professional dispositions necessary to help all students learn. Assessments indicate that candidates meet professional, state, and institutional standards.

**Standard 2: Assessment System and Unit Evaluation:** The unit has an assessment system that collects and analyzes data on applicant qualifications, candidate and graduate performance, and unit operations to evaluate and improve the performance of candidates, the unit, and its programs.

**Standard 3: Field Experiences and Clinical Practice:** The unit and its school partners design, implement, and evaluate field experiences and clinical practice so that teacher candidates and other school professionals develop and demonstrate the knowledge, skills, and professional dispositions necessary to help all students learn.

**Standard 4: Diversity:** The unit designs, implements, and evaluates curriculum and provides experiences for candidates to acquire and demonstrate the knowledge, skills, and professional dispositions necessary to help all students learn. Assessments indicate that candidates can demonstrate and apply proficiencies related to diversity. Experiences provided for candidates include working with diverse populations, including higher education and P-12 school faculty, candidates, and students in P-12 schools.

**Standard 5: Faculty Qualifications, Performance, and Development:** Faculty are qualified and model best professional practices in scholarship, service, and teaching, including the assessment of their own effectiveness as related to candidate performance. They also collaborate with colleagues in the disciplines and schools. The unit systematically evaluates faculty performance and facilitates professional development.

**Standard 6: Unit Governance and Resources:** The unit has the leadership, authority, budget, personnel, facilities, and resources, including information technology resources, for the preparation of candidates to meet professional, state, and institutional standards.

**BOX 8-4**
**Professional Associations That Provide Input to the National**
**Council for the Accreditation of Teacher Education**

*Teacher Education Associations*
American Association of Colleges for Teacher Education (AACTE)
Association of Teacher Educators (ATE)

*Teacher Associations*
American Federation of Teachers (AFT)
National Board for Professional Teaching Standards (NBPTS)
National Education Association (NEA)
National Education Association (NEA) Student Program

*Child-Centered Associations*
Association for Childhood Education International (ACEI)
Council for Exceptional Children (CEC)
National Association for the Education of Young Children (NAEYC)
National Association for Gifted Children (NAGC)
National Middle School Association (NMSA)

*Subject-Matter Associations*
American Alliance for Health, Physical Education, Recreation and Dance
  (AAHPERD)
American Council on the Teaching of Foreign Languages (ACTFL)
International Reading Association (IRA)
International Technology Education Association (ITEA)
National Council for the Social Studies (NCSS)
National Council of Teachers of English (NCTE)
National Council of Teachers of Mathematics (NCTM)
National Science Teachers Association (NSTA)
North American Association for Environmental Education (NAAEE)
Teachers of English to Speakers of Other Languages (TESOL)

*Educational Leadership Associations*
American Association of School Administrators (AASA)
Association for Supervision and Curriculum Development (ASCD)
National Association of Elementary School Principals (NAESP)
National Association of Secondary School Principals (NASSP)

*Policy Maker Associations*
Council of Chief State School Officers (CCSSO)
National Association of State Boards of Education (NASBE)
National School Boards Association (NSBA)

SOURCE: Data from http://www.ncate.org/governance/MemberOrganizations.aspx [March 2010].

The study noted that in all of the other fields, candidates are required to pass a single national exam or a state exam with a national component before they are allowed to begin practicing. None of the other fields allows candidates to gain licensure through alternative routes or to begin practicing before they have met all licensure requirements. The authors also found that all of the six comparison fields have more consistent program approval mechanisms across the states than does education.

Most of the 50 countries that participated in the Third Trends in International Mathematics and Science Study (TIMSS) have the same basic elements in place for teacher education and certification (Mullis et al., 2008). For example, 42 require that candidates who wish to teach at the elementary or primary level earn a degree from a teacher education program, and more than 40 require some sort of practicum (opportunity to apply what was taught in the classroom). The requirements are somewhat different for mathematics and science teachers, but more than half of the countries also require passage of an exam and have a probationary period for new teachers. These comparisons, though limited, suggest that the United States is quite different from other countries in having such a highly variable approach to accountability for teacher education.

An analysis of teacher education and development policies in a smaller group of countries that participated in TIMSS (the United States, Australia, England, Honk Kong, Japan, Korea, the Netherlands, and Singapore) provides a more detailed analysis (Wang et al., 2003). This study found that the United States and Australia have the least centralized systems and are the only two that do not have a single national agency that oversees teacher preparation programs. The scope of the challenge of ensuring accountability in the United States is suggested by the sheer numbers of programs in the country: 1,500 according to the National Center for Education Statistics. In comparison, no other nation has more than a few hundred.[1] The United States and England are the only two countries in the study that allow alternative routes to teacher certification. It is also worth noting that some countries that perform at high levels on TIMSS, such as Singapore and Finland, provide financial support for teacher candidates and are recognized for their ability to recruit high-achieving students for teacher preparation programs.

---

[1]The Netherlands offers teacher preparation in 12 public universities and 13 professional colleges; Australia has 35 institutions; and England has 123. Japan has 138 institutions that offer preparation in mathematics and 149 that offer preparation in science (with some overlap).

## CONCLUSION AND RECOMMENDATION

It is clear from our review of accountability in teacher preparation that the existing evidence does not support a strong conclusion about the effectiveness of the current accountability process in teacher education. Thus, there would be significant value in investment in research and development to improve the research base and technical infrastructure for teacher education accountability. In addition, although empirical links between teacher preparation and student learning have not been established, current accountability mechanisms could likely use information that is available. Specifically, accountability systems could better integrate in their evaluations indirect evidence, such as consensus about the intellectual foundations and priorities in academic fields and findings about promising instructional approaches.

As part of the broader research agenda on teacher education (discussed in Chapter 9), we recommend research on developing valid means of establishing links between teachers' preparation and outcomes for students that could be used in accountability policies for teacher preparation programs. This research will require attention to conceptual, data, and measurement issues, with a particular focus on improving the development of measures and technologies that would make it possible to accurately measure the teaching knowledge and practices that are most closely associated with gains in K-12 student achievement. Such measures are particularly needed for accountability purposes.

The accountability systems now in use are haphazard. Not enough is known about the effectiveness of any of their major elements—certification, testing, program approval, and accreditation—either at promoting the practices and approaches that are supported by research and professional consensus or at assuring the public of the quality of programs. The senior leadership of NCATE offered this committee access to its accreditation reports to help us describe programs. However, because teacher preparation varies so much across and within states and because programs bring different—often unique—forms of evidence to bear as they make the case for meeting NCATE standards, we were not able to use these rich sources of information to compare approaches across programs. Yet policy makers need guidance as to how to address the politically difficult issue of accountability in the context of a wide variety of practices. If the Department of Education wishes to meet the serious lack of information about teacher preparation programs, a comprehensive evaluation is needed.

**Recommendation 8-1:** The U.S. Department of Education should sponsor an independent evaluation of teacher education approval and accreditation in the United States. The evaluation should describe the nature, influence, and interrelatedness of approval and accreditation processes on teacher education program processes and performance. It should also assess the extent to which existing processes and organizations align with best practices in accountability and offer recommendations for how they could do so more effectively in the future.

The evaluation should focus specifically on evidence of learning and effects on outcomes. On the first point, the recommended evaluation should focus on the nature and rigor of the evidence base used to inform approval and accreditation standards and processes. The evaluation should also include an assessment of the near- and long-term effects of these mechanisms on key processes and, especially, K-12 student outcome measures. On the second point, the evaluation should assess the extent to which the information gathered in accreditation reviews serves as a force for ongoing improvement at the program level and whether and how it could contribute to a broader knowledge base about teacher preparation.

Both further research and an evaluation of existing accountability mechanisms are critical. All teacher education programs should be able to demonstrate that their graduates can teach in ways that have been shown empirically to lead to gains in K-12 student learning. As research strengthens the knowledge base that can be used for accountability purposes, it will be possible to better examine many questions. In particular, as stronger indicators are developed, states and independent associations that are involved in teacher education program approval and accreditation will be able to use them as a basis for their accreditation standards and reviews.

Although the empirical basis for this sort of accountability is slim at present, the field is not starting at zero. As we discuss throughout this report, a growing body of literature has identified some of the behaviors and skills of teachers that boost K-12 student learning in core subjects, and that knowledge base can be tapped for teacher education accountability. And even in the short term, there are ways to focus current accountability systems on the best available evidence. The established, consensus- and research-based conclusions of the professional and academic communities associated with school subjects provide a critical source of guidance to programs and state accountability systems as to the kinds of content and knowledge and pedagogical content that benefit teachers.

We note as well that there is no reason that program accountability should not extend to all types of programs that prepare teachers, including newer programs that operate outside state postsecondary institutions. As we discuss in Chapter 3, the distinction between traditional and alternative pathways is problematic, but in most states programs described as traditional or alternative are subject to separate systems of accountability and quality control. Thus, requirements for teacher education programs not only vary across states, they vary within states as well. In our view, states should hold *all* preparation programs to the same standards.

Finally, we suggest that accountability ought to focus on assessments that show program graduates can practice effectively. Workforce trends across sectors reflect heightened demand for workers at all levels who can demonstrate their knowledge and skill; high-stakes teacher certification tests are an example of this phenomenon in the teacher labor market (National Research Council, 2002b). But passing a paper-and-pencil test is different from demonstrating effective teaching practices, and a few states are developing performance assessments that are or will be part of their teacher certification requirements (e.g., the Performance Assessment for California Teachers; see Pecheone and Chung, 2006).

Most relevant for our purposes, however, is the observation that, despite changes in the rhetoric, teacher education program accountability is still overly dependent on input and process requirements. Many states continue to require programs to offer particular courses, set minimum admissions standards, ensure minimum contact hours with faculty and student teacher supervisors, and the like. The national accrediting bodies have made progress toward implementing outcome-oriented standards, but much remains to be done. We envision an accountability system that is based primarily on the evaluation of program graduates' ability to use instructional practices that facilitate K-12 student learning in core subjects. Although such an approach is likely to be more difficult and expensive than the current one, it is a fundamental need if teacher education is to reflect the ultimate outcome, student learning.

More systematic information about the development and content of tests used for teacher accreditation or certification is needed. Accountability is a complex component of the education system and one that provokes strong opinions. Questions about the quality of the nation's teachers go to the heart of many contentious issues in education policy. For example, discussion of licensure, certification, and accreditation naturally suggests comparisons with other fields in which these issues arise, such as medicine, law, accounting, and various technical occupations. This comparison in turn raises questions about the status of teaching as a field. The purpose of this committee was not to determine whether teaching ought to be considered a profession, nor to rehash the arguments in that debate. Whatever the answer to that question, it seems reasonable to ask that teacher candidates and teacher preparation programs be held to high standards and that the accountability system used be both professionally responsible and publicly credible.

# 9

# Summary and Research Agenda

I n response to our broad charge, the committee examined many aspects of the complex and diverse set of institutions and programs through which the majority of the nation's teachers are prepared. The bulk of our report focuses on the first three questions in our charge, about the candidates who enter teacher preparation programs, the nature of the pathways and programs those candidates select, and the extent to which the content of teacher preparation is consistent with scientific evidence. The first part of this chapter provides a summary of our findings about teacher preparation in the United States.

There is no lack of writing on teacher preparation, yet there are many gaps in the research base. The fourth part of our charge was to make recommendations regarding future data collection that would provide useful, valid, and reliable information. The second section of this chapter presents our conclusions about the research base, and the final section presents our recommendations for future research.[1]

## SUMMARY: TEACHER PREPARATION IN THE UNITED STATES

We looked first for information about the first two parts of our charge, regarding the individuals who enter teacher preparation programs and their academic preparation, as well as the types of instruction and experiences

---

[1] The numbering of the conclusions and recommendations below follows that in the chapters.

they receive. There is no system in place to collect data across the myriad
teacher preparation programs and pathways in the United States. Thus, we
can say little about the characteristics of aspiring teachers, the programs
and pathways they follow, or the outcomes of their preparation. We found
some information about general elements that most teacher preparation
programs share, such as courses in pedagogy and the foundations of education and required fieldwork. We also found that both programs and pathways vary dramatically in their requirements, structure, and timing. Because
of the paucity of systematic research as well as the enormous variation in
virtually all aspects of teacher preparation programs and pathways, we
cannot draw any specific conclusions about the characteristics of current
teacher preparation programs.

Researchers have examined particular programs and pathways to look
for differences among the people who pursue different routes, as well as
differences in the effectiveness of graduates. The findings are slim. Some
research suggests that there are differences in the characteristics of teacher
candidates who are attracted to different pathways and types of programs.
There is also some research that compares the outcomes for graduates of
different kinds of programs. However, the distinctions among pathways and
programs are not clear-cut, and there is more variation within categories
such as "traditional" and "alternative"—and even within the category of
master's degree programs—than there is between the categories.

**Conclusion 3-1:** There is currently little definitive evidence that particular approaches to teacher preparation yield teachers whose students are
more successful than others. Such research is badly needed. We believe
that the highest priority research would be studies that examine three
critical topics in relation to their ultimate effect on student learning:

1. comparisons of programs and pathways in terms of their *selectivity*; their *timing* (whether teachers complete most of their training
   before or after becoming a classroom teacher); and their specific
   *components and characteristics* (i.e., instruction in subject matter,
   field experiences);
2. the effectiveness of various approaches to preparing teachers in
   classroom management and teaching diverse learners; and
3. the influence of aspects of program structure, such as the design and
   timing of field experiences and the integration of teacher preparation
   coursework with coursework in other university departments.

### Content of Teacher Preparation Programs: Research Evidence

The question of the extent to which the required course work and experiences in reading, mathematics, and science across teacher preparation programs are consistent with converging scientific evidence presented a somewhat different challenge for the committee. Within each of the three fields there is a range of material that is potentially relevant. This material includes a relatively small body of empirical studies that provide some evidence about the effects of particular kinds of instruction; it also includes an even smaller amount of evidence about the effects of particular approaches to teacher preparation.

The other kinds of research that are available include descriptive and qualitative studies, which explore many aspects of teaching and learning in the three subjects, as well as a substantial body of empirical work on learning and cognition, which has had an important influence on practice within each discipline. In addition, the professional organizations that provide leadership in the fields of reading, mathematics, and science have drawn on the available research and their own intellectual traditions and experience as educators to develop content and achievement standards for students, standards for teachers, and, in some cases, guidance or standards for teacher education.

Substantial work by educators and researchers has identified some strong arguments about the factors that are likely to influence teacher quality and student learning. Yet this work is only a starting point because the empirical evidence supporting the impact of these factors is limited. The research base varies across the three school subjects, and our conclusions about preparation in each field reflect these differences. Our discussions of the state of knowledge in these three areas also reflect the fact that we found no evidence in the literature that undermines the current recommendations of disciplinary experts, or calls into question the tradition, common to many fields besides education, of basing some decisions about professional education on such recommendations.

## Reading

**Conclusion 5-1:** Successful beginning readers possess a set of foundational skills that enable them not only to continue growing as readers but also to progress in all academic subjects. A variety of instructional approaches that address these foundational skills can be effective when used by teachers who have a grounding in the foundational elements and the theory on which they are based.

**Conclusion 5-2:** It is plausible that preparation in the nature of the foundational reading skills and research-based instructional approaches would improve teachers' practice to a degree that would be evident in learning outcomes for their students. However, there is currently no clear evidence that such preparation does indeed improve teacher effectiveness or about how such preparation should be carried out.

**Conclusion 5-3:** There are very few systematic data about the nature of the preparation in reading that prospective teachers receive across the nation. The limited information that exists suggests that the nature of preparation of prospective teachers for reading instruction is widely variable both across and within states.

**Conclusion 5-4:** Little is known about the best ways to prepare prospective teachers to teach reading. Systematic data are needed on the nature and content of the coursework and other experiences that constitute teacher preparation in reading.

## Mathematics

**Conclusion 6-1:** It is plausible that to provide students with the instructional opportunities they need to develop successfully in mathematics, teachers need preparation that covers knowledge of mathematics, of how students learn mathematics, and of mathematical pedagogy and that is aligned with the recommendations of professional societies.

**Conclusion 6-2:** Many, perhaps most, mathematics teachers lack the level of preparation in mathematics and teaching that the professional community deems adequate to teach mathematics. In addition, there are unacceptably high numbers of teachers of middle and high school mathematics courses who are teaching out of field.

**Conclusion 6-3:** Both quantitative and qualitative data about the programs of study in mathematics offered and required at teacher preparation institutions are needed, as is research to improve understanding of what sorts of preparation approaches are most effective at developing effective teachers.

## Science

**Conclusion 7-1:** Systematic data are needed on the nature and content of the coursework and other experiences that currently constitute teacher preparation in science. Research is also needed to examine the propositions regarding the teaching and learning of science contained in professional recommendations that have not been adequately examined empirically.

## Accountability

This was the picture of what converging evidence suggests about teacher preparation, against which one might measure what is currently happening. However, there is very little systematic research about current practice in the preparation of reading, mathematics, and science teachers. The limited information we found does not support broad conclusions about the nature and content of current teacher preparation programs.

As we describe in Chapter 8, our investigations of these issues led us to consider the accountability system, which is designed to ensure the high quality of teacher preparation programs. The accountability measures in place are diverse, and the gaps in the data available are large. If accountability for teacher preparation is to become more effective, a major assessment of the current situation would be needed.

**Recommendation 8-1:** The U.S. Department of Education should sponsor an independent evaluation of teacher education approval and accreditation in the United States. The evaluation should describe the nature, influence, and interrelatedness of approval and accreditation processes on teacher education program processes and performance. It should also assess the extent to which existing processes and organizations align with best practices in accountability and offer recommendations for how they could do so more effectively in the future.

## RESEARCH AGENDA

The last part of our charge was to make recommendations regarding a model for data collection that would provide valid and reliable information about the content knowledge, pedagogical competence, and effectiveness of graduates from the various kinds of teacher preparation programs. The base of empirical knowledge about teacher preparation is thin. We believe the way forward is to build on what has been done by drawing on the professional consensus in each academic field for promising hypotheses about which features of teacher preparation are most promising and to subject those hypotheses to rigorous research. We were asked to develop an approach to future research that would provide a firmer foundation for policy and practice in the future. We organized our response around two overarching needs:

1.  improved understanding of the relationships between characteristics of teachers' preparation and students' learning, and
2.  a comprehensive, coherent system for collecting data about teacher preparation.

In discussing these two needs, we offer our assessment of the most important questions to pursue and the most productive means for doing so. Our discussion and recommendations draw on a study we commissioned (Crowe, 2007) to examine the current status and quality of data systems, as well as analysis of the available data related to the questions in our charge.

## The Relationship Between Characteristics of Teacher Preparation and Student Learning

An obvious question to ask about teacher education is whether particular ways of preparing teachers lead to measurable improvements in student learning. Many researchers have worked hard to establish such connections. In Chapter 2 we discuss why it is difficult to establish clear causal links between aspects of teacher preparation and outcomes for the students teachers teach after they have completed their training. Programs may differ in the types of candidates they attract and in the types of knowledge and skills that candidates acquire. Programs may also differ in whether and where their graduates teach (e.g., what kinds of schools; urban or rural) and how long they remain teachers. And programs almost certainly graduate people who have different capacities to use their knowledge and skills to improve their students' learning. Some programs may produce graduates who are more effective in some settings than others. We repeat as Figure 9-1 the model used in Chapter 2 to portray the complex interactions among different elements that influence teacher quality and student achievement.

Thus far, some attempts have been made to compare the learning of students whose teachers were prepared in one way to that of students whose teachers were prepared in a different way. Unfortunately, we found that the existing studies have generally been insensitive to the details of teacher preparation that are most likely to result in differences in quality. Theoretically, the best way to do this sort of investigation would be experimental field trials, in which teacher candidates are randomly assigned to different programs and students are randomly assigned to program graduates. When randomization is not possible, however—which is frequently the case in studies of education and other complex human behaviors (see Chapter 2) —other means of estimating the effects that programs have on participants and their students can provide valuable information. Other approaches include regression discontinuity designs, instrumental variables, or natural

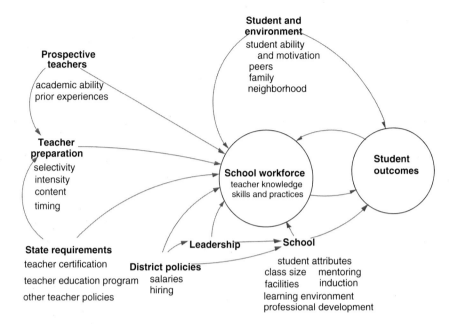

**FIGURE 9-1** A model of the effects of teacher preparation on student achievement. SOURCE: Adapted from Boyd et al. (2006, p. 159).

experiments with appropriate controls. Researchers are still in the process of working out an array of practical approaches to providing reliable answers to questions about teacher preparation.

Research in teacher preparation would also be much easier to conduct if researchers had better measures of student outcomes than standardized achievement scores in mathematics and reading. Although scores are readily available and easy to use, they provide incomplete measures of both students' learning and the effects of teachers (though assessment issues differ across the school subjects). We also believe there is much to be learned regarding the links between teacher preparation and the knowledge and skills teachers display in the classroom. Recently, there has been substantial interest in the development of observational protocols that measure various domains of teaching that have been linked to student outcomes (e.g., Mashburn et al., 2007; Matsumara et al., 2008; Grossman et al., 2009). Observational protocols offer a vehicle for exploring the contributions of teacher preparation and evaluating teachers' effectiveness.

A strong research program designed to illuminate the ways teacher preparation influences outcomes for students would include evidence drawn from a variety of different perspectives, with the goal of establishing not only whether a particular feature of preparation is important to student outcomes, but also why it is important. At present, research has provided only a fragmented and limited picture of how characteristics of teacher preparation improve student outcomes.

In our judgment, the simplest and most effective way to produce a clearer picture would be to focus research on the aspects of preparation that have the highest potential for effects on outcomes for students. Existing research provides some guidance on three aspects of teacher preparation that are likely to have the strongest effects: content knowledge, field experience, and the quality of teacher candidates.

## Content Knowledge

There are strong reasons to believe that teachers need relevant content knowledge to be effective. Nevertheless, there is surprisingly little research that establishes clear and strong connections between teacher content knowledge and student learning. Throughout the report we discuss the challenges of isolating these connections—not only that the measures of both content knowledge and student learning are weak, but also that the relationships among learning, learners, classroom practice, and teacher preparation are complex. Nevertheless, we believe understanding how content knowledge influences student outcomes is very important.

The conclusions we drew about the research that was needed related to preparation in reading, mathematics, and science focus on this point. Looking across these three fields, we note several topics that would be fruitful for research:

- Clarify what is meant by teacher knowledge and how that construct can best be measured, and how content knowledge interacts with knowledge of the pedagogical application of that knowledge.
- Develop better measures of student learning of academic content.
- Establish the extent to which measures of teacher content knowledge can predict student learning.
- Conduct intervention studies in which teacher content knowledge is enhanced and the intervention group is compared with one or more control groups established by a rigorous research design, such as randomized trials.

## Field Experience

Most observers agree that aspiring teachers should have field experience as part of their training. Yet reviews of previous research have failed to reveal any distinct relationships between the way field experiences are structured and implemented and teacher effectiveness. Recent work suggests that teachers benefit from preparation programs that provide significant oversight of field experiences and from field experiences that are congruent with candidates' eventual teaching positions (e.g., Boyd et al., 2008a). Although this research is suggestive, there is no systematic causal evidence on what aspects of field experiences have the greatest effect on teacher effectiveness.

A substantial research program could be built around hypotheses regarding field experiences. A program that included theoretical work, qualitative analysis, statistical analysis, and randomized experiments could provide strong causal evidence of the effects and mechanisms by which various components of field experiences—such as coplanning, coteaching, scaffolded entry into practice, seminars with mentors, a mentor with relevant content and grade level experience, and the like—affect teachers' classroom practices and student achievement. For example, each primary component of field experiences could be systematically manipulated in a randomized control field trial to examine the relative effects on teacher classroom practices and student achievement outcomes.

It is also likely that statistical analysis that exploits the substantial differences in current practice would yield insights on relative effectiveness, although this analysis would require controls for selection effects. Qualitative analysis that examined the implementation of the field experience components would provide important insights on how and why these components may influence teacher effectiveness and could offer some suggestions on whether there may be important interactive effects. For example, one interactive effect that is worth examining is whether teachers who work in low-performing schools benefit more from certain field experiences than others.

## Quality of Teacher Candidates

The quality of new teachers entering the field depends not only on the quality of the preparation they receive, but also on the capacity of preparation programs to attract and select academically able people who have the potential to be effective teachers. Attracting able, high-quality candidates to teaching is a critical goal, and there is reason to believe that some pathways and programs are much more attractive than others for such potential teachers. Less clear are the factors that attract the best candidates, the way program selectivity and preparation interact and the effect of each on student learning, and the extent to which the importance of these factors vary depending on the attributes (such as grade level and ability) of the students whom these teachers ultimately teach. That is, though some programs are more selective and attractive to academically accomplished candidates, researchers have not clearly established whether those candidates make the best teachers.

## A Comprehensive Data Collection System

A primary obstacle to investigating these and many other important aspects of teacher preparation is the lack of systematic data collection, at both the national and state levels. Crowe (2007) found that, apart from the methodological problems we have discussed, there is a problem with the "availability and quality of data about nearly everything having to do with teacher preparation" (p. 2).

The many basic questions that are at present difficult to answer systematically include the following:

- What are the characteristics of candidates who enter teacher preparation programs?
- How do those characteristics vary by program or pathway?
- Where do entrants and graduates of preparation programs ultimately teach?
- How long do teachers with different types of preparation continue to teach? Are differences in preparation associated with differences in teachers' career trajectories?
- Where do teachers with different types of preparation teach?
- How do the knowledge and teaching practices of teachers with different types of preparation differ?
- What have been the effects of states' policies regarding program approval and teacher certification?

A more comprehensive approach to data collection would provide both baseline monitoring of the status of teacher preparation (and improved opportunities to link that information with other aspects of the public education system) and a common foundation on which to build research efforts that investigate important aspects of teacher preparation. Moreover, it would provide the basis for much-needed national attention to the importance of teacher preparation and the urgency of improving it.

What would a more comprehensive approach look like? A comprehensive data system for teacher preparation would provide meaningful information about teacher candidates, preparation programs, practicing teachers, the schools in which those teachers teach, and the students they teach. For example, with respect to teachers, observational measures of their skills and practice would provide information about the content of preparation that goes beyond degree title, courses taken, or certifications attained. Similarly, with respect to students, the standardized performance measures that many states currently use provide important information, but it will be essential to bring other kinds of information about student learning into the systems used to track trends and evaluate the effects of teachers. The assessment community has made important strides in developing richer measures of achievement, such as portfolios of student work and assessments that are embedded in classroom instruction and in developing ways to standardize them. Measures of other important aspects of learning, such as persistence and motivation, are also important, but at present these issues have a very limited presence in large-scale data collection efforts and accountability systems.

The new data would be integrated so that information about teacher candidates and their preparation could be connected with the knowledge, teaching practices, career paths, school environments, and student outcomes of the teachers who are prepared in different ways. One key to integration will be consistent definitions of key indicators. At present, states each develop their own teacher licensure categories (which may change from year to year), determine which assessments teachers must pass—and most use many different ones—and what performance level will constitute passing. States differ in the way they define teaching assignments and identify out-of-field teachers, and they even have differing ways of counting years of teaching experience. There are countless other sources of variation that make it extremely difficult for researchers to compare across states or generalize from the available information. Some information is also needed on a national basis because substantial numbers of teachers move among states during their careers.

A few states have developed exemplary systems for capturing data. Florida, for example, has the PK20 Education Data Warehouse (see http://edwapp.doe.state.fl.us [October 2009]), which is a nationally recognized model. This system collects comprehensive information about the entire educational system and has built-in linkages so that researchers do not need to create cross-files to investigate specific questions. Texas, Utah, and Louisiana are developing similar systems. Unfortunately, few states collect a significant amount of data about the teacher preparation programs and pathways that are not based in their university systems (Crowe, 2007).

The U.S. Department of Education has focused on the problem of education data. The Institute for Education Sciences (IES) awarded grants to 14 states in 2005 to develop "well-designed, comprehensive statewide longitudinal data system[s] with the capacity to follow individual students' performance over time, to transmit student information both within and between States, and to provide educators and education researchers with the data needed to improve outcomes for students" (see http://nces.ed.gov/Programs/SLDS/ [October 2009]). High-quality research on teacher education will require extending those data systems to information about teachers, their background and education, preparation, and career paths across and within school systems.

At the national level, there are other data sources available, though none are linked to each other. They include a website maintained by the National Student Clearinghouse, which provides electronic verification of enrollment, degrees earned, and other information; the website of the National Association of State Directors of Teacher Education and Certification (NASDTEC), which lists approved college and university teacher preparation programs; a website mandated as part of the Title II of the 1998 Higher Education Amendments accountability system; the National Center for Education Information, which collects information on alternative routes; and the Core of Common Data (CCD), a project of the National Center for Education Statistics that collects a variety of relevant data on schools and students (Crowe, 2007).

The Data Quality Campaign (see http://www.dataqualitycampaign.org/ [February 2010]) has examined the data collection systems in every state and developed a set of recommendations to guide states in collecting comprehensive longitudinal data from the entire educational system (preschool through higher education) and using it to improve student achievement. To provide trustworthy answers to the questions about the connections between teacher preparation and student learning for which this committee could not find answers, data collection related to teacher preparation that is integrated into this type of system would be extremely valuable. Useful data collection will cover all levels of the education enterprise, from local school districts to states and the federal government. This means that a data network, rather than a single monolithic data system is needed. The federal government can play a critical role in coordinating definitions and standards and helping to ensure that measures are common across the nation.

Ideally, there would be a high-quality, well-defined state data system in every state that gives explicit attention to collecting baseline information about teacher education and its effects. Each state data system would use variables defined in the same way and measured in the same way. The network would include data analysis files that allow researchers to perform secondary analyses to look for causal relationships among the natural variation in approaches to teacher preparation captured in the data file. Most states are now building such databases, and with a reasonably modest expenditure of money and effort they could be expanded to collect data on the individuals who enter different types of teacher preparation programs and the achievement of the students they later teach. A significant sum of federal money has recently been targeted for state data systems related to education as part of the American Recovery and Reinvestment Act of 2009. A key goal for this federal funding is to make data collection more efficient and integrated so that it can better support improvement: thus, it is an ideal time to ensure that states incorporate information related to teacher preparation in their data collection efforts.

Finally, a targeted longitudinal nationally representative study—similar to those that the National Center for Education Statistics has conducted in other areas—would make it possible to track individuals from before they enter teacher education through their teacher education experiences and into the classroom. We recognize that designing such a study would be difficult, primarily because it is difficult to anticipate which high school students will ultimately pursue teacher education and become teachers. But the feasibility of such a study could be explored: if it proved feasible, it would provide important information that could not be learned from either a national indicator system or existing state databases.

### Recommendations

In order for policy makers and teacher educators to have a stronger empirical basis for decisions about teacher preparation, a much clearer and more detailed picture is needed of teacher candidates and how teacher preparation is delivered, as well as a means of tracking changes in this picture over time. A body of evidence, developed from multiple perspectives and using an array of research designs, that establishes links between teacher preparation and learning—both teachers' learning and K-12 students' learning—would also be of great value to those who are responsible for teacher preparation. Some evidence would come from research intended to identify causal links between specific aspects of preparation and students' achievement. Other evidence would come from more systematic collection and analysis of both data about teacher candidates and the steps they take as they work to become teachers, and descriptive information about programs and pathways (such as analysis of accreditation materials, syllabi, course descriptions, and other program documents, as well as interviews and other observations).

Research on the link between preparation and teachers' knowledge of content and research-based instructional practices and frameworks and between preparation and teachers' skills and performance in classrooms would also be valuable. Some of this research would also examine the contexts in which teachers from various programs and pathways are more or less able to use the knowledge and research-based skills they develop during preparation and the conditions that support or constrain their capacity to use what they know.

There is currently almost no nation that is *not* concerned about teacher quality and teacher preparation. The conviction is widely shared that the economic health of a nation depends on the quality of its education system, which in turn depends directly on how teachers are selected, prepared, supported, and evaluated. The U.S. Congress has asked for answers to important questions about teacher candidates and the nature and quality of the preparation they receive. We offer two recommendations for building an empirical base to provide more complete answers to these questions:

> **Recommendation 9-1:** The U.S. Department of Education should take the lead in coordinating existing data collection efforts and encouraging new ones, with the goal of developing a national education data network that incorporates comprehensive data related to teacher education.

Such a network would provide both baseline monitoring of the status of teacher preparation (and improved opportunities to link that information with other aspects of the public education system) and a common foundation on which to build research efforts that investigate important aspects of teacher preparation.

Ultimately, the kind of network we are recommending would include

- systems that provide integrated data within states using common definitions across states;
- a short-term national indicator system to monitor the status of teacher education; and
- a longitudinal, nationally representative study of teachers' career pathways beginning with their undergraduate education.

> **Recommendation 9-2:** Researchers and those who fund research related to teacher preparation should focus on topics that have the highest potential effects on outcomes for students, specifically, research that explores the benefits of particular kinds of teacher knowledge and clinical experiences and the factors that affect the quality of entering teacher candidates.

Teacher preparation is a key element in the K-12 education system, not an isolated enterprise. It is affected by and affects every other element in the system. The logic of systemic standards-based reform of public education is very clear in calling for each element of the system to be aligned to consistent state standards. Data collection and accountability at the state level are critical to this alignment as well. Teacher preparation has not yet been brought into this alignment at the state level, but high expectations for teachers and for teacher preparation programs are a critical aspect of an aligned system.

The quality of the nation's teachers has been the subject of blistering critiques, as have the institutions that prepare teachers. Moreover, the preparation offered to aspiring teachers has long been characterized by inequity in both resources and opportunities. This report begins by highlighting how much teacher preparation matters, both to the long-term success of efforts to improve public education and to immediate outcomes for students. Policy makers, educational researchers, and scholars in relevant fields have shown a growing awareness of its importance and of the gaps in the knowledge base.

The critical questions about teacher preparation cannot be answered without the kind of nationwide coordination we call for. Clearer understanding of the content and character of effective teacher preparation is critical to improving it and to ensuring that the same critiques and questions are not being repeated 10 years from now.

# References

Aaronson, D., Barrow, L., and Sander, W.L. (2003). *Teachers and student achievement in the Chicago public high schools.* (WP 2002-28). Research Department Federal Reserve Bank of Chicago.

Abell, S.K., and Lederman, N.G. (Eds.). (2007). *Handbook of research on science education.* Mahwah, NJ: Lawrence Erlbaum Associates.

Allen, M. (2003). *Eight questions about teacher education. What does the research say?* Denver, CO: Education Commission of the States.

American Association for the Advancement of Science. (1991). *Science for all Americans.* Washington, DC: Oxford University Press. Available: http://www.project2061.org/publications/sfaa/online/sfaatoc.htm [accessed March 2010].

American Association for the Advancement of Science. (1993). *Benchmarks for science literacy.* Washington, DC: Oxford University Press.

Anderson, C.W. (2007). Perspectives on science learning. In S. Abell and N.G. Lederman (Eds.), *Handbook of research on science education.* Mahwah, NJ: Lawrence Erlbaum Associates.

Applebee, A., Langer, J., Nystrand, M., and Gamoran, A. (2003). Discussion-based approaches to developing understanding: Classroom instruction and student performance in middle and high school English. *American Educational Research Journal, 40*(3), 685-730.

August, D., and Calderón, M. (2006). Teacher beliefs and professional development. In D. August and T. Shanahan (Eds.), *Developing literacy in second-language learners: Report of the national literacy panel on language-minority children and youth.* Mahwah, NJ: Lawrence Erlbaum Associates.

August, D., and Shanahan, T. (Eds.) (2006). *Developing literacy in second-language learners: Report of the national literacy panel on language-minority children and youth.* Mahwah, NJ: Lawrence Erlbaum Associates.

August, D., and Shanahan, T. (Eds.) (2008). *Developing reading and writing in second language learners: Lessons from the report of the national literacy panel on language minority children and youth.* New York: Rutledge.

August, D., Carlo, M.S., Calderón, M., and Nuttall, M. (2005a). Developing literacy in English-language learners: An examination of the impact of English-only versus bilingual instruction. In P. McCardle and E. Hoff (Eds.), *Childhood bilingualism*. Clevedon, England: Multilingual Matters.

August, D., Carlo, M.S., Calderon, M., and Proctor, P. (2005b). Development of literacy in Spanish-speaking English-language learners: Findings from a longitudinal study of elementary school children. *The International Dyslexia Association, (31)*2, 17-19.

August, D., Carlo, M.S., Dressler, C., and Snow, C. (2005c). The critical role of vocabulary development for English-language learners. *Learning Disabilities Research and Practice, 20*, 50-57.

August, D., Beck, I.L., Calderón, M., Francis, D.J., Lesaux, N.K., and Shanahan, T. (2008). Instruction and professional development. In D. August and T. Shanahan (Eds.), *Developing reading and writing in second language learners: Lessons from the report of the national literacy panel on language-minority children and youth*. New York: Rutledge.

Bacolod, M. (2007). Do alternative opportunities matter? The role of female labor markets in the decline of teacher supply and teacher quality. *Review of Economics and Statistics, 89*(4), 737-751.

Ball, D.L. (1990). Prospective elementary and secondary teachers' understandings of division. *Journal for Research in Mathematics Education, 21*, 132-144.

Ball, D.L. (1991). Research on teaching mathematics: Making subject matter part of the equation. In J. Brophy (Ed.), *Advances in research on teaching* (vol. 2, pp. 1-48). Greenwich, CT: JAI Press.

Ball, D.L. (1993). Halves, pieces, and twoths: Constructing representational contexts in teaching fractions. In T. Carpenter, E. Fennema, and T. Romberg (Eds.), *Rational numbers: An integration of research* (pp. 157-196). Hillsdale, NJ: Lawrence Erlbaum Associates.

Ball, D.L., Lubienski, S., and Mewborn, D. (2001). Research on teaching mathematics: The unsolved problem of teachers' mathematical knowledge. In V. Richardson (Ed.), *Handbook of research on teaching* (4th ed.). New York: Macmillan.

Ball, D.L., Hill, H.C., and Bass, H. (2005). *Who knows mathematics well enough to teach third grade and how can we decide?* Washington, DC: American Educator.

Banks, J., Cochran-Smith, M., Moll, L.C., Richert, A., Zeichner, K.M., and LePage, P. (2005). Teaching diverse learners. In L. Darling-Hammond and J. Bransford (Eds.), *Preparing teachers for a changing world: What teachers should learn and be able to do* (pp. 232-274). San Francisco, CA: Jossey-Bass.

Beck, I.L., McKeown, M.G., and Kucan, L. (2002). *Bringing words to fife: Robust vocabulary instruction*. New York: Guilford.

Beckman, S. (2004). What mathematicians should know about teaching math for elementary teachers. *Mathematicians and Education Reform Newsletter, 16*(2).

Beckmann, S. (2008). *Mathematics for elementary teachers* (2nd ed.). Boston, MA: Addison-Wesley Higher Education.

Bestor, H. (1953). *Educational wastelands: The retreat from learning in our public schools*. Champaign, IL: University of Illinois Press.

Betts, J., Reuben, K.S., and Danenberg, A. (2000). *Equal resources, equal outcomes? The distribution of school resources and student achievement*. Public Policy Institute of California. Available: http://www.ppic.org/content/pubs/report/R_200JBR.pdf [accessed September 2009].

Biancarosa, G., and Snow, C.E. (2006). *Reading next—A vision for action and research in middle and high school literacy: A report to the Carnegie Corporation of New York*. Washington, DC: Alliance for Excellent Education.

Bloom, H.S., Kemple, J., Gamse, B., and Jacob, R. (2005). *Using regression discontinuity analysis to measure the impacts of reading first.* Paper presented at the annual conference of the American Education Research Association, Montreal, Canada.

Boyd, D., Grossman, P., Lankford, H., Loeb, S., and Wyckoff, J. (2005). How changes in entry requirements alter the teacher workforce and affect student achievement. *Education Finance and Policy, 1*(2), 176-216.

Boyd, D., Grossman, P., Lankford, H., Loeb, S., Michelli, N., and Wyckoff, J. (2006). Complex by design: Investigating "Pathways into Teaching in New York City Schools." *Journal of Teacher Education, 57,* 155-166.

Boyd, D., Grossman, P., Lankford, H., Loeb, S., Rockoff, J., and Wyckoff, J. (2008). The narrowing gap in New York City: Teacher qualifications and its implications for student achievement in high-poverty schools. *Journal of Policy Analysis and Management, 27*(4), 793-818.

Boyd, D., Grossman, P., Lankford, H., Loeb, S., and Wyckoff, J. (2009). *Teacher preparation and student achievement.* Available: http://www.teacherpolicyresearch.org/portals/1/pdfs/EEPATeacherPrepVA.pdf [accessed May 2010].

Calderón, M. (2007). *Teaching reading to English language learners, grades 6–12: A framework for improving achievement in the content areas.* Thousand Oaks, CA: Corwin Press.

Calderón, M., August, D., Slavin, R., Cheung, A., Durán, D., and Madden, N. (2005). Bringing words to life in classrooms with English language learners. In A. Hiebert and M. Kamil (Eds.), *Research and development on vocabulary.* Mahwah, NJ: Lawrence Erlbaum Associates.

California Council on Science and Technology and the Center for the Future of Teaching and Learning. (2007). *Critical path analysis of California's science and mathematics teacher preparation system.* Available: http://www.cftl.org/documents/2007/TCPA.pdf [accessed September 2009].

Campbell, D.T., and Stanley, J.L. (1963). *Experimental and quasi-experimental designs for research.* Chicago: Rand McNally.

Capps, R., Fix, M., Murray, J., Ost, J., Passel, J.S., and Herwantoro, S. (2005). *The new demography of America's schools: Immigration and the no child left behind act.* Washington, DC: The Urban Institute.

Carlsen, W.S. (1992). Closing down the conversation: Discouraging student talk on unfamiliar science content. *Journal of Classroom Interaction, 27,* 15-21.

Carlsen, W.S. (1998). Engineering design in the classroom: Is it good science education or is it revolting? *Research in Science Education, 28*(1), 51-63.

Carnegie Corporation of New York and Institute for Advanced Study. (2009). *The opportunity equation: Transforming mathematics and science education for citizenship and the global economy.* New York: Carnegie Corporation of New York.

Carnegie Corporation of New York's Council on Advancing Adolescent Literacy. (2010). *Time to act: An agenda for advancing adolescent literacy for college and career success.* New York: Carnegie Corporation of New York.

Carnegie Task Force on Teaching as a Profession. (1986). *A nation prepared: Teachers for the 21st century.* Hyattsville, MD: Carnegie Forum on Education and the Economy.

Clifford, G.J., and Guthrie, J.W. (1988). *Ed school: A brief for professional education.* Chicago: University of Chicago Press.

Clift, R.T., and Brady, P. (2005). Research on methods courses and field experiences. In M. Cochran-Smith and K. Zeichner (Eds.), *Studying teacher education: The report of the AERA panel on research and teacher education.* Mahwah, NJ: Lawrence Erlbaum Associates.

Clotfelter, C.T., Ladd, H.F., Vigdor, J.L., and Wheelter, J. (2006). High poverty schools and the distribution of teachers and principals. *North Carolina Law Review, 85*(5), 1345-1379.

Clotfelter, C.T., Ladd, H.F., and Vigdor, J.L. (2007). Teacher credentials and student achievement in high school: A cross-subject analysis with student fixed effects. *Economics of Education Review, 26*(6), 673-782.

Cochran-Smith, M., and Fries, K. (2005). Researching teacher education in changing times: Paradigms and politics. In M. Cochran-Smith and K. Zeichner (Eds.), *Studying teacher education: The report of the AERA panel on research and teacher education.* Mahwah, NJ: Lawrence Erlbaum Associates.

Cochran-Smith, M., and Zeichner, K. (Eds.). (2005). *Studying teacher education: The report of the AERA panel on research and teacher education.* Mahwah, NJ: Lawrence Erlbaum Associates.

Cohen, D.K., and Spillane, J.P. (1992). Policy and practice: The relationship between governance and instruction. *Review of Research in Education, 18*, 3-45.

Cohen, D.K., Raudenbush, S.W., and Ball, D.L. (2003). Resources, instruction, and research. *Educational Evaluation and Policy Analysis, 25*(2), 1-24.

Cohen-Vogel, L., and Smith, T.M. (2007). Qualifications and assignments of alternatively certified teachers: Testing core assumption. *American Educational Research Journal, 44*(3), 732-753.

Commission on Teacher Credentialing. (2007). *Accreditation framework: Educator preparation in California.* Sacramento, CA: Author.

Conant, J. (1963). *The education of American teachers.* New York: McGraw-Hill.

Conference Board of the Mathematical Sciences. (2001). *The mathematical education of teachers.* Available: http://www.cbmsweb.org/MET_Document/index.htm [accessed September 2009].

Constantine, J., Player, D., Silva, T., Hallgren, K., Grider, M., and Deke, J. (2009). *An evaluation of teachers trained through different routes to certification.* Final report, U.S. Department of Education, NCEE 2009-4044. Available: http://ies.ed.gov/ncee/pubs/20094043/pdf/20094044.pdf [accessed May 2010].

Cook, T.D., and Campbell, D.T. (1986). The causal assumptions of quasi-experimental practice. *Synthese, 68*, 141-180.

Corcoran, S.P. (2007). Long-run trends in the quality of teachers: Evidence and implications for policy. *American Education Finance Association, 2*(4), 395-407.

Corcoran, S., Evans, W.N., and Schwab, R. (2004). Changing labor market opportunities for women and the quality of teachers, 1957-2000. *American Economic Review, 92*(2), 230-235.

Coulter, T., and Vandal, B. (2007). *Community colleges and teacher preparation: Roles, issues, and opportunities.* Denver, CO: Education Commission of the States.

Cremin, L. (1978). *The education of the educating profession.* Washington, DC: American Association of Colleges of Teacher Education.

Crowe, E. (2007). *An effective system of data collection on teacher preparation.* Paper prepared for the Committee on Teacher Preparation Programs, Division of Behavioral and Social Sciences and Education, National Research Council, Washington, DC.

Darling-Hammond, L., and Bransford, J. (2005). *Preparing teachers for a changing world: What teachers should learn and be able to do.* San Francisco, CA: Jossey-Bass.

Darling-Hammond, L., Hammerness, K., Grossman, P., Rust, F., and Shulman, L. (2005). The design of teacher education programs. In L. Darling-Hammond and J. Bransford (Eds.), *Preparing teachers for a changing world.* Washington, DC: National Academy of Education.

Davis, E.A., Petish, D., and Smithey, J. (2006). Challenges new science teachers face. *Review of Educational Research, 76*(4), 607-651.

Dole, J.A., Duffy, G.G., Roehler, L.E., and Pearson, P.D. (1991). Moving from the old to the new: Research on reading comprehension instruction. *Review of Educational Research, 61,* 239-264.

Druva, C.A., and Anderson, R.D. (1983). Science teacher characteristics by teaching behavior and student outcome: A meta-analysis of research. *Journal of Research in Science Teaching, 20*(5), 467-479.

Ebert-May, D., and, Hodder, J. (Eds.) (2008). *Pathways to scientific teaching.* Sunderland, CT: Sinauer Associates.

Editorial Projects in Education. (2000). *Lessons of a century: A nation's schools come of age.* Bethesda, MD: Author.

Editorial Projects in Education. (2006). *Quality counts at 10: A decade of standards-based education.* Bethesda, MD: Author.

Editorial Projects in Education. (2008). *Technology counts 2008: STEM-The push to improve science, technology, engineering, and mathematics.* Bethesda, MD: Author.

Education Development Center. (2003). *Science education in rural America: A snapshot.* Newton, MA: Author.

Education Trust. (1999). *Not good enough: A content analysis of teacher licensing examinations. How teacher licensing tests fall short.* Washington, DC: Author. Available: http://www. eric.ed.gov/ERICDocs/data/ericdocs2sql/content_storage_01/0000019b/80/19/42/30.pdf [accessed May 2010].

Elsbree, W.S. (1939). *The American teacher: Evolution of a profession in a democracy.* New York: American Book.

Feistritzer, C.E. (2006). *Alternative teacher certification: A state-by-state analysis 2005.* Washington, DC: National Center for Education Information.

Feistritzer, C.E. (2007). *Preparing teachers for the classroom: The role of the higher education act and no child left behind.* Testimony presented to the Subcommittee on Higher Education, Lifelong Learning and Competitiveness, Committee on Education and Labor; United States House of Representatives.

Feistritzer, C.E., and Haar, C. (2008). *Alternative routes to teaching.* Columbus, OH: Pearson.

Fillmore, L.W., and Snow, C.E. (2000). What teachers need to know about language. In C.T. Adger, C.E. Snow, and D. Christian (Eds.), *What teachers need to know about language* (pp. 7-54). McHenry, IL: Delta Systems.

Floden, R., and Meniketti, M. (2005). Research on the effects of coursework in the arts and sciences and in the foundations of education. In M. Cochran-Smith and K. Zeichner (Eds.), *Studying teacher education: The report of the AERA panel on research and teacher education.* Mahwah, NJ: Lawrence Erlbaum Associates.

Fowler, R.C. (2001). What did the Massachusetts teacher test say about American education? *Phi Delta Kappan, 82,* 773-780.

Fraser, J.W. (2007). *Preparing America's teachers: A history.* New York: Teachers College Press.

Gabel, D.L. (1994). *Handbook of research on science teacher and learning.* New York: Macmillan.

Gitomer, D.H. (2007). *Teacher quality in a changing policy landscape: Improvements in the teacher pool.* Princeton, NJ: Educational Testing Service.

Glazerman, S., Meyer, D., and Decker, P. (2006). Alternative routes to teaching: The impacts of teach for America on student achievement and other outcomes. *Journal of Policy Analysis and Management, 25*(1), 75-96.

Goldhaber, D.D., and Brewer, D.J. (1997). Why don't schools and teachers seem to matter? Assessing the impact of unobservables on educational productivity. *Journal of Human Resources, 32*(3), 505-523.

Gonzales, P., Williams. T., Jocelyn, L., Roey, S., Kastberg, D., and Brenwald, S. (2008). *Highlights from TIMSS 2007: Mathematics and science achievement of U.S. fourth- and eightgraders in an international context.* Available: http://nces.ed.gov/pubsearch/pubsinfo. asp?pubid=2009001 [accessed May 2010].

Goodlad, J.I. (1994). *Teachers for our nation's schools.* San Francisco, CA: Jossey-Bass.

Goodlad, J.I., Soder, R., and Sirotnik, K.A. (Eds.).(1990). *Places where teachers are taught.* San Francisco: Jossey-Bass.

Graham, P.A., Lyman, R.W., and Trow, M. (1995). *Accountability of colleges and universities: An essay.* New York: The Accountability Study. Available: http://eric.ed.gov/ERICDocs/ data/ericdocs2sql/content_storage_01/0000019b/80/14/4f/0b.pdf [accessed May 2010].

Graham, S., and Perin, D. (2007). *Writing next: Effective strategies to improve writing of adolescents in middle and high schools.* A report to Carnegie Corporation of New York. Washington, DC: Alliance for Excellent Education.

Greenberg, J., and Walsh, K. (2008). *No common denominator: The preparation of elementary teachers in mathematics by America's education schools.* Washington, DC: National Council on Teacher Quality.

Greenleaf, C., Schoenbach, R., Cziko, C., and Mueller, F. (2001). Apprenticing adolescent readers to academic literacy. *Harvard Educational Review, 71*(1), 79-129.

Grigg, W., Donahue, P., and Dion, G. (2007). *The nation's report card: 12th-grade reading and mathematics 2005.* (NCES 2007-468). U.S. Department of Education, National Center for Education Statistics. Washington, DC: U.S. Government Printing Office.

Gross, P.R., Goodenough, U., Lawrence, L.S., Haack, S., Schwartz, M., Schwartz, R., and Finn, C.E. Jr. (2005). *The state of state science standards.* Washington, DC: Fordham Foundation. Available: http://www.edexcellence.net/doc/Science%20Standards.FinalFinal. pdf [accessed May 2010].

Grossman, P.L. (1990). *The making of a teacher: Teacher knowledge and teacher education.* New York: Teachers College Press.

Grossman, P.L., Schoenfeld, A., and Lee, C. (2005). Teaching subject matter. In L. Darling-Hammond and J. Bransford (Eds.), *Preparing teachers for a changing world.* Washington, DC: National Academy of Education.

Grossman, P.L., Brown, M., Cohen, J., Loeb, S., Boyd, D., Lankford, H., and Wyckoff, J. (2009). *Measure for measure: A pilot study linking English language arts instruction and teachers' value-added to student achievement.* Paper presented at the annual meeting of AERA, San Diego CA.

Handelsman, J., Ebert-May, D., Beichner, R., Bruns, P., Chang, A., DeHaan, R., Gentile, J., Lauffer, A., Stewart, J., Tilghman, S.M., and Wood, W.B. (2004). Scientific teaching. *Science, 304*(5670), 521-522.

Hanushek, E.A. (2003). The failure of input-based resource policies. *Economic Journal, 113*(485), F64-F68.

Hanushek, E.A., Kain, J.F., O'Brien, D.M., and Rivkin, S.G. (2005). *The market for teacher quality.* (NBER working paper no. W11154). Available: http://ssrn.com/abstract=669453 [accessed May 2010].

Harris, D.N., and Sass, T.R. (2008). *Teacher training, teacher quality, and student achievement.* (Working Paper No. 3). Washington, DC: National Center for Analysis of Longitudinal Data in Education Research. Available: http://www.caldercenter.org/PDF/1001059_ Teacher_Training.pdf [accessed May 2010].

Hashweh, M.Z. (1987). Effects of subject-matter knowledge in the teaching of biology and physics. *Teaching and Teacher Education, 3*(2), 109-120.

Haynes, M. (2007). *From state policy to classroom practice: Improving literacy instruction for all students.* Alexandria, VA: National Association of State Boards of Education.

Heaton, R.M. and Lewis, J. (2002). *Strengthening the mathematics education of elementary teachers.* Proceedings of the National Summit on Mathematical Education of Teachers. Washington, DC: Conference Board of Mathematical Sciences. Available: http://www.cbmsweb.org/NationalSummit/WG_Speakers/heaton_lewis.htm [accessed May 2010].

Heller, R., and Greenleaf, C. (2007). *Literacy in the content areas: Getting to the core of middle and high school improvement.* Washington, DC: Alliance for Excellence in Education.

Henningsen, M., and Stein, M.K. (1997). Mathematical tasks and student cognition: Classroom-based factors that support and inhibit high-level mathematical thinking and reasoning. *Journal for Research in Mathematics Education, 28*(5), 524-549.

Herbst, J. (1989). *And sadly teach: Teacher education and professionalization in American culture.* Madison: University of Wisconsin Press.

Hess, F.R. (2002). *Tear down this wall: The case for a radical overhaul of teacher certification.* Washington, DC: The American Enterprise Institute.

Hickock, E.W. (1998). Higher standards for teacher training. *Policy Review,* 91.

Hill, H., Schilling, S., and Ball, D. (2004). Developing measures of teachers' mathematics knowledge for teaching. *Elementary School Journal, 105,* 11-30.

Hill, H.C., Rowan, B., and Ball, D.L. (2005). Effects of teachers' mathematical knowledge for teaching on student achievement. *American Educational Research Journal, 42*(2), 371-406.

Hollins, E., and Guzman, M.T. (2005). Research on preparing teachers for diverse populations. In M. Cochran-Smith and K. Zeichner (Eds.), *Studying teacher education: The report of the AERA panel on research and teacher education.* Mahwah, NJ: Lawrence Erlbaum Associates.

Humphrey, D.C., and Weschler, M.E. (2005). *The status of the teaching profession.* Santa Cruz, CA: Center for the Future of Teaching and Learning. Available: http://eric.ed.gov/ERICDocs/data/ericdocs2sql/content_storage_01/0000019b/80/29/dd/8e.pdf [accessed May 2010].

Humphrey, D.C., Weschler, M.E., and Hough, H.J. (2008). Characteristics of effective alternative teacher certification programs. *Teachers College Record, 110*(4). Available: http://policyweb.sri.com/cep/publications/AltCert_finalTCversion.pdf [accessed May 2010].

Ingersoll, R. (2003). *Out-of field teaching and the limits of teacher policy.* A research report cosponsored by Center for the Study of Teaching and Policy. Available: http://depts.washington.edu/ctpmail/PDFs/LimitsPolicy-RI-09-2003.pdf [accessed May 2010].

Ingersoll, R. (2008). *Core problems: Out-of-field teaching persists in key academic courses and high-poverty schools.* Washington, DC: Education Trust. Available: http://www.edtrust.org/dc/press-room/press-release/core-problems-out-of-field-teaching-persists-in-key-academic-courses-esp [accessed May 2010].

International Association for the Evaluation of Educational Achievement. (2009). *Teacher education and development study in mathematics: TEDS-M 2008.* Available: http://www.iea.nl/teds-m.html [accessed November 2009].

International Reading Association. (2003a). *Prepared to make a difference: An executive summary of the national commission on excellence in elementary teacher preparation for reading instruction.* Newark, DE: Author.

International Reading Association. (2003b). *Standards for reading professionals.* Newark, DE: Author.

International Reading Association. (2007). *Teaching reading well: A synthesis of the International Reading Association's research on teacher preparation for reading instruction.* Newark, DE: Author.

International Reading Association and the National Middle School Association. (2002). *Supporting young adolescent literacy learning: Joint position statement by the International Reading Association and the National Middle School Association.* Newark, DE: Author. Available: http://www.reading.org/downloads/positions/ps1052_supporting.pdf [accessed May 2010].

Interstate New Teacher Assessment and Support Consortium Science Standards Drafting Committee. (2002). *Model standards in science for beginning teacher licensing and development: A resource for state dialogue.* Washington, DC: Council of Chief State School Officers.

Jencks, C., and Reisman, D. (1969). *The academic revolution.* Garden City, NY: Doubleday.

Johnson, S.M., Birkeland, S.E., and Peske, H.G. (2005). *A difficult balance: Incentives and quality control in alternative certification programs.* Project on the Next Generation of Teachers. Harvard Graduate School of Education.

Judge, H. (1982). *American graduate schools of education: A view from abroad.* New York: The Ford Foundation.

Kamil, M.L. (2003). *Adolescents and literacy: Reading for the 21st century.* Washington, DC: Alliance for Excellent Education. Available: http://www.all4ed.org/files/AdolescentsAndLiteracy.pdf [accessed May 2010].

Kamil, M.L., Borman, G.D., Dole, J., Kral, C.C., Salinger, T., and Torgesen, J. (2008). *Improving adolescent literacy: Effective classroom and intervention practices.* Washington, DC: What Works Clearinghouse.

Kane, T.J., and Staiger, D.O. (2002). The promise and pitfalls of using imprecise school accountability measures. *The Journal of Economic Perspectives.* Available: http://www.dartmouth.edu/~dstaiger/Papers/KaneStaiger_jep2002.pdf [accessed May 2010].

Kane, T.J., Rockoff, J.E., and Staiger, D.O. (2006). *What does certification tell us about teacher effectiveness? Evidence from New York City.* (Working paper no. 12155). Cambridge, MA: National Bureau of Economic Research.

Katz, R., and Singer, B. (2007). Can an attribution assessment be made for yellow rain?: Systematic reanalysis in a chemical-and-biological weapons use investigation. *Politics and the Life Sciences, 26*(1), 24-42.

Kennedy, M.M. (1998). *Learning to teach writing: Does teacher education make a difference?* New York: Teachers College Press.

Kilburn, M.R., and Karoly, L.A. (2008). *The economics of early childhood policy: What the dismal science has to say about investing in children.* Santa Monica, CA: RAND. Available: http://www.rand.org/pubs/occasional_papers/2008/RAND_OP227.pdf [accessed May 2010].

Kilpatrick, J., Martin, W.G., and Schifter, D. (Eds.) (2003). *A research companion to principles and standards for school mathematics.* Reston, VA: National Council of Teachers Mathematics.

Klein, D. (2005). *The state of state math standards.* Washington, DC: Thomas B. Fordham Foundation.

Koerner, J.D. (1965). *The miseducation of American teachers.* Sarasota, FL: Pelican Press.

Labaree, D.F. (2004). *The trouble with ed schools.* New Haven, CT: Yale University Press.

Lagemann, E.C. (1989). *The politics of knowledge: The Carnegie Corporation, philanthropy, and public policy.* Middletown, CT: Wesleyan University Press.

Lagemann, E.C. (2002). *An elusive science: The troubling history of education research.* Chicago, IL: University of Chicago Press.

Lankford, H., Loeb, S., and Wyckoff, J. (2002). Teacher sorting and the plight of urban schools: A descriptive analysis. *Educational Evaluation and Policy Analysis, 24*(1), 37-62.

Leal, D. (2004). Assessing "traditional" teacher preparation. In F.M. Hess, A. Rotherham, and K. Walsh (Eds.), *A qualified teacher in every classroom?* Cambridge, MA: Harvard Education Press.

Lederman, N.G., Schwartz, R.S., Abd-El-Khalick, F., and Bell, R.L. (2001). Preservice teachers' understandings and teaching of the nature of science: An intervention study. *Canadian Journal of Science, Mathematics, and Technology Education, 1*(2), 135-160.

Lee, J., Grigg, W., and Donahue, P. (2007). *The nation's report card: Reading 2007.* (NCES 2007-496). Washington, DC: National Center for Education Statistics, U.S. Department of Education.

Leigh, A. (2009). What evidence should social policymakers use? *Economic Roundup,* (1), 27-43.

Lemann, N. (1997). The reading wars. *The Atlantic Monthly, 280*(5), 128-134. Available: http://www.theatlantic.com/past/docs/issues/97nov/read.htm [accessed May 2010].

LePage, P., Darling-Hammond, L., Akar, H., Gutierrez, C., Jenkins-Gunn, E., and Rosebrock, K. (2005). Classroom management. In L. Darling-Hammond and J. Bransford (Eds.), *Preparing teachers for a changing world.* San Francisco, CA: Jossey-Bass.

Levine, A. (2006). *Educating school teachers. The Education Schools Project.* Available: http://www.edschools.org/pdf/Educating_Teachers_Report.pdf [accessed May 2010].

Loucks-Horsley, S., Carlson, M.O., Brink, L.H., Horwitz, P., Marsh, D.P., Pratt, H., Roy, K.R., and Worth, K. (1989). *Developing and supporting teachers for elementary school science education.* Andover, MA: National Center for Improving Science Education.

Loucks-Horsley, S., Brooks, J.G., Carlson, M.O., Kuerbis, P., Marsh, D.P., Padilla, M., Pratt, H., and Smith, K.L. (1990). *Developing and supporting teachers for science education in the middle years.* Andover, MA: National Center for Improving Science Education.

Lucas, T., and Grinberg, J. (2008). Responding to the linguistic reality of mainstream classrooms: Preparing all teachers to teach English language learners. In M. Cochran-Smith, S. Feiman-Nemser, and D.J. McIntyre (Eds.), *Handbook of research on teacher education: Enduring questions in changing contexts.* New York: Routledge Group.

Lundmark, C. (2002). The FIRST project for reforming undergraduate teaching. *BioScience, 52*(7), 553.

Lutzer, D.J., Maxwell, J.W., and Rodi, S.B. (2005). *Statistical abstract of undergraduate programs in the mathematical sciences in the United States.* Washington, DC: Conference Board of the Mathematical Sciences. Available: http://www.ams.org/cbms/full-report.pdf [accessed May 2010].

Ma, L. (1999). *Knowing and teaching elementary mathematics: Teachers' understanding of fundamental mathematics in China and the United States.* Mahwah, NJ: Lawrence Erlbaum Associates.

Mashburn, A., Hamre, B., Pianta, R., and Downer, J. (2007). *Building a science of classrooms: Three dimensions of child-teacher interactions in PK-3rd grade classrooms.* Paper presented at the Biennial Meeting of the Society for Research in Child Development, Boston, MA.

Massell, D. (2008). *The current status and role of standards-based reform in the United States.* Paper prepared for the NRC Workshop on Assessing the Role of K-12 Academic Standards in States. Available: http://www7.nationalacademies.org/cfe/Massell%20State%20Standards%20Paper.pdf [accessed May 2010].

Matsumara, L.C., Garnier, H., Slater, S.C., and Boston, M.D. (2008). Toward measuring instructional interactions "At-Scale." *Educational Assessment, 13*(4), 267-300.

Mayer, D., Decker, P.T., Glazerman, S., and Silva, T.W. (2003). *Identifying alternative certification programs for an impact evaluation of teacher preparation.* Washington, DC: Mathematica Policy Research.

McCaffery, D.F., Lockwood, J.R., Koretz, D.M., and Hamilton, L.S. (2003). *Evaluating value-added models for teacher accountability.* Santa Monica, CA: RAND.

McCrory, R., and Cannata, M. (2007). *The mathematical education of elementary teachers: The content and context of undergraduate mathematics classes for teachers.* Paper presented at the annual conference of the Association of Mathematics Teacher Educators, Irvine, CA.

McKeown, M., Beck, I., and Blake, R. (in press). Toward more meaningful decisions about comprehension instruction through comparison of standardized instruction for strategies and content approaches. *Reading Research Quarterly.*

Milgram, J.R. (2005). *The mathematics pre-service teachers need to know.* Palo Alto, CA: Stanford University, Department of Mathematics.

Mitchell, R., and Barth, P. (1999). How teacher licensing tests fall short. *Thinking K-16, 3*(1), 3-23.

Monk, D. (1994). Subject area preparation of secondary mathematics and science teachers and student achievement. *Economics of Education Review, 13*(2), 125-142.

Monk, D.H., and King, J.A. (1994). Multilevel teacher resource effects on pupil performance in secondary mathematics and science: The case of teacher subject-matter preparation. In R.G. Ehrenberg (Ed.), *Choices and consequences: Contemporary policy issues in education.* Ithaca, New York: Cornell University Press.

Morgan, S.L., and Winship, C. (2007). *Counterfactuals and causal inference: Methods and principles for social research.* Cambridge: Cambridge University Press.

Mullis, I.V.S., Martin, M.O., Olson, J.F., Berger, D.R., Milne, D., and Stanco, G.M. (Eds.) (2008). *TIMSS 2007 encyclopedia: A guide to mathematics and science instruction around the world.* Chestnut Hill, MA: TIMSS and PIRLS International Study Center, Boston College.

Murnane, R.J., and Nelson, R.R. (2007). Improving the performance of the education sector: The valuable, challenging, and limited role of random assignment evaluations. *Economics of Innovation and New Technology,* (16)5, 307-322.

Murray, F.B. (2001). From consensus standards to evidence of claims: Assessment and accreditation in the case of teacher education. *New Directions for Higher Education, 2001*(113), 49-66.

National Academy of Sciences, National Academy of Engineering, and Institute of Medicine. (2007). *Rising above the gathering storm: Energizing and employing America for a brighter economic future.* Committee on Prospering in the Global Economy of the 21st Century: An Agenda for American Science and Technology. Washington, DC: The National Academies Press.

National Association of State Directors of Teacher Education and Certification. (2000). *NASDTEC'S report on how the states respond to NBPTS-certified teachers.* Washington, DC: Author.

National Center for Education Statistics. (1998). *Pursuing excellence: A study of U.S. twelfth-grade mathematics and science achievement in international context.* (NCES 98-049). Washington, DC: U.S. Government Printing Office.

National Center for Education Statistics. (1999). *Teacher Quality: A report on the preparation and qualifications of public school teachers.* (NCES 1999080). Washington, DC: U.S. Government Printing Office.

National Center for Education Statistics. (2002). *The condition of education.* Available: http://nces.ed.gov/pubs2002/2002025.pdf [accessed May 2010].

National Center for Education Statistics. (2003a). *The condition of education 2003.* (NCES 2003-067). Washington, DC: U.S. Government Printing Office. Available: http://nces.ed.gov/programs/coe/2003/pdf/28_2003.pdf [accessed May 2010].

National Center for Education Statistics. (2003b). _Teachers' familiarity with standards and their instructional practices: 1995 and 1999._ (NCES 2003-022). Available: http://nces.ed.gov/pubs2003/2003022.pdf [accessed May 2010].

National Center for Education Statistics. (2003c). _Teaching mathematics in seven countries: Results from the TIMSS video study._ Washington, DC: U.S. Department of Education.

National Center for Education Statistics. (2005). _The NAEP reading achievement levels by grade._ Washington, DC: U.S. Government Printing Office.

National Center for Education Statistics. (2007). _Master's degrees conferred by degree-granting institutions, by field of study: Selected years, 1970–71 through 2006–07._ Available: http://nces.ed.gov/programs/digest/d08/tables/dt08_272.asp [accessed April 2010].

National Center for Education Statistics. (2009). _The nation's report card: Mathematics 2009._ http://nces.ed.gov/nationsreportcard/pubs/main2009/2010451.asp [accessed May 2010].

National Center for Education Statistics. (2010). _Trends in International Mathematics and Science Study (TIMSS)._ Available: http://nces.gov/timss/results07.asp [accessed April 2010].

National Center for Research on Teacher Learning. (1991). _Findings from the teacher education and learning to teach study: Final report._ (Office of Education Research and Improvement NCRTL-SR-6/91).

National Commission on Excellence in Education. (1983). _A nation at risk: The imperative for educational reform._ A Report to the Nation and the Secretary of Education, United States Department of Education. Washington, DC: U.S. Department of Education.

National Council for Accreditation of Teacher Education. (2008). _Professional standards for the accreditation of teacher preparation institutions._ Washington, DC: Author.

National Council of Teachers of Mathematics. (1991). _Professional standards for mathematics teachers._ Reston, VA: Author.

National Council of Teachers of Mathematics. (2000). _Principles and standards for school mathematics._ Reston, VA: Author. Available: http://standards.nctm.org/ [accessed November 2008].

National Council of Teachers of Mathematics. (2006). _Curriculum focal points for prekindergarten through grade 8 mathematics: A quest for coherence._ Reston, VA: Author.

National Council on Teacher Quality. (2007). _State teacher policy yearbook: Progress on teacher quality._ Washington, DC: Author.

National Institute of Child Health and Human Development. (2000). _Report of the national reading panel, teaching children to read: An evidence-based assessment of the scientific research literature on reading and its implications for reading instruction._ (NIH Publication No. 00-4769). Washington, DC: U.S. Government Printing Office.

National Mathematics Advisory Panel. (2008). _Foundations for success: The final report of the national mathematics advisory panel._ Washington, DC: U.S. Department of Education.

National Research Council. (1996). _National science education standards._ National Committee on Science Education Standards and Assessment. Washington, DC: National Academy Press.

National Research Council. (1998). _Preventing reading difficulties in young children._ Committee on the Prevention of Reading Difficulties in Young Children. C.E. Snow, M.S. Burns, and P. Griffin (Eds.). Washington, DC: National Academy Press.

National Research Council. (2000a). _How people learn: Brain, mind, experience, and school._ Committee on Developments in the Science of Learning. J.D. Bransford, A.L. Brown, and R.R. Cocking (Eds.). Washington, DC: National Academy Press.

National Research Council. (2000b). *Inquiry and the national science education standards.* Committee on the Development of an Addendum to the National Science Education Standards on Scientific Inquiry. S. Olson and S. Loucks-Horsley (Eds.). Washington, DC: National Academy Press.

National Research Council. (2001a). *Adding it up: Helping children learn mathematics.* Mathematics Learning Study Committee. J. Kilpatrick, J. Swafford, and B. Findell (Eds.). Washington, DC: National Academy Press.

National Research Council. (2001b). *Classroom assessment and the national science education standards.* Committee on Classroom Assessment and the *National Science Education Standards,* Center for Education. J.M. Atkin, P. Black, and J. Coffey (Eds.). Washington, DC: National Academy Press.

National Research Council. (2001c). *Understanding dropouts: Statistics, strategies, and high-stakes testing.* Committee on Educational Excellence and Testing Equity. A. Beatty, U. Neisser, W.T. Trent, and J.P. Heubert (Eds.). Washington, DC: National Academy Press.

National Research Council. (2002a). *Scientific research in education.* Committee on Scientific Principles for Education Research. R.J. Shavelson and L.Towne (Eds.). Washington, DC: National Academy Press.

National Research Council. (2002b). *The knowledge economy and postsecondary education: Report of a workshop.* Committee on the Impact of the Changing Economy on Post-secondary Education. Division of Behavioral and Social Sciences and Education. Center for Education. P.A. Graham and N.G. Stacey (Eds.). Washington, DC: The National Academies Press.

National Research Council. (2004). *Keeping score for all: The effects of inclusion and accommodation policies on large-scale educational assessment.* Committee on Participation of English Language Learners and Students with Disabilities in NAEP and Other Large-Scale Assessments. J.A. Koenig and L.F. Bachman (Eds.). Washington, DC: The National Academies Press.

National Research Council. (2005). *How students learn: History, mathematics, and science in the classroom.* Committee on How People Learn, A Targeted Report for Teachers. M.S. Donovan and J.D. Bransford (Eds.). Washington, DC: The National Academies Press.

National Research Council. (2006). *Systems for state science assessment.* Committee on Test Design for K-12 Science Achievement. M.R. Wilson and M.W. Bertenthal (Eds.). Washington, DC: The National Academies Press.

National Research Council. (2007). *Taking science to school: Learning and teaching science in grades K-8.* Committee on Science Learning, Kindergarten Through Eighth Grade. R.A. Duschl, H.A. Schweingruber, and A.W. Shouse (Eds.). Washington, DC: The National Academies Press.

National Research Council. (2008a). *Assessing accomplished teaching: Advanced-level certification programs.* Committee on Evaluation of Teacher Certification by the National Board for Professional Teaching Standards. M.D. Hakel, J.A. Koenig, and S.W. Elliott (Eds.). Washington, DC: The National Academies Press.

National Research Council. (2008b). *Common standards for K-12 education?: Considering the evidence.* Committee on State Standards in Education: A Workshop Series. A. Beatty (Ed.). Washington, DC: The National Academies Press.

National Research Council. (2010). *Getting value out of value-added.* Committee on Value-Added Methodology for Instructional Improvement, Program Evaluation, and Educational Accountability. H. Braun, N. Chudowsky, and J. Koenig (Eds.). Washington, DC: The National Academies Press.

National Science Teachers Association. (2003). *Standards for science teacher preparation.* Washington, DC: Author.

Neville, K.S., Sherman, R.H., and Cohen, C.E. (2005). *Preparing and training professionals: Comparing education to six other fields.* New York: The Finance Project. Available: http://www.financeproject.org/Publications/preparingprofessionals.pdf [accessed May 2010].

Noell, G. (2008). *Teacher preparation program and pathway analyses for Louisiana for 2004-2005.* Paper prepared for the National Research Council Committee on Teacher Preparation Programs in the U.S.

Ogren, C.A. (2005). *The American state normal school: An "instrument of great good."* New York: Palgrave Macmillan.

Organisation for Economic Co-operation and Development. (2007). *Science competencies for tomorrow's world.* Available: http://www.oecd.org/document/2/0,3343,en_32252351_ 32236191_39718850_1_1_1_1,00.html#ES [accessed March 2010].

Parker, T.H., and Baldridge, J. (2003). *Elementary mathematics for teachers, Volume 1.* Okemos, MI: Sefton-Ash.

Pecheone, R.L., and Chung, R.R. (2006). Evidence in teacher education: The performance assessment for California teachers. *Journal of Teacher Education, 57*(1), 22-36.

Peske, H., and Haycock, K. (2006). *Teaching inequality: How poor and minority students are shortchanged on teacher quality. A report and recommendations by the Education Trust.* Washington, DC: Education Trust. Available: http://eric.ed.gov/ERICDocs/data/eric docs2sql/content_storage_01/0000019b/80/27/fa/aa.pdf [accessed May 2010].

Phelps, G., and Schilling, S. (2004). Developing measures of content knowledge for teaching reading. *Elementary School Journal, 105*, 31-48.

Porter, A., Polikoff, M., and Smithson, J. (2008). Is there a de facto national intended curriculum? evidence from state content standards. *Educational Evaluation and Policy Analysis, 31*(3), 238-268.

Pugach, M.C. (2005). Research on preparing general education teachers to work with students with disabilities. In M. Cochran-Smith and K. Zeichner (Eds.), *Studying teacher education: The report of the AERA panel on research and teacher education.* Mahwah, NJ: Lawrence Erlbaum Associates.

Raimi, R., and Braden, L.S. (1998). *State mathematics standards: An appraisal of math standards in 46 states, the District of Columbia, and Japan.* Washington, DC: Thomas B. Fordham Foundation.

Rickover, H.G. (1959). *Education and freedom.* New York: E.P. Dutton.

Risko, V., Roller, C., Cummins, C., Bean, R., Block, C.C., Anders, P., and Flood, J. (2008). A critical analysis of research on reading teacher education. *Reading Research Quarterly, 43*(3), 252-289.

Rivkin, S.G. (2007). *Value added analysis and education policy.* Washington, DC: Urban Institute, Center for the Analysis of Longitudinal Data in Education Research.

Rivkin, S.G., Hanushek, E.A., and Kain, J.F. (2005). Teachers, schools, and academic achievement. *Econometrica, 73*(2), 417-458.

Rockoff, J.E. (2004). The impact of individual teachers on student achievement: Evidence from panel data. *American Economic Review, 94*(2), 247-252.

Rothstein, J. (2009). *Student sorting and bias in value-added estimation: Selection on observables and unobservables.* (NBER Working Paper No. w14666). Available: http://cpre-wisconsin.org/news/events/VAM%20Conference%20FInal%20Papers/StudentSorting&Bias_ JRothstein.pdf [accessed May 2010].

Rothstein-Fisch, C., and Trumbull, E. (2008). *Managing diverse classrooms: How to build on students' cultural strengths.* Alexandria, VA: Association for Supervision and Curriculum Development.

Rowan, B., Chiang, F.S., and Miller, R.J. (1997). Using research on employees' performance to study the effects of teachers on students' achievement. *Sociology of Education, 70*(4), 256-284.

Sackett, D.L., Rosenberg, W.M.C., Gray, J.A.M., Haynes, R.B., and Richardson, W.S. (1996). Evidence based medicine: What it is and what it isn't. *BMJ, 13*(312), 71-72.

Sanders, L.R., Borko, H., and Lockard, J.D. (1993). Secondary science teachers' knowledge base when teaching science courses in and out of their area of certification. *Journal of Research in Science Teaching, 30*, 723-736.

Sanders, W.L., and Rivers, J.C. (1996). *Cumulative and residual effects of teachers on future student academic achievement.* Knoxville: University of Tennessee Value-Added Research and Assessment Center. Available: http://www.mccsc.edu/~curriculum/cumulative%20and%20residual%20effects%20of%20teachers.pdf [accessed May 2010].

Sass, T. (2008). *Teacher preparation pathways, institutions, and programs in Florida.* Paper prepared for the Committee on Teacher Preparation Programs, Division of Behavioral and Social Sciences and Education, National Research Council, Washington, DC.

Schmidt, W.H., Tatto, M.T., Bankov, K., Blomeke, S., Cedillo, T., Cogan, L., Han, S.I., Houang, R., Hsieh, F.J., Paine, L., Santillan, M., and Schwille, J. (2007). *The preparation gap: Teacher education for middle school mathematics in six countries.* Michigan: MSU Center for Research in Mathematics and Science Education.

Sedlak, M.W. (1989). Let us go and buy a schoolmaster: Historical perspectives on the hiring of teachers in the United States, 1750-1980. In D. Warren (Ed.), *American teachers: Histories of a profession at work* (pp. 257-291). New York: Macmillan.

Sedlak, M.W. (2008). Competing visions of purpose, practice, and policy: The history of teacher certification in the United States. In M. Cochran-Smith, S. Feiman-Nemser, and D.J. McIntyre (Eds.), *Handbook of research on teacher education: Enduring questions in changing contexts, 3rd edition.* New York: Routledge.

Shadish, W., Cook, T., and Campbell, D. (2002). *Experimental and quasi-experimental designs for generalized causal inference.* Boston: Houghton Mifflin.

Short, D., and Fitzsimmons, S. (2007). *Double the work: Challenges and solutions to acquiring language and academic literacy for adolescent English language learners. A report to Carnegie Corporation of New York.* Washington, DC: Alliance for Excellent Education.

Shroeder, C.M., Scott, T.P., Tolson, H., Huang, T.Y., and Lee, Y.H. (2007). A meta-analysis of national research: Effects of teaching strategies on student achievement in science in the United States. *Journal of Research in Science Teaching, 44*(10), 1436-1460.

Shulman, L. (1986). Those who understand: Knowledge growth in teaching. *Educational Researcher, 15*(2), 4-14.

Shulman, L. (1987). Knowledge and teaching: Foundations of the new reform. *Harvard Educational Review, 57*, 1-22.

Singer, B. (2008). Comment: Implication analysis as abductive inference. *Sociological Methodology, 38*(1), 75-83.

Smagorinsky, P., and Whiting, M.E. (1995). *How English teachers get taught: Methods of teaching the methods class.* Urbana, IL: National Council of Teachers of English.

Smith, C., Wiser, M., Anderson, C.W., and Krajcik, J. (2006). Implications of research on children's learning for assessment: Matter and atomic molecular theory. *Measurement: Interdisciplinary Research and Perspectives, 14*(1&2), 1-98.

Smith, M.B. (1954). *The diminished mind: A study of planned mediocrity in our public schools.* Chicago: Henry Regnery.

Stahl, S.A. (2003). Vocabulary and readability: How knowing word meanings affects comprehension. *Topics in Language Disorders, 23*(3), 241-247.

Stecher, B., and Naftel, S. (2006). Implementing standards based accountability (ISBA). Working paper series, RAND Education. Available: http://www.rc.rand.org/pubs/working_papers/2006/RAND_WR380.pdf [accessed May 2010].

Stein, M.K., Grover, B., and Henningsen, M. (1996). Building student capacity for mathematical thinking and reasoning: An analysis of mathematical tasks used in reform classrooms. *American Educational Research Journal, 33*(2), 455-488.

Stigler, J.W., and Hiebert, J. (2004). Improving mathematics teaching. *Educational Leadership, 61*(5), 12-16.

Strickland, D., Snow, C., Griffin, P., and McNamara, P. (2002). *Preparing our teachers: Opportunities for better reading instruction.* Washington, DC: Joseph Henry Press.

Stotsky, S. (2006). Why American students do not learn to read very well: The unintended consequences of Title II and teacher testing. *Third Education Group Review, 2*(2). Available: http://www.tegr.org/Review/Articles/vol2/v2n2.pdf [accessed May 2010].

Trow, M. (1996). Trust, markets and accountability in higher education: A comparative perspective. *Higher Education Policy, 9*(4), 309-324.

U.S. Census Bureau. (2009). *Statistical abstract of the United States.* Available: http://www.census.gov/compendia/statab [accessed April 2010].

U.S. Department of Education, Office of Postsecondary Education. (2006). *The secretary's fifth annual report on teacher quality: A highly qualified teacher in every classroom,* Washington, DC: Author.

U.S. Office of Special Education Programs. (no date). *History: 25 years of progress educating children with disabilities through IDEA.* Washington, DC: Author. Available: http://www.ed.gov/policy/speced/leg/idea/history.pdf [accessed January 2010].

Valdés, G., Bunch, G., Snow, C.E., Lee, C., and Matos, L. (2005). Enhancing the development of students' language(s). In L. Darling-Hammond and J. Bransford (Eds.), *Preparing teachers for a changing world: What teachers should learn and be able to do* (pp. 126-168). San Francisco, CA: Jossey Bass.

Venezky, R. (1984). The history of reading research. In P.D. Pearson (Ed.), *Handbook of reading research, volume III.* Mahwah, NJ: Lawrence Erlbaum Associates.

Walsh, K., and Jacobs, S. (2007). *Alternative certification isn't alternative.* Washington, DC: Thomas B. Fordham Foundation and the National Council on Teacher Quality.

Wang, A.H., Coleman, A.B., Coley, R.J., and Phelps, R.P. (2003). *Preparing teachers around the world.* Princeton, NJ: Educational Testing Service.

Wayne, A.J., and Youngs, P. (2003). Teacher characteristics and student achievement gains: A review. *Review of Educational Research, 73*(1), 89-122.

Wenglinsky, H. (2002). How schools matter: The link between teacher classroom practices and student academic performance. *Education Policy Analysis Archives, 10*, 12. Available: http://epaa.asu.edu/ojs/article/view/291 [accessed May 2010].

Wilson, S., and Youngs, P. (2006). Research on accountability processes in teacher education. In M. Cochran-Smith and K. Zeichner (Eds.), *Studying teacher education: The report of the AERA panel on research and teacher education.* Mahwah, NJ: Lawrence Erlbaum Associates.

Wilson, S.W, Floden, R.E., and Ferrini-Mundy, J. (2001). *Teacher preparation research: Current knowledge, gaps, and recommendations.* Research report prepared for the U.S. Department of Education. Seattle, WA: Center for the Study of Teaching and Policy. Available: http://depts.washington.edu/ctpmail/PDFs/TeacherPrep-WFFM-02-2001.pdf [accessed May 2010].

Wu, H. (2002). *What is so difficult about the preparation of mathematics teachers?* Available: http://www.cbmsweb.org/NationalSummit/Plenary_Speakers/Wu_Plenary.pdf [accessed May 2010].

Wu, H. (2007). The mathematics K-12 teachers need to know. Plenary session presentation at the Mathematical Sciences Research Institute Conference on Critical Issues in Education: Teaching Teachers Mathematics, May 30-June 1, Berkeley, CA.Xu, Z., Hannaway, J., and Taylor, C. (2008). *Making a difference? The effect of Teach for America in high school*. Washington, DC: Urban Institute. Available: http://www.urban.org/Uploaded-PDF/411642_Teach_America.pdf [accessed May 2010].

Zehler, A., Fleischman, H., Hopstock, P., Stephenson, T., Pendzick, M., and Sapru, S. (2003). *Descriptive study of services to LEP students and LEP students with disabilities, Volume 1A: Research report*. Arlington, VA: Development Associates.

Zeichner, K.M., and Conklin, H.G. (2005). *Teacher education programs*. In M. Cochran-Smith and K.M. Zeichner (Eds.), *Studying teacher education: The report of the AERA panel on research and teacher education*. Mahwah, NJ: Lawrence Erlbaum Associates.

Zumwalt, K., and Craig, E. (2005). Teachers' characteristics: Research on the demographic profile. In M. Cochran-Smith and K.M. Zeichner (Eds.), *Studying teacher education* (pp. 111-156). Washington, DC: American Educational Research Association.

# Appendix A

# Dissent, *Michael Podgursky*

This report goes beyond our charge from Congress. We were not asked to make recommendations about how teachers ought to be prepared or the necessary preparation of teachers. We were not asked to make recommendations to states about how they should approve teacher training programs. There is simply no scientific research basis for making these recommendations.

Congress asked us to assess available data on teacher preparation programs in the United States and whether the training teachers receive is consistent with scientifically based research. If reliable data are lacking (as they clearly are), we were to make recommendations regarding data collection.

Since the body of scientifically based research on teacher preparation is very thin, the committee chose to rely heavily on descriptive and qualitative studies, as well as the opinions of panels of teachers and teacher educators. This evidence is then reported in ways that obfuscate the weak research base for the recommendations. The report frequently asserts that these various types of evidence are consistent, but it fails to provide supporting documentation.

The proposals for data collection are not well thought out. Clearly it would be useful to know more about what teacher training programs do. However, the rather nebulous language used to describe elements of such a database are not helpful or practical. The proposal for a national longitudinal survey on teacher candidates is not well developed.

# Appendix B

# How Teachers Learn Critical Knowledge and Skills: Tracing One Example

**Learning Objective**

Reading diverse text with understanding.

**Student's Opportunity to Learn**

Develop and enhance language and meta-cognitive skills to meet the demands of specific printed texts.

Experience supported opportunities to learn to interpret diverse kinds of texts for diverse purposes.

**Teacher Study**

Linguistic and psychological studies:

- development of oral and written language abilities, including relations among meta-cognitive abilities, print processing abilities, and comprehension abilities
- theories of text-comprehension

Pedagogy of reading (teaching and assessing):

- activities to develop and practice comprehension and metacognition strategies on oral language, on written text read aloud, and as the student reads independently
- activities to develop concepts and words (oral and written)
- activities to develop the skills needed to lead text-based discussions focused on constructing the meaning of text and engaging in knowledge building with text

### Teacher's Opportunity to Demonstrate Knowledge

Suppose a linguistically/culturally diverse student in your classroom has excellent decoding skills but has trouble comprehending the texts you assign. What are some reasons why comprehension may be a problem for this student?

Describe the interplay between prior knowledge and reading strategies as students read and comprehend a text on a particular topic.

Analyze a text for its affordances and challenges and identify probing questions that will assess students' understanding of the content.

Discuss the purpose and use of comprehension strategies. When do readers use them? How do they contribute to reading comprehension?

Discuss how readers' perspectives influence what they comprehend and interpret from a text.

### Teacher's Opportunity to Demonstrate Practice

Select a text that you or your cooperating teacher uses as part of the regular curriculum—this could be a selection in a basal reading program or a leveled text or a trade book. Read through the text and identify the likely areas where your linguistically/culturally diverse student may have trouble comprehending the text. Plan a lesson that builds or activates prior knowledge to build a bridge between what your student knows and the new information the student needs to understand the text better.

Select two different, but relatively easy, texts for your students to read, one on a familiar topic and one on an unfamiliar topic. Develop, conduct, and evaluate a lesson in which you show students how you can read texts on a familiar topic by activating and using prior knowledge. Then show them how you often use comprehension strategies to comprehend a text on the unfamiliar topic since you do not have much background information on which to rely.

Select a text that will be used in content instruction (a text book or trade book). Identify a set of learning goals appropriate to the use of that text; identify semantic and linguistic features that might impede students' comprehension of the text, script how you will launch the discussion of the text, and script a set of probing questions that you will use to guide a discussion of the text so that the discussion is consistent with your learning goals and reflects the textual challenges.

Read a text on a topic with which you are very unfamiliar. As you read, think about and list the different comprehension strategies you use to assist you in making sense of this difficult text. In a small group, discuss with your peers the strategies you used and the reasons why you used them. Next use a think-aloud to assess a typical third-grader's comprehension abilities as the student reads a text. Make a list of the specific strategies the student uses. Compare and contrast these lists with your peers. Develop a profile of a typical third-grade reader's strategies for comprehending text.

Develop, implement and evaluate a comprehension lesson where students learn how to revisit a story from a different perspective. Then, ask students to write a story of their choosing from a perspective that is different from the one taken by the author of the story.

# Appendix C

# Biographical Sketches of Committee Members

**Ellen Condliffe Lagemann** (*Cochair*, 2007-2009, *Chair*, 2009-2010) is the Levy Institute research professor and a senior scholar at the Levy Economics Institute at Bard College in New York. Previously, she was the Charles Warren professor of the history of American education at Harvard University and former dean of the Harvard Graduate School of Education. She also served as the president of the Spencer Foundation, as a professor of history and education at New York University, and as a professor of education at the Teachers College at Columbia University. She is a past president of the National Academy of Education and the History of Education Society, and has served on the boards of the Teaching Commission, Jobs for the Future, the Russell Sage Foundation, and the Center for Advanced Study in the Behavioral Sciences. She has written widely on many topics, including education reform, education research, philanthropy in education, women's history, and nursing. She has an undergraduate degree from Smith College, an M.A. in social studies from Teachers College, and a Ph.D. in history and education from Columbia University.

**Herbert K. Brunkhorst** is professor in the Department of Biology in the College of Natural Sciences and chair of the Department of Science, Mathematics, and Technology Education in the College of Education at the California State University at San Bernardino. He previously taught at the precollege level. He has served as a senior faculty researcher for the U.S. Department of Education's Salish Consortium, a multidimensional collaborative research effort for improving science and mathematics teacher education. He is a fellow of the American Academy for the Advancement of Science, and was elected director of the preservice teacher preparation division of the National Science Teachers Association. He has a B.A. in biology from Coe College, an M.A.S. in science education and a Ph.D. in science education and plant physiology from the University of Iowa.

**Margarita Calderón** is a senior research scientist at the Center for Data-Driven Reform in Education at Johns Hopkins University. She is a co-principal investigator on a randomized evaluation of English immersion, transitional, and two-way bilingual programs for the Institute for Education Sciences of the U.S. Department of Education. She is also conducting longitudinal research and development projects in El Paso, Texas, on teachers' learning communities, bilingual staff development, and adult English-language learners. Other research topics include ESL reading, Spanish-English transitional reading, two-way bilingual reading, and the transition from Spanish reading into English reading. She has a B.A. in English, French, and journalism, an M.A. in applied linguistics from the University of Texas, El Paso, and a Ph.D. in educational management, sociolinguistics, and organizational development from Claremont Graduate School and San Diego State University.

**Marilyn Cochran-Smith** is the John E. Cawthorne professor of teacher education for urban schools at the Lynch School of Education of Boston College where she directs the doctoral program in curriculum and instruction. She is the immediate past president of the American Educational Research Association and has also served as the co-chair of the organization's National Consensus Panel on Teacher Education. Her research has concentrated on teacher education across the professional lifespan; teaching and issues of race, class, culture, and gender; teacher research/practitioner inquiry; children's early language and literacy learning, and outcomes, teaching quality, and competing agendas for education reform. She has a B.A. in sociology from the College of Wooster, an M.Ed. in curriculum and instruction from Cleveland State University, and a Ph.D. from the University of Pennsylvania.

**Janice Dole** is in the Department of Teaching and Learning at the University of Utah. After several years as an elementary teacher, she held positions at the University of Denver, the Center for the Study of Reading at the University of Illinois at Urbana-Champaign, and Michigan State University. She has written for many different audiences, including teachers, administrators, and reading researchers and other educational researchers. She is currently a member of the Reading Development Panel for the National Assessment of Educational Progress and working for the research and development section of the American Federation for Teachers. Her current research focuses on comprehension instruction at the K-3 level and reading professional development for K-3 teachers in at-risk schools. She has M.A. and Ph.D. degrees from the University of Colorado.

**Donald N. Langenberg** is chancellor emeritus of the 13-institution University System of Maryland. Previously, he was a professor of physics and then chancellor of the University of Illinois at Chicago. He served as deputy director of the National Science Foundation under President Jimmy Carter. His research has been primarily in experimental condensed matter physics and materials science, with a major focus on the study of superconductivity. He has served as chair of the American Association for the Advancement of Science and of the National Association of State Universities and Land Grant Colleges, as president of the American Physical Society, and on the boards of the Alfred P. Sloan Foundation and the University of Pennsylvania. As chair of the National Reading Panel in 1998-2000, he headed the committee that issued *Teaching Children to Read*. He has a B.S. from Iowa State University, an M.S. from the University of California at Los Angeles, and a Ph.D. from the University of California at Berkeley, all in physics. He also has received honorary degrees from the University of Pennsylvania and the State University of New York.

**Ronald Latanision** is the corporate vice president and practice director of the Mechanical Engineering and Materials Science Center at Exponent Consulting, Inc. He is the author or co-author of more than 200 scientific publications, and he has been a consultant to industry and government. He served as a science adviser to the Committee on Science and Technology of the U.S. House of Representatives, and he served on the Nuclear Waste Technical Review Board under President George W. Bush. He is a member of the National Academy of Engineering and of the American Academy of Arts and Sciences. He has a B.S. in metallurgy from the Pennsylvania State University and a Ph.D. in metallurgical engineering from Ohio State University.

**James Lewis** is a professor in the Department of Mathematics and director of the Center for Science, Mathematics, and Computer Education at the University of Nebraska at Lincoln. He previously served as department chair, and during that tenure the department won the university-wide Departmental Teaching Award and a Presidential Award for Excellence in Science, Mathematics, and Engineering Mentoring. He served as the coprincipal investigator for the Nebraska Math and Science Initiative and led a study to revise the mathematics education of future elementary school teachers at the university. He has M.S. and Ph.D. degrees in mathematics from Louisiana State University.

**David H. Monk** is professor of educational administration and dean of the College of Education at the Pennsylvania State University. Previously, he was a professor at Cornell University, and he has also been a 3rd-grade teacher and a visiting professor at the University of Rochester and the University of Burgundy in Dijon, France. He serves on the editorial boards of *The Economics of Education Review*, *The Journal of Education Finance*, *Educational Policy*, and the *Journal of Research in Rural Education*. He consults widely on matters related to educational productivity and the organizational structuring of schools and school districts and is a past president of the American Education Finance Association. He has an A.B. in economics from Dartmouth College and a Ph.D. in educational administration from the University of Chicago.

**Annemarie Sullivan Palincsar** is the Jean and Charles Walgreen Jr. professor of reading and literacy in the School of Education at the University of Michigan. Her research focuses on the design of learning environments that support self-regulation in learning activity, especially for children who experience difficulty learning in school. She studies how children use literacy in the context of guided inquiry science instruction, what types of text support children's inquiry, and what support students who are identified as atypical learners. She is a member of the Reading Study Group at RAND, the National Education Goals Panel, and the National Advisory Board to Children's Television Workshop. She is the coeditor of *Cognition and Instruction*. She has a B.S. in special education from Fitchburg State College and M.S. and Ph.D. degrees in education from the University of Illinois at Urbana-Champaign.

**Michael Podgursky** is Middlebush professor of economics at the University of Missouri at Columbia. Previously, he served on the faculty of the University of Massachusetts at Amherst. He has published numerous articles and reports on education policy and teacher quality and coauthored a book titled *Teacher Pay and Teacher Quality*. He is a member of the advisory boards of the National Center for Teacher Quality and the American Board for Certification of Teacher Excellence. Podgursky served on the faculty of the University of Massachusetts at Amherst. He has a B.A. degree in economics from the University of Missouri at Columbia and a Ph.D. degree in economics from the University of Wisconsin at Madison.

**Andrew Porter** is dean of the Graduate School of Education and the George and Diane Weiss Professor of Education at the University of Pennsylvania. He has published widely on psychometrics, student assessment, education indicators, and research on teaching. His current work focuses on curriculum policies and their effects on opportunity to learn, and includes serving as codirector of System-Wide Change for All Learners and Educators, as the principal investigator of studies on the use of longitudinal designs to measure effects of professional development and on improving effectiveness of instruction in mathematics and science with data on enacted curriculum, and aas a member of the Consortium for Policy Research in Education. He is an elected member and former officer of the National Academy of Education, a lifetime National Associate of the National Academies, and past president of the American Educational Research Association. He has a B.S. in education from Indiana University and M.A. and Ph.D. degrees in educational psychology from the University of Wisconsin.

**Kenneth Shine** is Executive Vice Chancellor for Health Affairs of the University of Texas System and professor of medicine emeritus at the University of California at Los Angeles. He is the former president of the Institute of Medicine at the National Academies and was the founding director of the RAND Center for Domestic and International Health Security. A cardiologist and physiologist, he is a fellow of the American College of Cardiology and American College of Physicians and a member of many other honorary and academic societies, including the Institute of Medicine. He has served as chair of the Council of Deans of the Association of American Medical Colleges and as president of the American Heart Association. He has an A.B. in biochemical sciences from Harvard College and an M.D. from Harvard Medical School.

**Edward Silver** is William A. Brownell collegiate professor of Education and professor of mathematics at the School of Education at the University of Michigan. Previously, he was a senior scientist at the Learning Research and Development Center and professor at the University of Pittsburgh. His research interests focus on the teaching, learning, and assessment of mathematics, particularly mathematical problem solving. He is also actively involved in efforts to promote high-quality mathematics education for all students, particularly Hispanic students. He has served on a number of editorial boards and has published numerous articles and several books in the field of mathematics education. He has a B.A. in mathematics from Iona College, an M.S. in mathematics from Columbia University, and M.A and Ed.D. degrees in mathematics education from Teachers College of Columbia University.

**Dorothy Strickland** is the Samuel DeWitt Proctor professor of education at Rutgers, the State University of New Jersey. Previously, she was a classroom teacher in the New Jersey public schools, the Arthur I. Gates professor at Teachers College of Columbia University, and a faculty member at Kean University and New Jersey City University. She is a past president of both the International Reading Association and its Reading Hall of Fame, and she has held several elected positions in the National Council of Teachers of English. She is also active in the National Association for the Education of Young Children and was a member of the panel that produced *Becoming a Nation of Readers*. She has a B.S. in elementary education from Newark State College (now Kean University) and an M.A. in educational psychology a Ph.D. in early childhood and elementary education from New York University.

**Suzanne Wilson** is a university distinguished professor and chair of the Department of Teacher Education and director of the College of Education's Center for the Scholarship of Teaching at Michigan State University. Her work spans several domains, including teacher learning, teacher knowledge, and the connection between educational policy and teachers' practice. She has also conducted research on history and mathematics teaching. Her current work focuses on developing sound measures for tracking what teachers learn in teacher preparation, induction, and professional development. She has a B.A. and teaching certificate in American History and American civilization from Brown University and an M.S. in statistics and a Ph.D. in educational psychology from Stanford University.

**Hung-Hsi Wu** is a professor of mathematics at the University of California at Berkeley. His mathematics research focuses on differential geometry, and he has authored numerous research papers and monographs, as well as three graduate level textbooks in Chinese. He has also been involved in K-12 mathematics education, working on the development of California's Mathematics Professional Development Institutes and the California's Mathematics Framework. He served as a member of the Mathematics Steering Committee of the National Assessment of Educational Progress and Achieve. He has an A.B. from Columbia University and a Ph.D. in mathematics from the Massachusetts Institute of Technology.

**James Wyckoff** is a professor in the Curry School of Education at the University of Virginia. He has written widely on issues of education finance, including teacher compensation and teacher recruitment and retention of teachers in New York State. Currently, he examining attributes of teacher preparation programs and pathways and induction programs that are effective in increasing the retention of teachers and the performance of students.

He directs the Education Finance Research Consortium and serves on the editorial boards of *Education Finance and Policy* and the *Economics of Education Review*. He is a past president of the American Education Finance Association. He has a B.A. in economics from Denison University and a Ph.D. in economics from the University of North Carolina at Chapel Hill.